Praise for

"*Tender Paws* will be especiall[...] [...]ting new puppies or adopting traum[...] [...]ffers lots of positive, gentle methods for working effectively with dogs."

—**Temple Grandin,** author of *Animals Make Us Human* and *Animals in Translation*

"I love this book! Not only will it help transform the relationship the reader has with their dog, but it has the potential to change how they relate to other humans and even with themselves. This is no ordinary training manual! *Tender Paws* gives an insight into the importance of understanding the individual's lived experience, with a heavy focus on safety (physical and emotional) and the importance of fostering secure social attachments. This book will support the reader to give their dogs the best gift of all—a voice! I highly recommend this book, and I know dogs everywhere will too."

—**Andrew Hale,** founder of Dog Centred Care

"I'm so glad Wendy Sunshine—a best-selling child development author—suddenly began to wonder about dogs. In her new book *Tender Paws,* she pulls off something extraordinary: an exploration into parenting and dog-raising techniques that is both wonderfully readable and fully grounded in well-cited science. The author focused her considerable research skills on the topic, and dozens of poignant case studies and examples of hard-won wisdom shared by thoughtful fellow travelers (including some famous names!) really give *Tender Paws* its powerful emotional punch. I'm so grateful this book now exists!"

—**Kathy Callahan,** author of *Welcoming Your Puppy from Planet Dog* and *101 Rescue Puppies*

How
Science-Based
Parenting Can
Transform Our
Relationship
with Dogs

*Tender*paws

Wendy Lyons Sunshine

Health Communications, Inc.
Boca Raton, Florida

www.hcibooks.com

Disclaimer: This book is intended for educational purposes only. To clarify how the principles discussed here may impact your specific situation, consult a qualified professional who is well-versed in the latest scientific understanding of canine behavior, training, and welfare. No claim is made to any trademark or registered mark of any individual or organization.

Library of Congress Cataloging-in-Publication Data
is available through the Library of Congress

©2024 Allison Wendy Lyons Sunshine

ISBN-13: 978-07573-2495-6 (Paperback)
ISBN-10: 07573-2495-9 (Paperback)
ISBN-13: 978-07573-2496-3 (ePub)
ISBN-10: 07573-2496-7 (ePub)

Publisher: Health Communications, Inc.
301 Crawford Boulevard, Suite 200
Boca Raton, FL 33432-3762

Back cover photo by Nancy Guth.
Photo montage courtesy of Larissa Hise Henoch; photos courtesy of Norm and Wendy Sunshine.
Line drawing illustrations by Ethan Kocak and used with permission.
Cover, interior design, and formatting by Larissa Hise Henoch.

To little ones,
human and canine,
who need an
advocate

contents

Introduction 1

PART ONE
Can We Parent a Dog? 5

Chapter 1: **My Puppy Problem** 7

Chapter 2: **The Science of Family** 21

Chapter 3: **The Meaning of Parenting** 31

PART TWO
The Science and HEARTS of Parenting 43

Chapter 4: **HEARTS Principles** 45

Chapter 5: **Parenting Styles** 91

Chapter 6: **HEARTS and Parenting Styles to Guide Us** 105

PART THREE
HEARTS-Friendly Practices 115

Chapter 7: **Consider Their Developmental Stage** 117

Chapter 8: **Practice Attunement** 127

Chapter 9: **Help Little Ones Feel Safe** 147

Chapter 10: **Nurture at Every Opportunity** 157

Chapter 11: **Show Respect, Expect Respect** 165

Chapter 12: **Water the Seeds You Want to Grow**....................... 173

Chapter 13: **Use Play Creatively** 181

Chapter 14: **Avoid a Head-On Collision**................................. 195

Chapter 15: **Honor Their Talents** 203

Chapter 16: **Help Them Self-Regulate**................................. 209

Chapter 17: **Set Everyone Up for Success** 219

PART FOUR
HEARTS to the Rescue—Three Case Studies 233

Chapter 18: **Case Study 1—Duke and Dr. Rudy De Meester**... 235

Chapter 19: **Case Study 2—High Performance
            Sports and Mr. Grin** 243

Chapter 20: **Case Study 3—Changing the Lens on Cooper** 251

PART FIVE
Embracing HEARTS 273

Chapter 21: **Become a Detective of Unmet Needs**..................... 275

Chapter 22: **Restore Balance** 291

Notes 299

Acknowledgments.. 341

About the Author 343

introduction

I NEVER EXPECTED to help write an award-winning, best-selling parenting book that's been translated into multiple languages and continues, more than a decade later, to be recommended by adoption agencies and child protective organizations across the country.

But luck was on my side when then-editor of the *Fort Worth Weekly* Gayle Reaves, asked me to write an article about child development expert Dr. Karyn Purvis, her mentor Dr. David Cross, and their groundbreaking work at Texas Christian University with struggling adopted children. The professors invited me to attend their "Hope Connection" camp, where at-risk kids ran sensory obstacle courses, participated in Theraplay sessions, and sat wide-eyed on the floor as Dr. Purvis blew bubbles, lit sparklers, and engaged with them playfully. Parents told me, damp-eyed, about the miraculously positive shifts that occurred as a result of their child's participation in the camp and through personal interactions with Dr. Purvis. Kids once thrown out of school for aggressive outbursts were now complimented by their teachers. Young children who were once bundles of defiance, unable to focus or learn, could now sit and practice their alphabet and numbers.

The professors yearned to help even more struggling families and asked me to partner on a book. During this process, I became their honorary graduate student. The professors personally tutored me in Dr. John Bowlby's attachment theory, the Ainsworth Strange Situation, Dr. Bruce Perry's work on trauma, stages of child development, neurobiology, and concepts of positive reinforcement. Karyn herself administered the Adult Attachment Inventory to me and explained how the findings played out in my own life. She and I spent hours together, me tapping on a laptop while she play-acted scenarios to demonstrate practical application of their approach.

This extraordinary experience gave me a glimpse of their wisdom, but I couldn't yet appreciate its full dimension and power. I had no experience in real-life parenting challenges—the frustration, the endless responsibility, the guesswork, the fear, the guilt, the power struggles. I remained blissfully unaware of these stresses until right around the time that *The Connected Child: Bring Hope and Healing to Your Adoptive Family* went to the publisher. And that's when my husband and I adopted a small, brown puppy.

A puppy of indeterminate lineage.

A puppy born behind a gas station.

A puppy taken from her mother and littermates too soon.

A puppy with worms and anemia.

A special-needs puppy.

My first puppy.

And I was in way over my head.

In short order, puppy training guides failed me. Nothing in their pages explained what to do with a scrambling, out-of-control bundle of teeth and claws. I would have sent the blasted creature back to the shelter so that someone more qualified could raise her, but my husband refused.

Desperate for help and grasping at straws, I got a crazy idea.

Could a book written for struggling parents help me with a fanged, four-legged toddler? Could lessons in raising happy, well-adjusted kids transfer to a puppy?

On my very first try, *The Connected Child* transformed my relationship with her. From that point forward, I secretly used a parenting book as my compass for puppy-rearing. It helped me see my challenging puppy, not as a demon out to get me, but as an at-risk child struggling with invisible, unmet needs. Those needs were complicated by developmental challenges, neglect, abuse, or trauma, and I would need compassion, patience, and a therapeutic mindset to meet those needs.

Years afterward, when I began collaborating on a different parenting book (*Raising the Challenging Child: How to Minimize Meltdowns, Reduce Conflict, and Increase Cooperation*, with Karen Doyle Buckwalter and Debbie Reed of Chaddock), my husband and I happened to take home our next rescue dog, who had his own background of trauma. And sure enough, parenting wisdom again offered useful insights for our jittery new arrival.

Was this a lucky fluke, or did the seeming similarities between child-rearing and dog-rearing have a basis in science? To find out, I began reaching out to animal behavior experts—such as Temple Grandin, PhD, who affirmed that attachment mechanisms did indeed work across species—and other researchers, and I scoured scientific literature. I attended Kelley Bollen's dog behavior workshops at my local shelter and began attending specialized webinars and conferences, reporting and blogging about dogs and people for PsychologyToday.com, and speaking with experts such as Suzanne Clothier and Denise Fenzi. I found my way to Kim Brophey's L.E.G.S. Applied Ethology Family Dog Mediation program and became part of the team at Positively, founded by progressive dog trainer Victoria Stilwell. The more I learned, the more I saw that advances in dog handling and research had close parallels in the fields of child development, trauma, and attachment psychology.

This book incorporates terminology from a cross section of disciplines and includes a variety of analogies and metaphors. My language choices will at times intentionally veer away from precise academic, medical, psychological, or industry definitions, but I will do my best to show where and how these concepts and practices fit together to benefit dogs of all types.

Whether your puppy or dog was rescued from a background of harm or deprivation or has developed perplexing behaviors, recognizing the hidden needs that drive behavior can make it easier to brainstorm creative solutions. It is my deepest hope that the insights shared here will help you and your dog thrive in your journey together.

PART ONE

Can We Parent a Dog?

CHAPTER 1:
My Puppy Problem

A FEW YEARS into our marriage, my husband decided that what our home needed—beyond the big-screen TV dominating our living room or the second rescue cat he'd convinced me to adopt—was a puppy.

Yes, a puppy.

Others might have greeted this prospect with delight or at least confident understanding of the next steps, but not me.

I had lived with easygoing grown dogs and enjoyed walking and caring for them, but I had never raised a puppy or infant of any kind and frankly was not eager to try. I was busy racing toward a work deadline, and if past experience with my night-owl husband and our distribution of cat box duties was any indication, the less glamorous, more hands-on aspects of puppy care would fall to me.

My protests slammed right up against Norm's sentimentality for his late beloved hound. The dog was long gone, but his likeness festooned my husband's office. There were images of Flash as a puppy in Norm's arms, as a teenager sprawled on a couch, as a mature basset with long ears draped across a field of Texas bluebonnets. I never really stood a chance.

Finally, I agreed to visit a breeder. We were welcomed by a pair of drooling basset hounds with plate-sized paws and yards of ears, eager to greet us. Outside on the back porch, we sidestepped yellow puddles and scattered brown piles to meet the pups. They were friendly and cute enough, but I kept thinking about those massive, drooling adults. So much slobber, and one false turn of a stout creature like that would torpedo my bad knee. We thanked the breeder and went on our way.

My husband took the rejection of his beloved breed in stride. If a puppy was involved, he was flexible. So we browsed possibilities, oohing and aahing at standard poodles and Wheaten terriers. Somehow, each time we took an interest, further research revealed that the breed had a reputation for killing cats, was prohibitively expensive, or both.

Keeping our cats safe added anxiety to the choice. I didn't intend to put little Sven or Gracie in harm's way. But we were at a loss for a clear breed winner, so decided to explore local shelters for a small, mixed-breed puppy—preferably something that would grow to less than thirty pounds to give my knee and the cats a fighting chance.

Visiting shelters near Dallas took a strong stomach. Harsh barking echoed the hallways. Antiseptic, musky smells enveloped us. Row after row of sad faces squinted in the dim hallways, many lethargic and indifferent, even earless, hulking survivors of the fighting ring. Some of the animals, penned together, began snarling and snapping at one another when I approached.

These visits were so depressing that Norm didn't have the heart to join me. It was like looking for a needle in a gloomy haystack. Then one day, I discovered a squirmy, dappled dachshund mix awaiting release for adoption. Let out to meet me, she wriggled and licked my hand and rolled over in friendly greeting. Suddenly I was all in on the puppy adventure.

Norm and I awoke early the next morning and dashed out to be first in line to adopt her. On arrival, we learned someone else had beaten us to her.

Weeks later, Norm and I met a litter of strays. Their mother had fled when animal control came, and her puppies were being housed in a foster home instead of the city shelter to protect them from germs.

We entered a living room dominated by a pen and settled ourselves cross-legged on the floor, surrounded by a riot of life.

Puppies—some black and fluffy, others brown and velvety—trotted, chased, and pounced among themselves, just out of reach. Norm and I made kissy noises and wiggled fingers, luring them to us, but they hardly even noticed.

At last, one finally trotted forward but veered away at the last second. Minutes ticked by. We sat, ignored, while the puppies wrestled and scrimmaged together. Finally, out of nowhere, a potato-sized, fuzzy brown lump appeared. It tottered and climbed—unbidden—into my husband's lap, curled up, and went to sleep.

Norm and I looked at each other. This creature was a deep caramel color with undistinguished features. She had a pleasing earthy odor, like truffles and toast.

We discussed the dozing puppy. She seemed mild mannered and reasonably small. Maybe twenty or thirty pounds full grown? Short-haired, probably wouldn't shed too much. She was nothing like her rowdy littermates, we decided. Plus, she had chosen us.

"Okay," we told the foster parent, "we'll take this one."

The first clue that I was unprepared for what lay ahead arrived the following morning in the shape of Karyn Purvis, PhD, a child development professor from Texas Christian University. She set her laptop on my kitchen table, swung aside her long, gray hair, and knelt to greet the as-yet unnamed puppy.

She turned to me and asked, "Has she pooped yet?"

The question unnerved me. I mean, who arrives at another person's home and inquires about bowel habits? I wasn't sure I'd heard correctly.

"What?"

"Has she pooped yet? She's so little, her system can't work by itself. She needs her mama to lick her belly and help her go."

"Oh, goodness. Now that you mention it, I don't recall seeing—"

"Get me a warm washcloth and some olive oil, and I'll show you what to do."

Karyn lifted the puppy onto her lap and demonstrated how to stroke its round underside with a warm, moist cloth, mimicking what the mother would do by tongue. On its nose went a spot of oil, to be licked off and to ease internal machinery.

Lesson complete, Karyn—a newly minted PhD—and I went back to revising our manuscript. We were working on a book for families with at-risk adoptive kids, written in collaboration with Karyn's mentor, David Cross. I smiled and thought, *Well, that's a stroke of good luck. Not only does this woman have the magic touch with special-needs children "from hard places," she's a puppy expert too!*

The next morning, Karyn arrived carrying a giant tote. Out came a pack of swizzle rawhide chews for our puppy. Then two gigantic hand-me-down feeding bowls.

I burst out laughing.

This animal was barely six inches long. If stretched, her muzzle might reach the lip of the bowls. How would we use these bowls? Bathe her in them? I thanked Karyn for the kind gesture, then packed the bowls away in a closet, snickering. What a joke! This animal would never grow big enough to use them.

That night, as the puppy gnawed on a twizzle chew, a thought prickled at the back of my head: *Did Karyn know something I didn't?*

During the next couple of days, we focused on giving the puppy a name. I wanted something fresh and special. That put choices like "Flash" and "Missy" and "Brownie" out of the running.

Norm tossed out an exhaustive list of choices that I continued to nix, and finally asked, "How about Hazel?"

I giggled, visualizing the stout, middle-aged woman who starred as a housekeeper in the eponymous 1960s TV show. Her name was so silly for a puppy. It was irresistible.

So the puppy was pronounced "Hazel," and we took commemorative photos. The puppymoon phase, however, was short-lived.

Within weeks, I was ranting to my husband, listing little Hazel's offenses. Her teeth were too sharp. She was too wild, too nippy, too uncooperative. She rocketed around the house, leaping onto any cat in sight. One of our cats had gone into hiding. The other crouched in ambush, tail twitching, waiting for the chance to—whack!—bring a paw down on the puppy's head. Our household was in chaos, and we were harboring a future assassin. Visions of Petageddon kept me up at night.

We had to act fast.

"Please," I begged my husband, fighting back tears, "this puppy is too much for me. She's going to grow into a cat killer. We should take her back to the shelter—right away."

I had tried to be a good mama to our puppy. I had massaged her round, constipated belly with a warm, wet washcloth and gotten her plumbing flowing. I had fed her and protected her from harm. When Karyn, David, and I squeezed around my kitchen table for our final book editing session, I could barely focus on the screen, completely distracted by David's massive boots threatening to flatten little Hazel.

First thing in the morning, hours before my night-owl husband awoke, I would race downstairs to attend Hazel. I'd hold her gingerly with my fingertips, arms stiff and outstretched like I was holding a lobster to drop into the cooking pot, and rush her outside to relieve herself. She would blink, sniff the air, and inspect blades of grass that brushed her face. Then she would lumber toward a patch of green ground cover, climb into the thick of it, battling leaves that tickled her round belly, and search for the perfect spot.

When she finally squatted to do her business, I sang out, "Go potty, Hazel! Go potty," as one of the training books advised. Business complete, she would nose around for a twig and, finding one, meticulously chew it to sawdust.

Even after Karyn, David, and I hit "send" on our manuscript and they returned to their teaching and research, I continued working in the kitchen so I could monitor the puppy. The afternoon when

Hazel tumbled through the wrought-iron railing from our kitchen into the sunken den a few feet down—fortunately onto a couch and not the hard floor below—I realized my error and sprang into action. I dashed around the house dismantling picture frames to repurpose their plexiglass panels, clipping them as a barrier across the problem railing. Then I remembered the backyard and spent hours lashing yards of nylon netting to the wrought-iron fence with twist ties. At night, I would fall asleep exhausted while Norm and the puppy snuggled in front of the TV together until the wee hours.

On the first day it seemed safe to leave Hazel alone for a little while, Norm and I set her outside in the yard where she could pee and chew to her heart's delight. But when we returned, the yard was empty. I went into shock. *Oh my god, how did she get out? Did somebody snatch her? Could it have been a hawk? Why didn't we think of that? What if she got to the road?*

Paralyzed with fear and self-recrimination, I stood in the yard and shouted, "Hazel, Hazel, Hazel!" over and over. There was no sign of her, and I had no idea where to start looking. I stood frozen, shouting. A few minutes later, a rustling in the far corner of the yard caught my attention. I went to investigate. There, at ground level, amid some leaves, did I see a tiny nose poking in my direction? *Hazel?* More rustling, and our puppy wriggled back into full view to rejoin us in the yard. I was beyond relieved.

"Good girl, Hazel," I cried. "Good girl!"

Norm and I bragged to each other about picking such a great dog. Who else came back after she escaped? Who else learned to go potty on command? I was as proud as if she earned an A in class or her first trophy. Plus, her medical test results were improving, and she would soon be cured of intestinal parasites and anemia.

But once the medical problems disappeared, so did our small, docile puppy.

Gone was the malleable muffinhead we had adopted. Gone, for that matter, was any resemblance to any of the easygoing adult dogs I had ever lived with in the past.

This creature was mushrooming in size and greeted each new day like the crack from a starter's gun. She ricocheted around the house, skidding into furniture and doors, pawing at all in her path. If I bent to pet her short velour coat, she sprang and snapped like an angry jack-in-the-box. Attempts to leash her for a walk were met with lashing teeth and sharp nails. Red welts laced my arms. Little Hazel had transformed from a fuzzy lump of putty into a demon out to get me.

I thumbed through puppy-training manuals, searching for clues on how to handle an animal that behaves like a downed electrical wire. I found nothing.

I was sapped, frustrated, and drowning in a river of chaos. Didn't this puppy understand that we rescued her from foster care, took her to the vet, cured her of worms, gave her food, shelter, chew toys? She had been born behind a gas station, for God's sake. What an ingrate!

Before long, I snapped.

"No!" I shouted in pain after the latest nip. I rolled up a newspaper into a baton and whacked the puppy square on the nose. She yelped and backed away, whirling in circles, biting at her tail.

Oh, my god, I thought, *what have I done? I don't believe in beating animals.*

That was the last straw. Effective immediately, I decided, I was finished. No more nipping teeth or scrabbling paws for me. No more arms checkered in red welts and scrapes. No more sleepless nights worrying about the cats' welfare.

We needed to bring her back to the shelter and get an adult dog instead: a calm, mature, appreciative creature. Not some scary clown shot from a cannon.

"I can't manage her," I told Norm tearfully. "I don't want to hit her again. The shelter is her best choice." Privately, though, I understood returning her to the shelter was a gamble. A puppy's chances of getting adopted shrink with every passing day. Hazel was closing in on three months old and was not a purebred, flashy animal who would attract a lot of takers. Adopters want the youngest, cutest puppies. Even our kind vet described her as "a generic brown dog." We couldn't be certain that another family would choose her. She might easily be left to languish at the shelter—or worse, be euthanized.

Brushing aside a guilty twinge, I clung to the hope that someone more qualified would rescue her. I refused to remember how Hazel had learned the potty command or found her way back into our yard. Of course I didn't remind Norm that she was the only pup who approached us while her littermates scrimmaged on the foster parent's floor or how she snored in his armpit while he watched TV every evening. Instead, I said that if we brought her back to the shelter right now, while she was still young, she had a good chance of being adopted again.

On and on I pleaded. I reasoned. I implored. I cried.

It was futile.

My husband listened sympathetically and heard me out, but he couldn't be swayed. When all the talking was done, he still believed in Hazel's goodness. The puppy stayed.

Seriously.

I was screwed.

How preposterous to be a grown-ass woman at the mercy of a creature hardly one-tenth my size. How humbling to feel so helpless.

What was I going to do?

After I finished hyperventilating, the irony washed over me. Here I was, a forty-something woman who had never raised a child, being held hostage by a fanged, juvenile delinquent. I'd become a struggling parent.

And I had just helped write a book for struggling parents.

On a whim, I went to my computer and brought up the file for *The Connected Child: Bring Hope and Healing to Your Adoptive Family.* I had worked on the manuscript for a year and its pages were familiar, but that evening I read with fresh eyes.

Faint as a wisp of smoke from a genie's lamp, Karyn and David's compassion and calm and confidence wound around me.

parenting pearl

The beauty of a re-do is that it catches an inappropriate action in progress and says, "Whoa! Let's go back and do this again differently." Immediate practice is an aid to developing mastery, just like in any skill—whether it's riding a bicycle, learning to read, or playing a game. By actively replacing misbehavior with correct behavior in your child's memory banks, you can help the child encode competency. A re-do "erases" the muscle memory of the failed behavior and gives the child the physical and emotional experience of substituting a successful one in its place.

—The Connected Child[1]

The next morning when I bent over and tried to pet the puppy, she sprang and snapped like I had electrocuted her. Sharp teeth caught my fingers.

"Ow!" I cried. But this time, Karyn's words whispered in my ear and I curbed my anger. I stepped back. Took a centering breath. Collected myself and gently knelt. The puppy took a break from snapping at her tail to eye me.

I reached out an arm and extended relaxed fingers in her direction. In a calm voice, I said, "Do-over."

Hazel cocked her head and studied my fingers. I stayed crouched on the floor and kept my hand steady. I repeated in a mild, warm tone, "Do-over."

The puppy stepped nearer, sniffed, and then—for the first time ever—licked my hand. No nips, no scratches, no snapping at her tail. One lick. Then she waited and watched.

I nearly swooned.

"Good girl!" I cooed. "Good girl!"

In my ignorance, I had assumed life with a puppy would be a straight trajectory, an easy transition to maturity. After some rambunctious chewing and piddling, the animal would transform directly into a docile family pet. Neat. Simple. Straight line. No zigs or zags.

It never dawned on me that a rescue puppy who had introduced herself by climbing into my husband's lap and going to sleep might be waving a red flag of malnutrition or illness, that her early inability to move bowels might signal developmental or sensory needs, that being taken too soon from her biological family would deprive her of basic social skills, or that her small size could signal an early stage of life or trauma and medical problems rather than her final, mature stature—which eventually peaked at sixty-five pounds, more than double what we had hoped.

No, it hadn't even crystalized yet that we had a special-needs puppy on our hands when I revisited *The Connected Child* and was inspired to offer the puppy a redo, a mulligan, a do-over.

But little Hazel's lick arrived like a miracle, a clear sign of goodwill. This was not an act of violence or aggression. There were no teeth involved. Her tongue touch was measured and deliberate and gentle.

I had not yet heard of the term "appeasement behavior," the technical term for when dogs try to "make nice" or "suck up" to another,[2] but all the same, the puppy's intention was clear.

In that split second, I understood she wasn't the devil's spawn or a malicious sprite out to torment me. She was a young, unformed creature who didn't understand what was expected of her. Hazel wanted to connect with me. She just didn't know how.

The do-over cast my role in a new light. More than simply feed her, care for her physical needs, or string safety barriers across the house to protect her from injury, I needed to become this animal's guide. Her teacher. Her coach. This puppy and I didn't have to be adversaries. It was time for a fundamental shift in my attitude.

The do-over affirmed the promise my husband saw in her. It offered hope that I, too, could one day bond with this challenging puppy. Just maybe, if I could help Hazel calm her wildest impulses, she might even one day live peacefully with our two cats.

reflections from the field

What made the "do-over" strategy work? Here's what Kelley Bollen, a certified animal behavior consultant and former director of behavior programs for the Maddie's Shelter Medicine Program at Cornell University College of Veterinary Medicine, told me:

> What you call the "do-over" was just so great because you came to a place where you knew you had to change. It wasn't about the puppy changing, it was about you changing. You finally realized, look, this is a baby. This is an infant. This is what I try to teach people: you are a grown adult human. This is an infant animal, and it's doing puppy things. If you want to teach it, you have to guide it and be patient with it.
>
> Your "do-over" worked because the puppy was still weeks old and very young. You were lucky because you made this decision when the puppy was still open to learning. If the puppy was too much older, it wouldn't have been as receptive.
>
> You also learned from your own experience that your demeanor is going to affect the animal's demeanor. This is true when I work with clients who have a dog who shows aggressive behavior and we're trying to modify the aggressive behavior. Part of my work is to teach them how to change their attitude and emotions and behavior so that they're not inadvertently feeding right into what the dog's doing. You were feeding into the puppy. You were feeding into the puppy's mouthiness and inability to calm down because you were getting so agitated by it.

Your energy was feeding her energy, and it was just this horrible cycle you were in. When you finally realized, *I'm going to take a breath, I'm going to calm down, I'm going to be quiet and calm with this puppy,* the puppy in turn was able to do the same.[3]

CHAPTER 2:
The Science of Family

FOR THE LONGEST TIME, I wouldn't admit to anyone that a parenting book was helping me with our puppy. But privately, *The Connected Child* became my touchstone. Whenever Hazel's behavior posed a problem, I scanned our book for inspiration about how to proceed. Of course, I also consulted dog behavior books and experts—it would have been silly to ignore species-specific and practical knowledge—but I weighed what they recommended against parenting best practices to make sure they aligned.

In a sense, I was asking myself, *What would an expert parent do?* I had watched Karyn Purvis detect subtle impairments and signs of trauma in a child and respond precisely to individual needs in real time. Her style was consistently calm, exceptionally kind, playful, and yet unflappably firm, demanding of respect and clear about expectations.

Her example transformed my relationship with our puppy and made it easier for me to support and advocate for Hazel as she grew. By the time Hazel passed away at eleven years old, my husband and I—along with our male cat, who grew to love his canine sister dearly—grieved a well-adjusted and beloved family member.

Eventually, intellectual curiosity overtook my earlier embarrassment, and I wanted to know if there was a scientific basis in transferring parenting principles to dogs. One of my first steps in that journey was speaking with the renowned Temple Grandin, PhD,
author of *Animals Make Us Human*,[1] about the feasibility of interspecies attachment. She confirmed that yes, it's entirely possible. She even shared how it was hard for her to say goodbye to a little piglet she had hand raised. As a result, I went on to speak to other experts, read journal articles, and piece together the underlying biology of the human–dog connection.

How Nature Brings Us Together

A friend who became a pediatrician once pointed out to me that if babies weren't so darn cute, no one would ever willingly undertake all the hard work that's required to care for them and raise them.

Is it any different with puppies?

Think of those chunky little heads and chubby limbs.

The big round eyes[2] and button nose. The wriggling. The comic antics.

We can't help but respond.

Puppies' and dogs' babylike features compel us to behave in ways we don't necessarily realize.[3] For example, we do something special with babies and dogs that we don't do with one another. We offer an especially enthusiastic and intense, natural smile—pulling our lips up and crinkling our eyes—only to babies and dogs. This goofy, happy grin shows up five times more often than other facial expressions when parents play with their baby or their dog. This exaggerated smile is almost never given adult to adult.[4]

In a similar vein, what do you think makes a dog most appealing to potential adopters? Is it because they . . .

a. approach us for attention?

b. wag their tail?

c. raise their inner eyebrow?

If you chose (c), you'd be correct. The eyebrows have it. Researchers tracked a group of twenty-seven "bully"-type dogs to see which ones were adopted most quickly from the shelter.[5] Dogs adopted most quickly were the ones that raised their inner eyebrow muscle most often. That one small facial movement mattered more than how frequently the dog approached the front of the kennel to greet the people and more than how often they wagged their tail. Although the study was small, the results are provocative.

One simple eyebrow movement might cut the length of shelter stays nearly in half!

This is an example of how dogs' physiology has evolved to appeal to us. Wild dogs typically cannot move their inner eyebrow, but domesticated dogs can. Small muscles on the forehead between a dog's eyes, called the *levator anguli oculi medialis*, raise the inner eyebrows and create a soulful expression. This tiny muscle is the puppet master that pulls our heart strings by creating "puppy dog eyes" that trigger our protective parenting response.[6]

Our instinctive attraction to baby faces contributes to the popularity of flat-faced breeds like the pug, French bulldog, and American bulldog.[7] These dogs do not resemble wild dogs for the simple reason that they are bred to look more like baby humans, with large heads, big eyes, and small, flat noses. Unfortunately, achieving these features in dogs requires malformations of the skull that obstruct normal breathing and cause chronic health problems.[8, 9]

But no matter what type of baby canine you prefer, you're bound to find one to your taste. Maybe you feel parental toward dogs but draw the line at using such direct language—at least publicly. One study found that Americans describe their dog as a "child" or "kid" almost twice as often in private with family and friends as they do in public with strangers and coworkers.[10] Dog owners in India, by contrast, appear to be more consistent in their language choices. In my own informal survey of more than one hundred American dog owners, 45 percent admitted to calling their dog "my child," and a full 65 percent confessed to calling their dog "my baby."

Our affinity for dogs is more than a personal choice; it is nature stacking the deck toward survival. Puppies' babylike cuteness is the magic power that renders us deaf and blind to all the challenges and demands that raising them will likely cause down the road. We end up cooing and speaking baby talk to them, and like human infants, dogs respond.[11]

From earliest history, dogs and people seem to have understood that partnering together led to greater success in locating and securing food. We began huddling together for warmth on cold nights, alerting each other to danger, and sharing living spaces. If you consider the close relationship we humans have enjoyed with canine mammalian brethren over millennia and the many ways our species' biologies have evolved to complement each other, approaching them through a parenting lens becomes a natural extension.

The Pull of Attachment Biology

Relationships are vital to humans and to dogs in a deep, biological way. For both our species, offspring are born helpless and vulnerable. They need more than food and shelter to survive: They need tender touch and responsive caregiving to spark neural activity in the brain and activate healthy development. Neurochemicals wash through the mother's body after she gives birth, stimulating her feeding and caregiving behaviors; the infant's corresponding responses stir the mother's neurological reward centers.

Scientists call this constellation of mechanisms "attachment," the powerful, emotional force integral to social and familial connections. Attachment pulls us toward children, partners, and friends and it can pull us toward our dog. For example, we may feel a rush of happiness when we stroke their fur or hand them a treat. It's nature's way of rewarding us for connecting. When our dog appears to smile or engage in proximity-seeking behavior, it stimulates our own feel-good neurochemical pathways that reinforce caregiving behavior.

Mammalian caregiving and attachment are orchestrated through neurochemical messengers called neurotransmitters.[12-15] These neurotransmitters are influenced by the vagus nerve system, which connects our brain to our gut and beyond, significantly linking our internal bodily state to social interactions with others.[16, 17] Neurotransmitters naturally ebb and flow within our cells and nervous system throughout the day, influencing our emotional state and responses. Three neurotransmitters common to mammals are oxytocin, dopamine, and cortisol.

- **Oxytocin** has been called the "love hormone" and is linked to prosocial behaviors and emotional responses. Oxytocin regulates basic life functions, including reproductive systems and neurological connections through the senses. It is involved in mothering, fathering, coparenting, romance, and friendship. Working in tandem with other hormones and neurochemical systems, oxytocin contributes to females' "tend and befriend" impulse in reaction to stress.[18] Some researchers propose that oxytocin contributes to the emotion of compassion, making us more attentive to cues of pain and distress.[19] Oxytocin helps explain the domestication of dogs and their bond with humans.[20] Even petting could have played a role, as areas of mammalian skin with hair contain specific receptors that are stimulated by gentle stroking, and these in turn raise oxytocin levels.[21-25] In both dogs and infants, oxytocin helps reduce anxiety; as little as five minutes of friendly petting increases dogs' oxytocin levels.[26, 27] (In an interesting twist, high oxytocin levels are linked to greater aggressiveness in some individuals because the higher affiliative and caregiving impulse provokes an increased impulse to defend the "in group." In dogs, this phenomenon appears most prevalent when there is both raised oxytocin and another neuropeptide called vasopressin.[28, 29])

- **Dopamine** influences physical movement, plays a role in curiosity and learning, and affects habit formation and reward.[30-33] Dopamine also influences information-seeking behavior, by providing a reward signal for finding something pleasurable and motivating.[34] Dopamine's role, like that of all neurotransmitters, is nuanced. High levels have been linked to increased movement while low levels are linked to attentional imbalances, such as ADHD-like behaviors in dogs.[35] Disturbances in dopamine circuitries have been linked to obsessive and compulsive behavior and other disorders.[36] Dogs that gaze at their owners for help in solving problems have been found to have higher dopamine levels.[37] Working in tandem with oxytocin, dopamine sparks and energizes attachment bonds.

- **Cortisol** is linked to stress management and regulation.[38] Levels of cortisol vary with the time of day and with the demands of the environment around us. At-risk children, such as those with a history of deprivation or harm, have reduced morning cortisol levels corresponding to their dysregulated response to stress.[39]

Oxytocin, dopamine, and cortisol work in tandem with other neurochemicals, such as serotonin and reproductive hormones, to influence mood, attachment, learning, and behavior.[40] Overall, our mammalian caregiving neurobiology encourages parenting behaviors, empathy for animal suffering, and attachment relationships with dogs.[41, 42]

Shared Needs

Humans have a habit of raising others' offspring. This phenomenon is called alloparenting and is seen in social species from dolphins and monkeys to humans.[43] Alloparenting usually occurs within a single species, such as when we adopt orphaned children, but it also occurs across species. It's reasonable to describe our life with dogs as a type of alloparenting, considering how often we invite dogs into our homes and the terms we choose to describe them.

People's relationship with pet dogs has much in common with the classic definition of parent–child attachment: We are drawn to be near each other, we gain comfort from the other's presence, and we feel distress at prolonged separation. With so much biological similarity and affinity between our species, it seems natural that we would care for a dog or puppy much like we would parent a child.

Of course, children and dogs are not the same. For starters, kids have opposable thumbs; dogs do not. Kids play using their fingers and hands; dogs play using their mouth. Kids travel on two limbs; dogs travel on four. Kids grow up to speak sophisticated language; dogs have limited options for vocal communication. The average human life span is multiple times that of a dog. Yet despite obvious differences, children and dogs share core biological needs. Here are a few:

Need for Adequate Food, Water, and Shelter

Life can only be sustained when an individual receives adequate nourishment, liquids, and protection from the elements. These are essentials of minimal existence.

Need to Develop in Stages

Infants are born in an immature state; with time and under correct conditions, they can grow and develop into optimal adulthood. This process occurs in sequential stages, with each stage providing the foundation for the next stage of maturity. (Admittedly, humans tend to limit the developmental trajectory, independence, and maturity of most pet dogs, rendering them comparable to grown children kept tied to a parents' apron strings.)

Need to Use the Senses

Specific cells throughout the body capture and process information about the world, enabling the individual to function and navigate successfully through the environment. External sensory inputs include hearing, vision, taste, smell, and touch. Internal sensory inputs also provide awareness of the bodily state and movement through processes known as proprioception and interoception.

Need to Repair and Regulate

The body operates best within certain ranges, so it's important to restore functioning so that it remains within those parameters. Healing from illness and maintaining normal blood pressure are familiar examples. Regulation in early life relies in large part on synchrony with caregivers in a process called co-regulation. As the individual grows and learns, they become able to practice greater self-regulation.

Need for Secure and Supportive Relationships

To improve the odds of survival, individuals are genetically programmed to establish and maintain multiple types of relationships. This includes close attachment relationships with family as well as wider circles of supportive interactions. Early life plays a key role in enabling these capacities to unfold.

Need for Scaffolded Guidance

To mature and develop optimally, individuals require assistance, leadership, and teaching from qualified others in a measured, incremental, and stage-appropriate manner.

Need to Feel Safe

During times of danger, the body diverts resources toward mounting a physical defense (the fight-or-flight response) or immobilization (the freeze response, also known as tonic immobility). Individuals who feel chronically under threat cannot adequately rest, digest, or restore themselves. Individuals learn from experience to predict what situations are likely to feel dangerous or safe.

Need to Move the Body

When the body moves, multiple systems are stimulated and regulated. The process of contracting and extending muscles

enhances blood flow, digestion, waste removal, mood stabiliza-
tion, cognition, and more.

Need to Seek, Pursue, and Attain

An individual's survival can depend on their ability to locate
and secure food, shelter, safety, social connections, and a mate,
so nature has provided impulses for exploring, hunting, and
gathering. The predatory sequence is one expression of this
need; both humans and dogs are natural predators.

Need to Express Their Unique Self

Individuals are constrained by their own unique combination of genetics, environment/epigenetics, early caregiving,
learning, and other circumstances. Each individual has a range
of potential that is inherently finite; their greatest opportunity
for well-being lies in an optimal early life combined with the opportunity to use and express their own unique combination of
preferences, aptitudes, and talents.

Humans and dogs have so many neurochemical pathways and
social skills in common that one scholar describes us as having
"amazingly similar social brains and minds" and "social kinship."
He almost sheepishly concludes that "anthropomorphically applying
human empathy to dogs in an educated manner may not be as inappropriate as previously thought."[44] Essentially, science now explains
what many of us instinctively felt: that approaching dogs from a
compassionate parenting perspective is actually quite reasonable.

CHAPTER 3:
The Meaning of Parenting

LET'S STEP BACK A MOMENT and consider the word "parent"—perhaps the most loaded, fraught, and comprehensive word in the dictionary. *Webster's Encyclopedic Unabridged Dictionary of the English Language* defines a parent in myriad ways: as a mother, a father, an ancestor, a protector, a guardian, and someone who contributes genetic material that enables new life. In casual conversation, most of us think of parenting as the responsibility to nourish and to protect. But the role can also involve being a mentor, a disciplinarian, a facilitator, a coach, a teacher, an advocate, and, during those early days of diapering, even a sanitation worker! Plus, there are the more emotional and fraught aspects. These include:

- taking joy in facilitating another's joy and success and gaining satisfaction from seeing a cherished one thrive and flourish;
- celebrating individuality as well as togetherness;
- weighing day-to-day options and decisions on behalf of the entire family, sometimes making difficult short-term choices on behalf of long-term goals and priorities; and

- making life-or-death decisions on behalf of a little one, such as having the final word in an emergency room.

The sheer scope of a parent's responsibilities boggles the mind. The very survival and well-being of individuals, groups, and species rest in significant measure on parenting. And how much deeper are those responsibilities when the little one struggles with special needs, early deprivation, or developmental delays? Science-based parenting can give us a framework for undertaking such challenges.

Whether we agree with these practices or not, humans routinely benefit from scientific experiments conducted on other mammalian species. Laboratory research conducted on monkeys, rats, rabbits, and yes, dogs yields knowledge that benefits humans. If we're such a good match with these other mammals, couldn't we reverse that knowledge flow?

Science has come far in understanding and helping at-risk children. Over the past few decades, experts have accumulated powerful insights into child development, trauma, neurobiology, attachment psychology, sensory development, and other fields and used them to inform evidence-based practices and interventions that benefit children and help them become their best selves. Why not harness these insights on behalf of our canine family members?

We already see this trend emerging in research and practice. Researchers are repurposing psychological instruments and studying attachment and parenting style in relation to domestic dogs. Practitioners continue to use operant-style training both with special needs children and with dogs, and many are moving beyond conventional behavioral modification toward more psychologically attuned, trauma-informed, and attachment-sensitive methods.

Interdisciplinary publications have been appearing at a breakneck pace, highlighting research into animal behavior, ethology, and welfare. While research into human–dog parallels yields limited meaningful conclusions at this point, we can still drill down to shared, core biological imperatives and benefit from that understanding.

Science-based dog parenting is not about dressing puppies in bows or staging funny scenes for social media or ruthlessly shaping dog behavior regardless of the cost to the animal. Instead, it is focused on understanding and respecting the needs of vulnerable little ones in our care and using evidence-based tools at our disposal to meet those needs while seeking mutually beneficial outcomes for the entire family and community.

Science-Based Parenting . . .
- encourages us to reconsider assumptions like "we've always done it that way" and "this was how I was raised, and I turned out okay" in light of statistically significant, meaningful research findings;
- empowers us to consider developmental needs and trauma and to seek diverse modalities for healing;
- reminds us to contemplate what drives behavior—both our dogs' behavior and our own—so that we can seek creative, win-win solutions for our lives together; and
- inspires us to approach four-legged little ones with tenderness born of informed compassion.

Seeing dogs through a parenting lens can fundamentally change the way we interact with them. Roman Gottfried of Holistic Dog Training puts it this way: "When we think of dogs as our children, we are more likely to be patient and understanding. We are also more likely to be willing to put in the time and effort to help them learn."

Adopting a Therapeutic Parenting Mindset

Some child welfare specialists use the term "therapeutic par-enting" in a very specific way.[1] They are referring to attachment-sensitive interventions designed to help children and youth who face great risk due to a history of trauma, harm, neglect, or abandon-ment. This book expands the meaning of "therapeutic parenting" to describe the totality of science-based and holistic methods and modalities available to optimize outcomes for little ones. All types of therapeutic parenting begin from these assumptions:

- if a little one could do better, they would;
- difficult behavior is an attempt to get needs met; and
- we can help the little one meet those needs more appropriately.

A therapeutic parent never says, "I'll give you something to cry about," or "I'll make you listen," or "Quit bothering me," or "I'll show you who's boss."

A therapeutic parent looks for appropriate, creative ways to solve behavioral problems. With therapeutic parenting, each interaction can become a fresh beginning, a new step in helping the little one progress toward wellness and learning.

A therapeutic parent is less concerned about "naughty" behavior and more about the vulnerability and trust placed in their care. A therapeutic parent sets aside preconceptions and evaluates situations neutrally, with curiosity, through the eyes of respect and appreciation and even love. They shift their mindset from "fixing" to "supporting."

With this mindset, the notion of obedience gets turned upside down. Parents no longer applaud or berate themselves based on how closely a little one complies to their every command or request. In-stead, a therapeutic parent views challenging behavior as a clue to the state of the little one and approaches it as a problem awaiting a solution.[2] A therapeutic parent approaches with compassion and gives little ones the benefit of the doubt.

For example, perhaps the little one was asked to do something but didn't comply. Then what? Therapeutic parents may feel frustrated inside, but instead of getting angry, they approach with curiosity and consider the following:

- What's preventing the little one from cooperating?
- Has the request been communicated in a way the little one can understand?
- Is the little one developmentally equipped to meet the request?
- Does unrecognized pain prevent them from meeting the request?
- Is the little one too distracted to focus right now?
- Is the little one too tired or stressed to cooperate?

Applying this therapeutic parenting mindset to dogs is not about excessive coddling or spoiling of "fur babies." It is about using best practices, meeting authentic needs, and empowering the little one to succeed. It is about looking deeply to find the root cause of a behavior. It is built on a recognition that behavior is affected by myriad circumstances, starting with the very setting from which a little one emerged.

Focused on Needs, Not "Naughty"

Effective therapeutic parents remind themselves to focus on little ones' underlying needs because this is the best route to supercharging and improving outcomes. When we recognize needs and respond to them in an appropriate, timely matter, we can make a world of difference. How do we pick up on needs without being told? We pause before jumping to conclusions. We watch, listen, and observe because long before babies develop the ability to express themselves through language, they communicate their needs through behavior. Dogs, too, communicate needs through behavior. Behavior—whether we label it "good" or "bad" or something in between—is an attempt to meet core needs.

reflections from the field

Justine Schuurmans of the Family Dog shares an amusing example from her own family about how managing child behavior and dog behavior can be surprisingly similar. She says:

When he was about 18 months, my son was diagnosed with reactive airway disease. He was getting scary episodes where he was struggling to breathe, and he needed to be on a nebulizer. Nebulizers are large, noisy machines with a big strap-on mask that go over the head. The first time I strapped it on him, he totally freaked out. He was terrified, crying, and having absolutely none of it.

My son was too young for me to explain to him just how urgent this treatment was. He could die without it and needed to accept the treatment. But what could I do?

Being a dog trainer, I thought, *What would I do with a dog that was petrified of something?* With a dog who was freaking out, you wouldn't put the scary thing so close, you wouldn't turn it on, and you wouldn't put it on their face to start. The scary thing would be further away, and you would gradually decrease the space when the dog felt comfortable.

So I sat my son down with a big tub of yogurt, which he loved, and took him through this tiny step by tiny step. We started with the machine turned off and far away, then brought it a little closer and closer. He got a spoonful of yogurt each step of the way. We got to the point where he would happily hold the mask up to his face for a second in return for a mouthful of yogurt.

Then my plan came to a standstill. The mask had to remain on for about ten minutes, so the yogurt wasn't going to work anymore.

I needed to change tactics. TV was a big treat when my kids were young, so I let my son watch while he was doing the nebulizer. Any time the mask was up to his face, the TV was on. As soon as he moved it off, I hit the remote and turned the TV off. Mask back on? TV back on! It was as if the mask was controlling the screen. Plus, we started calling it "doing bubbles!" My son not only accepted the treatment this way, he became comfortable and even really enjoyed doing it!

It was hilarious that I had to lean into dog training skills to help my child navigate something so tricky. But it also showed me that dogs and kids have the same needs—they need to feel safe and to go slow.

___

Whenever a child or a dog does something that seems crazy or annoying or "bad" to us, we can come back to that list of needs to feel more compassion and understand the motivation better. Dig deeply enough, and you'll see that needs and past learning play an oversized role in motivating virtually all behavior.

Puppy Hazel Through a Therapeutic Parenting Lens

If I look back at puppy Hazel from a therapeutic parenting perspective, her unruly and confusing behavior becomes more understandable.

She was born behind a gas station to a feral mother who was likely stressed and malnourished during pregnancy. The mother fled when rescue volunteers arrived, depriving Hazel of real mothering starting at around three weeks of age. As a very young pup, Hazel got transported with her litter to a shelter, then to a foster home, and finally to our house. Along the way she contracted a case of worms that caused anemia and malnutrition.

Given this start on life, it's no surprise she struggled. After the case of worms was healed and she was put on a consistently good diet, her system kicked into overdrive. I believe her reactive behavior was nothing more sinister than an explosion of internal and external growth. Sensory circuits and neurological systems were playing catch-up to more visible physical growth. (And in hindsight, I'm glad my husband let her sleep in his armpit because it gave her some of the sensory pressure and social support that she needed.)

When Hazel snapped and leaped and pawed wildly when I tried to leash her, it was easy to assume she was being intentionally defiant. After all, she already knew how to hold her bladder and relieve herself outside the house. If she was smart enough to become house-trained in a few days, then wearing a collar and walking on a leash should be a breeze too, right?

Maybe not. Consider that emptying bladder and bowels away from the den and sleeping quarters is behavior that happens naturally in dogs. Most puppies learn, and instinctively prefer, to keep their home clean. Those who resist housebreaking are likely to have an anatomical or medical problem or may have been so aggressively caged during early life that their developing brain never learned the sensory distinctions or rewards of doing their business away from their sleeping area.

The puppy training manual on my shelf had encouraged me to say, "Go potty," each time I whisked Hazel outside to relieve herself and also to praise her success. Even at weeks old she responded quickly to that technique and soon had virtually no accidents in the house. I felt like a proud parent at this accomplishment, but the credit really belonged to her. Hazel was developmentally ready to learn and genetically predisposed to become housebroken.

Graduating to collars and leashes, on the other hand, is not necessarily an easy leap and is certainly not part of instinctive, natural dog life. Collars and leashes are man-made tools and are not embedded in the canine genetic code. No mama dog is going to collar up her litter and walk the puppies by a leash around the block.

Seen from that perspective, Hazel's snapping and clawing and spasms of movement each time I tried to collar her made more sense. She was trying to figure out "What the heck is going on here?" and communicate, "Cut that out! That feels weird and unpleasant." Interestingly, just as teething puppies become nippy and "mouthy," young human children can go through a stage of biting. This is normal behavior and part of a feedback loop of sensory learning.

After Hazel's do-over, when she offered me that lick that showed her gentler side, I began to wonder if her live-wire act and tendency to put her teeth on me—what trainers call "mouthiness"—and re-activity were related to fear and sensory processing issues. Seen through a developmental lens, it made sense. The unfamiliar rub of a collar and the leash brushing against the short fur on her back, at seemingly random times, could have made her feel like she was being stung or assaulted, and she was reacting to protect herself. That meant she wasn't out to get me; my hands just happened to get in the way of her teeth. This perspective made it much easier to feel compassion and patience for her situation.

As a therapeutic parent, I could pay closer attention and notice when my actions were revving her up or calming her down. I could make development easier for Hazel by slowing down and taking things at her pace, with more of a focus on her needs.

Characteristics of a Healthy Family

Borrowing best practices of human parenting and using them with dogs feels obvious to some people: instinctive and ordinary and inevitable. But that's not true for everyone, especially those of us who had a less-than-ideal childhood and bear our own scars of early harm, loss, trauma, or deprivation.

When we invite a puppy or dog into our home, we are building a surrogate family relationship. The question is, will that relationship prove to be mutually supportive and productive, or will it feel oppressive or harmful?

Healthy families share certain characteristics. They:

- agree upon acceptable behaviors, rules, and limits;
- protect and support one another;
- appreciate the unique aptitude of each of the members; and
- balance individual needs against group needs.

Ideally, every child receives the unspoken message from their caregivers that "you are welcome here," "I am your ally and will help you stay safe," and "I will help you become the best you can be." In this environment, a little one can expect to:

- be treated with respect and tenderness;
- ask for what they need;
- have their needs met often; and
- understand what's expected of them.

PART TWO

The Science and HEARTS of Parenting

CHAPTER 4:
HEARTS Principles

WHAT'S THE IDEAL WAY to help a young child or dog grow into the best version of themselves? Experts around the world, particularly those serving at-risk, adoptive, and special-needs families, have identified science-based principles and best practices that can guide our way. A simple way to sum up their techniques and wisdom is by using the acronym HEARTS.

H = Heal the body

E = Enrich and optimize the brain

A = Appropriate environments with felt safety

R = Respectful and secure relationships

T = Teach sensitively and positively

S = Support the individual

These HEARTS elements fit together like slices of one large pie that contains multiple disciplines. Each slice overlaps and interacts synergistically with other slices. For example, without a healthy body, environments that feel safe, and respectful and secure relationships, we're unlikely to achieve an optimized brain.

HEARTS aligns neatly with research into animal welfare best practices and hands-on methods used by progressive dog professionals who consider a dog's ethological, emotional, medical, and other needs when formulating a plan for an individual puppy or dog. HEARTS mirrors or overlaps with elements of multiple child and animal welfare needs frameworks, including those from Abraham Maslow, Jaak Panksepp, and others. Chapter 6 provides more details about the parallels and alignment of various models and practices.

Remember that there is no single way to deliver HEARTS-based care. Practitioners have developed many strategies that adhere to these fundamental principles. In this book you'll hear from a variety of dog enthusiasts and professionals who use specific practices that align with HEARTS. As long as a technique aligns with these six goals and does not explicitly work against any of these goals, it is likely beneficial and unlikely to cause harm.

Let's take a brief look at the evidence behind each HEARTS slice and see how they impact kids and dogs. With this understanding, we can more easily find creative ways to deliver them to our own puppies and dogs.

HEARTS Therapeutic Parenting Principles

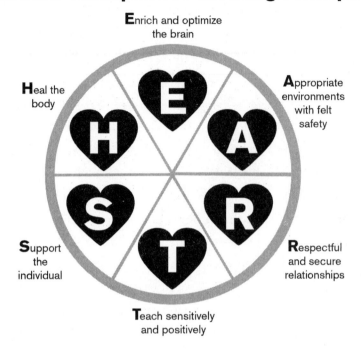

Enrich and optimize
the brain

Heal the
body

Appropriate
environments
with felt
safety

Support
the
individual

Respectful
and secure
relationships

Teach sensitively
and positively

Heal the Body

None of us would be at our best if we fell out of a tree and broke a leg or just spent hours in the bathroom with a bad reaction to food. These are extreme and obvious examples of injury or pain that reduce well-being, but less obvious and more ordinary physical issues affect behavior and welfare as well.

In simple terms, all of us—children, adults, puppies, and dogs—behave and perform better when our body is in good working order. A healthy body needs:

- timely food, water, and toileting;
- adequate sleep;
- optimal nutrition;

- treatment for medical issues; and
- freedom from pain.

Consider a toddler who is overheated from outdoor play, dehydrated, and dipping in blood sugar levels. That child is far more likely to have a tantrum than to excel in a classroom activity. Likewise, a depleted, exhausted dog may collapse or become hyperactive, growly, and reactive.[1]

Preverbal and nonverbal children have limited ways to express their bodily needs, and dogs have limited communication options too. The colicky baby screams and cries, while an uncomfortable young dog may become hyperactive, hide, snap, or growl. It's easy to notice if a dog limps or growls when touched in a certain area, but chronic conditions or lower levels of pain can also contribute to the problem.

One study found that dogs who suffered from itchy and irritated skin for more than three months behaved more aggressively, fearfully, and anxiously as compared to their healthy counterparts.[2] The dogs with skin conditions were more touch sensitive and excitable and sought more attention, perhaps because they were seeking soothing or assistance. Not surprisingly, these dogs were also less trainable. Correcting thyroid imbalances sometimes helps dogs with difficulty concentrating or that develop aggressive behaviors, while other problematic neurological behavior might reflect a tick-borne illness or encephalitis.[3-6]

Consider Hidden Pain

Pain is valuable because it signals an unmet physical need. When pain arises from an obvious cause, like a fresh wound, it's easier to identify in dogs. But less obvious underlying pain, such as pain from spinal misalignment, may require testing to identify. Consider that common training practices can contribute to muscular pain or musculoskeletal imbalance. For example, repeated practice of a heeling cue that requires the dog to continually look up and turn its head in a certain direction toward the handler may cause neck pain for some dogs. That pain may in time cause the dog to stop complying. Likewise, forcing a sitting position from breeds with an incompatible anatomy or from dogs with conditions like hip dysplasia simply adds to their discomfort and heightens the potential for cranky and uncooperative behavior. To fully support dogs, we need to consider potential pain and its myriad sources—such as arthritis, musculoskeletal imbalances, gut disturbance, illness, or inflammatory conditions—as the possible culprit behind behavioral issues.

In a special issue of the journal *Animals* called "Fundamentals of Clinical Animal Behaviour," an international group of veterinarians and researchers concluded that up to 80 percent of cases of problem behaviors in dogs can be traced back to pain. Given this high frequency, the authors conclude, "In general, it is better for veterinarians to treat suspected pain first rather than consider its significance only when the animal does not respond to behavior therapy."[7]

reflections from the field

Stephie Guy, known as the Shouty-Barky Dog Lady (UK), explains that being able to spot hidden pain has been a game changer for her dogs. She says:

> I've come to realize that pain is the single biggest cause of dogs' separation anxiety or chronic shouty-barkiness (reactivity) behaviors in the cases that I see.

Pain has often been missed because the dog can't show it in a veterinary setting where adrenaline is pumping and there's too much else going on; an "I can't see evidence of pain in this consultation" from the veterinarian turns into "my dog's not in pain" in the guardian's head; and many (possibly even most) dog trainers and behaviorists haven't been taught what to look for. Before I dove into specific courses around what proper movement looked like and how to identify pain and discomfort, I was one of them.

And as we all know, when a dog is in pain, no amount of training is going to "fix the problem."

The bottom line is that a rested, nourished, fortified body helps optimize outcomes. Healthier bodies contribute to healthier brains, which in turn improve learning and the emotional self-regulation that can reduce extreme and maladaptive behaviors.

❤ Enrich and Optimize the Brain

To support a little one's well-being, we need to pay special attention to that wondrous organ, the brain—the central control for the entire nervous system. The brain has unique potential to enhance every aspect of a little one's functioning. The ability to learn is essential to adapting to circumstances, but the brain does not work in isolation; it requires inputs and assistance from the rest of the body.[8]

Get Them Moving

Early in my career I worked in a public school system where administrators were gossiping about a new teacher. They were amazed at how well he was doing with a class of especially unruly kids—considering their previous teacher had quit in frustration.

What was the new teacher's secret? Aside from carrying himself like an elite athlete (which he was, having recently competed in the Winter Olympics), each time that a student participated well in class, the teacher invited the student to stand up, come forward, and shoot a basketball at the hoop installed along one of the class walls.

This instructor not only motivated his students with positive reinforcement, he got the students *moving their bodies*. He understood what science confirms: physical movement is among the essential pathways to enhancing and empowering the brain.[9, 10]

Movement is a brain superfood for everyone. It enhances neurogenerative and neuroprotective processes, improves learning, and helps the brain adapt to stress. Even one session of exercise delivers positive impacts that can last hours, including enhancing these brain functions:[11]

- attention,
- working memory,
- problem-solving,
- cognitive flexibility,
- decision-making, and
- inhibitory control.

The effect is heightened in the young. Cutting down on time spent sitting and increasing physical activity improves brain function, helps students perform better in subjects such as math,[12-14] improves their self-control, enables them to follow directions better,[15] and improves mental health, reducing symptoms such as anxiety.[16, 17]

Unfortunately, many little ones do not get adequate daily movement, including those who need it most, such as children with attention deficit hyperactivity disorder (ADHD).[18] The essential need for movement is why child welfare experts warn against keeping infants and toddlers strapped into hard carriers or strollers longer than necessary.[19] Growing brains need physical movement and sensory engagement with the world to develop optimally.

Dogs have a similar need for physical movement, and reduced movement is a behavioral risk factor. High impulsivity, hyperactivity, and inattention in dogs has some association with breed but research suggests it occurs most frequently in young male dogs who spend a lot of time alone at home and receive less than an hour of exercise daily. By contrast, dogs who get two or more hours of exercise a day are less likely to display these ADHD-type symptoms.[20] Low rates of daily exercise have also been linked to noise sensitivity and separation anxiety in dogs.[21] With physical movement comes better brain health for kids and dogs.

Touch Warmly and Gently During Early Life

Gentle and caring touch from the earliest days, such as cradling in a parent's arms during nursing, provides essential sensory stimulation that contributes to a child's healthy emotional balance throughout life. On a neurochemical level, this "affective touch" stimulates the release of oxytocin and opioids made by the child's own body, tones the vagal nerve, and lays the groundwork for a healthy nervous system that can self-regulate.[22]

Children raised in sterile environments, such as orphanages, suffer serious disadvantages. Without caring, affective touch in early life, children are unable to form healthy neural circuitry and instead can grow into emotionally reactive adults who struggle to form lasting emotional bonds.[23]

Puppies, too, need early touch provided by licking, grooming, and nursing to stimulate vital neurochemistry.[24] After birth, puppies receive sensory input from their mother's tongue and enjoy physical contact while nestled against her during feeding and when they are jostled by littermates. This physical contact—along with inputs from smell, taste, hearing, muscle and joint pressure, movement, and even breathing—provides sensory information that enables puppies to develop the ability to see and hear and explore the world around them.

The ideal timeframe for building neurological circuits corresponds to puppies' early life window of socialization. This period is not just about becoming habituated to specific environments; it's also about giving the sensory system the full range of inputs needed for a healthy nervous system. For puppies that will live with people, early human touch improves emotional self-regulation.

One study looked at forty-three puppies from seven litters of varying breeds.[25] Approximately half the puppies were raised in a commercial breeding kennel and the other half raised in a family atmosphere. Regardless of where they were raised, puppies that were handled gently from days three to twenty-one were significantly calmer, quieter, and more confident in exploring their environment than puppies who were not.

Stimulate Their Senses

Dogs that spend their early life in austere, kenneled settings are at a developmental disadvantage.[26] Confinement to a small, hard cage can contribute to sensory and developmental deficits, with unwelcome repercussions at any age of a dog's life.[27]

One study looked at working German shepherd police dogs in Santana do Parnaíba, Brazil. These dogs perform scent detection and guard functions for one-quarter of their time. The remaining time is spent resting inside austere concrete and mesh kennels of approximately 120 square feet, partially covered by a roof. Apart from maintenance staff and a view of the dog in the facing kennel, these dogs are entirely isolated during the rest periods. To varying degrees, they show stress by pacing, circling, spinning, or standing waiting in their kennels.[28]

These behaviors are called "stereotypies" and can be a response to the frustration and sensory deprivation of confinement. To explore ways to improve the dogs' welfare during the rest periods, the researchers compared two simple enrichment interventions. In one, the dogs remained in their kennel but received fifteen minutes of daily access to a "toy"—the same jute rag roll used during training sessions, hung about five feet off the ground. The other dogs were taken outside their kennel for fifteen minutes of daily access to a lawn area of approximately 3,800 square feet.

Despite the small sample size, researchers found the following:

- high levels of pacing, circling, and spinning dropped off noticeably while the dogs had lawn access but not while they had in-kennel toy access; and

- after more than six days of receiving enrichment, regardless of the type, all dogs showed a significant reduction in fecal stress markers.

Results suggest that all dogs can benefit from even a simple, steady diet of environmental enrichment. Particularly beneficial are sensory-rich, unstructured opportunities to sniff and explore outdoors.

Empower Self-Regulation

During early life, when the nervous system is still developing, little ones cannot self-regulate. They get easily overexcited, overstimulated, overtired, overstressed, and overwhelmed and need soothing, calming, and comforting from others to regain their equilibrium.

As they grow, they can be taught and helped to self-regulate. This essential life skill makes it possible to bounce back from adversity, gain resilience, and participate more effectively in social situations.[29-31] Self-regulation is the foundation of emotional stability and self-control.

For dogs, poorer self-control can correspond with higher levels of aggressive reactivity.[32] Greater self-control and emotional stability are desirable qualities in pet dogs and working dogs, such as those used for scent detection.[33] Expert handlers who work and compete with high-drive dogs are constantly on the alert to manage their animal's shifting level of arousal, excitement, energy, and stress and take steps to help the animal stay within an optimal range—not too high and not too low. They intentionally help a dog learn and practice escalation and de-escalation and self-control during calmer times so that this important skill is available in a crunch situation.

Typically, this involves practice in shifting between a high-energy activity and a low-energy one. For example, immediately following a high-energy agility run, Frisbee chase, or power tug, the handler asks for a quieter behavior, such as briefly lying down, weaving between the handler's legs, or selecting between two closed hands, one of which has a treat. Some handlers teach dogs a hand-touch cue[34] and use that cue as both a low-energy activity and a gauge to see how revved up the dog has become. Fine motor skills get diminished when the dog is going full throttle, and this is evident in the dog's hand touch becoming harder and more forceful. If the handler decides a dog needs more help dialing down excitement, they might quit the high-energy activity, at least temporarily, perhaps to take a simple sniffy walk away from the area or focusing instead on more advanced nose work, in which the dog hunts for a particular scented item. The added mental challenge of scent work can help flip the switch for some dogs that have difficulty switching gears.

Make Time for Natural Learning and Problem-Solving

Just as growing kids can get into mischief during their explorations, so can growing dogs, and if we don't provide appropriate outlets for their natural urge to seek and explore and interact with the world, they may discover their own ways. When a little one has freedom to interact at will with the world, perhaps playing in an unstructured way or exploring their surroundings, they are engaging in self-directed learning that builds brain circuitry.[35, 36]

We often underestimate dogs' need to use their brains. For a fun example, search social media for hidden camera videos that capture the ingenuity dogs display when left to their own devices. One enterprising hound, for example, opened a floor-level drawer, then another a little higher, and used these as steps to climb up onto the counter, finally reaching up to pull open a cabinet and nab a loaf of bread. A shrewd little Shih Tzu was caught on video dragging the foldable corner of a flexible wire mesh pen inward. Using this narrower angle, he levered and braced himself higher and higher to inch upward, then teetered along the top as well as any highwire acrobat before leaping away like a cartoon super dog. These impressive accomplishments were not trained by careful shaping, luring, and capturing of behaviors. These individual animals contemplated their own predicament and used their seeking and problem-solving capacities as nature intended.

When we empower the brain and senses, we empower the neurocircuitry that orchestrates all aspects of behavior, learning, and wellness.

reflections from the field

Michelle Stern of Pooch Parenting reminds us that even experts can overlook the power of allowing a dog to use its full faculties. She says:

> I recently worked with a client who is a veterinarian. She and her husband are expecting a child, and they wanted ideas for managing their fearful and reactive dog when family came to visit the new baby.
>
> Because this dog reacts so strongly to many triggers outside in the world, it has had a small life and doesn't get to enjoy a lot of dog things. So we talked about enrichment opportunities that were easy, safe, and wouldn't take much time. I suggested that instead of feeding the dog food from a bowl as usual, she could toss the kibble around the backyard so the dog has to hunt for the pieces to eat. It wouldn't take any extra time.
>
> So she tried scatter feeding in the backyard. It was the simplest suggestion, but she just sent me a note saying how it was so much more effective than she ever anticipated and how surprised she was. She said, "I can't believe how much of a difference that made for my dog. It was so easy. It was doable. And my dog felt better and has been less reactive." This client was really grateful,

and she's a vet. It's easy to assume that a veterinarian is an expert on everything about dogs, but not all vets have training in behavior and dog psychology. It's like asking your general practitioner to be a psychiatrist.

I was so excited that this vet was willing to try something that seemed too easy, too insignificant, to have an impact. And she did. I was so proud of her for that, and I want to celebrate these wins.

Appropriate Environments with Felt Safety

Imagine being tossed, alone and without equipment, into the deepest ocean. How would you feel? Confident or frantic?

You might know how to swim, you might even enjoy swimming, but how long would you survive in open waters without food or fresh water or protection from the elements? And what about sharks? Would you ever reach safety? Stuck in this challenging environment, every fiber of your mental and physical capacity would be strained and tested. This is an extreme example, but environment affects everyone's ability to feel safe and thrive.

Children and dogs, likewise, are impacted by their surroundings and circumstances. That's why caseworkers remove children from squalid, neglectful, and abusive living conditions and animal welfare agents confiscate dogs from similarly desperate circumstances.

Consider Resilience: Dandelions and Orchids

Children and dogs vary in their ability to adapt to their environmental circumstances. Experts use the familiar analogy of the orchid, dandelion, and violet.[37, 38] An orchid can thrive only under very specific nourishment, humidity, light, and temperature conditions. A dandelion, by contrast, blossoms and spreads easily across a broad range of locations and conditions to the point that it is often considered a weed. The violet falls somewhere in the middle, being neither as picky as the orchid nor as freewheeling as the dandelion.

Highly adaptable "dandelion" kids and dogs manage passably well under many circumstances across a variety of settings. They may not become their best selves, but they are less likely to fall into complete breakdown or collapse when faced with difficulty or hardship.

"Orchids," however, remain at risk. These highly sensitive kids and dogs have potential to blossom exquisitely but only if given the right treatment in the right environment.

For everyone—dandelions, orchids, and all points in between— the ideal and appropriate environment provides both *physical* safety and *emotional* safety.

- Physical safety is needed to protect the body from injury.
- Emotional safety is needed to enable restoration of bodily systems.

Feelings of safety tell our neurochemistry and nervous systems that it's okay to operate at optimal capacity. This is the signal to let our guard down, to rest and restore ourselves at a profound cellular level. Child welfare literature sometimes describes this condition as "felt safety," and it's integral to healing.[39]

Curating the environment is a direct way to improve a little one's well-being. By setting up an appropriate and optimal environment, we provide conditions that help a little one to thrive.

Increase Felt Safety in the Environment

Fear is not an intellectual emotion. Instead, polyvagal theory suggests that our bodies detect danger across multiple sensory levels in a process called neuroception, which is different from rational thinking.[40] During this heightened emotional and visceral reaction to danger, our brain shifts gears, and we actually lose the ability to communicate. That's why helping a little one feel safe can be an essential part of restoring their ability to think and reason.[41]

A vivid example comes from Karyn Purvis, who told me about her experience conducting a learning assessment on a little boy.[42] He was brought to the university by his adoptive mother, but at the very first test question, he shut down and could not speak or answer any questions. Rather than marking the test as failed, Karyn took a break and introduced the little boy to his environment.

He had spent years in an orphanage, and visiting this large institutional building with scary construction sounds made him frightened that he would be taken away again. Terror was hijacking this little boy's brain and preventing his compliance. Although the adults understood that this little boy was in no danger in the environment, the boy needed to grasp that for himself.

Karyn showed him how to operate the room's door and let him practice turning the key in the lock. Then she led him and his mother through the entire building, showing them where workers were banging with hammers, even allowing the boy to take a scrap nail as a souvenir. After this full introduction to the environment, they returned to the testing room. Now this little boy was able to settle and complete the testing. He had experienced "felt safety," the visceral understanding that indeed he was safe in this place with these people at this time. Then he could engage his full brain in answering the questions.

In a similar fashion, the American Society for the Prevention of Cruelty to Animals (ASPCA) has developed a protocol for helping dogs with a background of cruelty and abuse and who are extremely fearful in a shelter environment.[43] In addition to providing low-stress handling, behavioral modification, and pharmacological support that help them feel safe, these dogs are given an enriched environment that includes a rotation of toys, food puzzles, chews, and calming scents four times a day. They are housed in kennel runs that contain a portion of a plastic airline crate to hide behind. This object provides a visual barrier that allows the dog to retreat and emerge as their comfort allows. By using many HEARTS strategies, including environmental enhancements that help dogs feel safe, this intervention improves shelter dogs' quality of life and significantly reduces the need for behavioral euthanasia in severe cases.

We don't need to implement such comprehensive protocols to help most dogs. Sometimes a small change can make a huge difference.

reflections from the field

Sherry Steinlein of Paws for Success shares how one simple environmental shift can have a big impact. She says:

> I had a client with a shepherd mix rescue that was a very tense dog. I said, "Please just bring him to a big park with some trails, and on a long line of an eighteen-foot leash. Just take him for a half-hour walk and let him lead. Let him sniff and let him lead where there's not going to be other animals." They videoed it for me. They were so thrilled to see how this dog's body changed and how much this dog responded. They could see the

obvious change in this dog connecting to nature. And now science is showing how much scent work and sniffing work decompresses and relaxes dogs.

Beware of Sterile Environments

Like children raised in orphanages, dogs kenneled for extended periods risk harm from institutionalization. The chronic stress and fear they experience can become neurotoxic and damage and disrupt important biochemical processes.[44-46]

Extended physical restraint interferes with developing proprioceptive and muscular skills, and restraining puppies in tiny cages or isolating them and depriving them of sensory input can cause physical, mental, and emotional problems. Adult dogs kept penned up in small kennels for extended periods, even if they receive food and water, suffer from acute emotional and physical distress. Research shows that dogs under chronic stress have shorter telomeres, which are linked to shorter life spans.[46] Dogs kept in the following conditions have shorter telomeres:

- being used in a laboratory setting;
- kenneling overnight; and
- living with more than five animals.

Long-term kenneling—such as in animal shelters, large-scale commercial breeding establishments, experimental facilities, and training compounds—is deeply stressful and poses many risks to a dog. It contributes to hearing loss due to unsafe sound levels from constant barking,[47] compulsive behaviors from lack of enrichment, and fearfulness due to lack of positive human interactions or enrichment.[48] What's more, a dog's cognitive abilities and ability to control their own behavior are negatively affected by the kennel environment.[49] Combine a kennel environment with fear-inducing training methods (such as found in "board-and-train" facilities that use electronic collars to deliver punitive shocks), and a dog's welfare can really take a nosedive.

In chronically stressful and fear-inducing environments, children and dogs are apt to resort to self-serving, survival-driven behaviors that do not transfer well into other settings, such as domestic family life.[50, 51]

Seek the Right Fit

We can bring home a dog with the best of intentions, but our living environment may pose unforeseen challenges. Tara Stillwell discovered this when she brought home Eva, a high-performance border collie puppy, with the goal of raising her for agility competition.

"I realized pretty quickly I was in well over my head, like starting off with a Ferrari when you need a Honda," says Tara. "It was pretty hard-core." Unfortunately, at one year old, Eva suffered an injury, and a cycle of reinjuries followed. The dog's future in competitive agility was over. "That was a big adjustment in terms of expectations," says Tara. "I didn't get what I thought I was going to get."

With all the medical care, restricted movement, and rehabilitation, the dog became spooked about being handled, on top of an aversion she had developed to riding in a car. "It was the perfect storm for an already highly sensitive, high-drive dog," says Tara. "That restriction, the pain, and, frankly, a lot of trauma when Eva was quite young."

To help the young border collie, Tara learned sensitive handling practices and found a behavioral veterinarian to reduce the dog's skittishness and discomfort. She sought out low-impact activities, such as paddleboarding and hiking, that she and the dog could enjoy together.

Then, when Eva was two, another dog joined their household—a fourteen-month-old female border collie named Curri. That made a total of three dogs, including Duke, the miniature shepherd who was one when Eva arrived as a puppy. This newly expanded group seemed to work—at first—but friction developed between the two females. Periodically, their conflicts escalated into "fairly serious-looking fights, with snarling and gnashing and thrashing. It was not biting, but it was still alarming," Tara says. Both females were high-energy border collie personalities, both desperately wanting to control everything and neither dog themself being controllable.

"All six of us—me, my husband, my teenage son, and the three dogs—were intense beings in this house, all with our own stuff, and none of the three dogs were chill kind of dogs." Tara couldn't shake the feeling that if she found the right piece of the puzzle or tried harder, the problems in the home would fall away. She taught Eva cues that could give the dog reassuring distance in potentially triggering situations. The family purchased a van and transport kennel to help Eva feel more comfortable on the road. When they moved out of state, the family accepted a longer school commute to have acreage for the dogs.

In truth, Tara now sees that she was too fixated on a specific outcome, caught in the trap of trying harder, working harder. "In this culture we're taught to not quit. That caught me up into trying for too long and just extending the suffering," says Tara. "I finally started to see that none of us were feeling safe. That it really wasn't a fair, sustainable situation."

"There was so much behavior suppression going on in order for everyone to live together. We were just using discipline to hold this together—not obedience discipline, but everybody working hard to run a tight ship with all this management. Then things would fail or loosen up and we'd have a problem again. It just didn't feel sustainable."

To complicate matters, Tara's husband and the highly sensitive Eva did not communicate well. The dog's attempts at peacemaking were misunderstood and backfired. "She would present him with appeasing behaviors," says Tara. "But he didn't see them as that and would react in a way that further eroded her trust." Relationships in the home deteriorated while Tara struggled to quiet the warring parts of her brain. One side whispered that it was up to Tara to see this through and that nobody else would be willing to deal with Eva. The other side worried that rehoming could worsen the problem and become a path to euthanasia.

"It felt so confusing, so conflicting. One side said it's unfair to keep her; another said it's unfair to let her go. Heavy stuff put so much fear in my head, in my whole being," says Tara. "We get a dog primarily for us, and it's hard to not be selfish. I would picture myself letting her go and literally feel like I would die of a broken heart. How could I even survive this? We had so much fun when it was just the two of us.

"It took me a long time to really see how afraid Eva was of Curri. When one dog is aggressing, it's hard to see that they're doing it out of fear." Tara also came to recognize that "this wasn't a situation that we should be trying to make work, honestly." Finally, Tara recalled the weeks when just she, her teenage son, and Eva had stayed by themselves in a hotel room during the moving process. There, in a different environment with the ordinary stresses gone, the dog began to decompress and behaved differently.

This was the glimmer of hope Tara needed. "This was such a good indication that in a different environment Eva could be who she really is. I had seen how much love and joy she has to offer and wanted to let her have that." Tara found a couple about ninety miles away who was willing to meet and consider taking in the sensitive dog.

"Once they decided to try it, I actually went and stayed in their home with them and Eva for a few days," says Tara. "They did such a good job so quickly. They figured out how to play with her and had this philosophy of acceptance and joy for who the individual dog is and commitment to meeting her needs. I could have not curated better people for her."

Now at age five, Eva is living her best life as the solo dog in a new home. Tara visits weekly, taking the opportunity to enjoy a run with Eva and assist with her medical care. "I miss her. It's sad to not have her with me day in and day out, but it's so much easier for her. This is a great outcome—not only does it feel so supportive of her, but also of me. We're collaborating together to give Eva what she needs. There was a team involved in helping me try to make this work with her, and now I feel like there's a team in wanting her to have this best life."

The new family recently texted photos of the dog looking relaxed and comfortable in her new home. "Eva has a spot where she likes to lay upstairs, in a little bed by a floor-level window. She's lying there looking out into the backyard, and she's just happy.

"Rehoming really can be in the best interest of everyone," says Tara, who founded Glimmer Dog and now consults with families seeking help with their dogs. "By sharing this, I hope to remove some of the grief and the guilt and the shame around the process and maybe help someone not suffer quite as much as I did. I hope that people feel supported and not so alone, knowing that other people have made the decision and actually, this is a really happy story."

R Respectful and Secure Relationships

A newborn is extremely vulnerable and dependent, making the relationship with her mother or primary caregiver pivotal. This adult provides not only physical care, but the gentle rocking and caresses and mirroring back-and-forth interactions catalyze the child's developing senses and nervous system. Every interaction with an early caregiver is a learning experience about the importance of relationships, about getting needs met, and about agency in the world. This applies for children and for dogs.[52, 53]

Consider the experience of three infants, each crying because of hunger:

- the first is ignored;
- the second is met by angry shouts; and
- the third is given tender care and nurturing.

Which infant learns that the world is scary? Which one learns that the world is welcoming and loving? These infants cannot articulate it, but they have just received a life lesson in how vital social connections are to well-being and that without high-quality relationships, the world becomes a harsh and scary place.

Nurture Secure Attachment

The concept of "attachment" was introduced by British psychologist John Bowlby as a way of describing and categorizing an infant's relationship with their mother or primary caregiver.[54] This first primary attachment relationship serves as a kind of blueprint for future relationships—whether they are with other family members, friends, romantic partners, social groups, strangers, or even members of other species. Attachment falls into two main categories: insecure and secure.

Insecure

Children who are treated unpredictably, unreliably, neglectfully, or harmfully by their primary caregiver develop an insecure attachment style. Because these children lack the care and protection they crave and require, they learn to experience people as untrustworthy and the world as unsafe.

Insecurely attached children tend to behave in one of three ways, appearing either (1) anxious and clingy, (2) avoidant and remote, or (3) a conflicted combination of both those extremes. Insecurely attached children, especially those with an early history of multiple adverse experiences, are predisposed to physical, emotional, behavioral, and relational challenges throughout their lives.

Secure

Children who are treated attentively, consistently, and kindly by their primary caregiver develop a secure attachment bond. They feel confident because the caregiver acts as a safe haven and secure base from which to explore the world; when these children encounter a frightening situation, they can return to the caregiver for comfort and reassurance.

Securely attached children learn that it is safe to trust and count on other people and relationships. They benefit on a deep neurological level, enjoying more robust circuitry in the brain, improved resilience, improved emotional balance, and improved recovery from trauma.

Children learn what to expect from the world based on their first caregiving relationships.

Securely attached children go forward in life with a solid foundation, confident in the expectation that others will be responsive to their needs. Insecurely attached children go forward in life with caution or trepidation, uncertain if others will be responsive to their needs.

Psychologists gauge a young child's attachment style using a protocol known as the Ainsworth Strange Situation Procedure (SSP), in which a child interacts with a stranger. The child's reaction during separation and reunion with the parent illuminates the quality and style of the attachment relationship. SSP studies suggest that, worldwide, roughly 52 percent of all young children have a secure attachment relationship with their mother.[55]

Excess closeness	Relationship balance	Excess distance
Anxious	Confident and calm	Avoidant
Clingy/overly dependent	Capable of closeness and independence	Fearful/lonely/disengaged
Insecure attachment	*Secure attachment*	Insecure attachment

Securely attached children begin life with a clear advantage, enjoying stronger relationships and overall outcomes throughout life. By contrast, children with an insecure attachment style face long-term challenges; the more severely impacted among them grow up to become overrepresented in the criminal justice system and social services system.[56]

The early life adversity and poor-quality caregiving that contribute to insecure attachment are linked to anxiety and other negative physiological and behavioral outcomes in children and in dogs.
In dogs, early life adversity could include:

- living with an unreliable mother dog or caregiver who is
  unresponsive to the little one's needs, is slow to respond, or
  responds erratically and unpredictably;

- being deprived of sufficient and appropriate sensory stimulation and lacking exposure to a range of sights, sounds, and
  textures;

- being isolated or confined in a way that restricts their
  freedom to move, which prevents physical balance and coordination from developing appropriately;

- being deprived of gentle, nurturing physical touch and comfort during sensitive periods;

- living conditions that are neglectful, dangerous, overcrowded,
  filthy, or squalid, or being deprived of adequate food, shelter,
  or medical care;

- physical assault, harm, or injuries inflicted by a caregiver or
  companion, or by restraints or equipment. For example, a
  young dog might suffer punctures or abrasions from prong
  collars, lack of oxygen or brain damage from choke collars,
  and burns or trauma from electronic collars; and

- experiencing chronic fear following a profoundly traumatic event, exposure to violence, medical trauma, or
  abandonment.

Dogs from adverse early life environments show more fear, more
avoidance, and less affiliative engagement in shelters.[57-59] Excessive
stress during early life and punishment-based training methods contribute to poorer outcomes for dogs as well.

Nurture Secure Attachment and Relationships

Researchers have begun studying dog-to-human attachment from behavioral and cognitive angles, lately with help from functional magnetic resonance imaging, which tracks blood flow in the brain.[60] Although attachment findings can be complicated by study design, the dog's breed, temperament, age, gender, and reproductive status, along with the human caregiver's own attachment style, it's clear that a healthy relationship with a reliable caregiver builds trust and confidence in dogs. A securely attached dog is more likely to return—voluntarily—to its human caregiver and to seek that person out when it needs comfort. Dogs even sleep differently in the presence of owners to whom they are attached, consistent with the "safe haven" phenomenon.[61]

The SSP,[62] which helps reveal a child's attachment style, has been repurposed to explore how dogs react to being reunited with their human. Researchers note that dogs' interaction with their humans—upon whom they are dependent—resembles a parent-child relationship. Dog-to-dog relationships, in contrast, are more like sibling relationships.[63, 64]

High-quality relationships are therapeutic; they help improve outcomes and overcome early life relationship deficits.[65] Part of building healthy relationships is through positive body language, facial expressions, and vocal tones. Children's brain reward centers get activated when they hear their mother's voice, and a similar phenomenon occurs when securely attached dogs hear the speaking voice of a person to whom they are attached.[66] And if a dog is offered treats by someone unfamiliar, the dog is more likely to approach and accept the treat if the stranger gives a positive, friendly facial expression.[67] Similarly, a happy, upbeat, and playful higher tone of voice elicits a more positive response from dogs than neutral or harsher vocal tones.[68]

Whether we're talking about children or dogs, studies confirm that high-quality relationships increase cooperation and improve outcomes.[69–71] Gentle handling and rewards-based training can strengthen our relationships with dogs, which in turn makes dogs more willing to engage with us.[72] Through nurturing and positive relationships, we help little ones thrive and become their best self.

Encourage Two-Way Communication

Adults expect little ones to listen—most often because we want to deliver instructions or information. But we can also listen to the little ones. Through mindful, attentive listening and conversation, we become more open and receptive and able to glimpse the heart of what motivates that individual.[73] This in turn strengthens the relationship.

In a respectful and secure relationship, communication flows in two directions. Both members of the relationship have opportunities to express their needs and preferences as well as to listen to the other.[74] This dialogue improves social skills and supports wellness on multiple levels, and ideally, we engage in a similar give-and-take with dogs. Dogs "talk" to us constantly through their body language and vocalizations, such as barking, whining, growling, or squealing. However, the challenge to us human primates is to listen attentively and with attunement, as we are innately predisposed to interpret signals through the filter of our own species' types of body language and speech.

Modern dog trainers aren't limited to issuing instructions to dogs—they also engage with dogs in a nonverbal dialogue. This human-canine silent "conversation" can be fluid and informal, or it can be implicit in a specific training protocol. One such example is Leslie McDevitt's "Look at That," which purposely encourages the dog to look to the handler for reassurance and validation after the dog has noticed something of interest or concern in the environment.[75]

Dog behavior experts make a study of how dogs communicate, but some pet dogs have actually been taught to employ human language. Christina Hunger, for example, communicates with her dog using the same technology she uses as a professional speech language pathologist working with preverbal and nonverbal children. She taught her mixed breed dog, Stella, to operate paw-sized buttons that were programmed to broadcast prerecorded individual words. Stella steps on buttons to communicate to Christina, letting her know she'd like to go outside, get a drink of water, or have a belly rub and cuddle.[76]

♥T Teach Sensitively and Positively

Children and dogs learn a great deal without obvious parental intervention or formal teaching or training. They soak up a constant stream of life lessons based on natural, daily interactions. They learn about their world, how to influence outcomes, and how to get their needs met through experience.

But parents are a little one's first and most important teachers.[77] They offer a finger to hold onto when the child takes their first steps. Parents encourage and soothe when a little one stumbles or scrapes a knee, and they serve as a role model and provide a secure base to return to that empowers little ones to explore the world.

Still, to optimize outcomes, parents can take a lesson from the master teachers who encourage and motivate students by pointing out when students have done something correctly. In the field of operant training, this is called "positive reinforcement." A skillful teacher rewards the student's correct effort as well as correct outcomes. This teacher is sensitive to a student's inherent aptitudes and motivations and uses this understanding to selectively coach the individual through increasingly more advanced goals.[78]

Step-by-step, incremental "scaffolding" of lessons enables optimal wiring in a learner's brain, especially early in life. Jumping ahead with shortcuts is to be avoided, as this can undermine maximum success. For example, the toddler needs to crawl before she can properly walk or later run, just as she must first grasp a pencil in a fist and scribble before learning to use more fine motor skills and write her name.[79] Our puppy, Hazel, needed time to develop her tactile and physical senses and improve what's called "proprioception" (her body position awareness) before she could easily accept being collared and leashed or tolerate the feel of a leash randomly brushing against her back and flank.

Some specialists who work with traumatized and developmentally delayed children refer to Dr. Bruce Perry's "neurosequential model"[80] as a guide to decide at what point it is best to begin rehabilitation. This model emphasizes the need to build foundational neurological circuitry before pursuing more advanced capabilities. Skillful teachers, likewise, tailor lessons to the learner's current capacity and level, then advance through progressive stages with greater challenges. These teachers may "push" a student, but they do it with sensitivity and respect. They encourage the learner to operate within a sweet spot of stress where there's just enough challenge and difficulty in the task to heighten focus and engagement but little enough that success can be achieved and soon celebrated.

Encourage with Positive Reinforcement

"Positive trainers" typically modify animal behavior using force-free methods. Central to these is positive reinforcement. In positive reinforcement, the learner receives a pleasing reward for achieving a goal. For kids, the reward might be praise, affection, toys or stickers, treats, or other activities.[81] For dogs, the reward is often food but can be a tossed ball, a favorite game, social interaction, or physical affection.[82] "Clicker training," used with humans and animals, couples the treat with a clicking sound, and eventually the sound itself signals the reward.

Positive reinforcement can deliver wonderful outcomes, but it isn't foolproof. One challenge is pinpointing what, exactly, to reward because sometimes the learner makes the wrong association. Another challenge is timing; ideally, rewards should be given immediately after the correct behavior is performed. But there are other concerns, as well. Think about the kidnapper who uses treats to lure an unsuspecting child and you have one example of the potential downside of positive reinforcement. Another potential for misuse is when the desirable outcome is only offered for doing something repugnant.

Providing pleasing items and activities can help reduce fear when used thoughtfully. This technique is called "counterconditioning" because it couples something unpleasant with something pleasant. Counterconditioning can be highly beneficial to help dogs become less fearful, such as during fireworks or thunderstorms or in a shelter.[83-85] But optimal outcomes are only possible when we manage the learner's stress with sensitivity. A limited amount of stress can sometimes heighten performance, but chronically high levels of stress can be detrimental to long-term outcomes.

The problem occurs when dogs are asked to, in a sense, "hold their noses" and put up with the unpleasant situation to get the payoff for too long. If this happens over and over in the presence of something particularly loathsome or directly in opposition to their innate needs, the dog becomes highly conflicted, anxious, and even traumatized. The treat itself may become "poisoned." For example, a dog might deeply dislike the feel of a muzzle on whiskers and sensitive facial areas but tolerate wearing it in exchange for a tasty bit of meat. Once the dog realizes that the tasty treat leads to being trapped in a muzzle for extended periods, perhaps during which an uncomfortable medical procedure occurs, the animal could become highly conflicted and eventually reject both the treat and the muzzle.

If a sensitive animal has no choice but to tolerate a situation that they find deeply aversive—even if the reward stakes are raised to higher and higher levels to become more attractive—these triggers can "stack" and become cumulative. Then the dog develops an even more intense aversion than they started with in an unfortunate process called sensitization.[86] Dogs are particularly prone to sensitization when they aren't given enough time to recover between highly uncomfortable experiences, such as high-intensity noises or events like fireworks or explosions.

We see a parallel in the behavioral modification protocol known as Applied Behavioral Analysis (ABA). Although ABA is widely considered a standard of care for children on the autism spectrum, ABA also sparks controversy because individuals who went through these programs sometimes describe them as traumatizing, and there is discussion as to whether these methods are sensitizing and abusive, especially to lower-functioning individuals who are intentionally trained not to use self-soothing behaviors.[87] For some individuals on the autism spectrum, their innate auditory, visual, and tactile sensitivities make common ABA student–teacher interactions and "goals" deeply aversive. For example, being forced to make eye contact, which is part of certain ABA life skills curriculum, can feel like sensory punishment.[88–91]

Dogs, too, are prone to perceive eye contact as threatening or aversive. They are also nonverbal learners, with limited methods for expressing discomfort. Modern behavioral interventions are moving toward responding to the needs of individuals who are preverbal or nonverbal by giving them more control by providing mechanisms for ensuring student consent. Greater agency and choice benefit all learners, especially those who struggle. Progressive dog behavior specialists extend similar considerations, and choices, to dogs.

Take It Step-by-Step

Dog trainers talk about "splitting" tasks into tiny steps that can be taught separately and intentionally avoiding "lumping" too many steps together in a long string, which may cause a new learner frustration. Using lots of tiny steps multiplies the probability and opportunity for the dog to succeed and get praised and rewarded. This mirrors how skilled teachers work with young children.

Skillful elementary schoolteachers and positive dog trainers have a lot in common. They both:

- break things down into small steps;
- make activities inherently rewarding and fun;
- start with lessons that are guaranteed wins;
- don't overwhelm students with more information than they need;
- praise and celebrate student successes; and
- keep lessons short and focused.

Each of these strategies is applied by expert dog trainers and behaviorists who follow a positive reinforcement philosophy. Keeping a tight focus on the desired result means the learner doesn't get overloaded with more instruction or information than they need at one time. Plus, thanks to lots of wins and short lessons, the experience becomes rewarding. The dog learns to enjoy the training experience and cooperate more fully the next time.

Think of Little Ones as Learners

When we think about children and dogs as "learners," we acknowledge that each one is full of unique potential, driven by their needs, strengths, and experiences. Learners aren't empty brains waiting to be filled with knowledge. They aren't empty, static thumb drives waiting for data to be uploaded. Learners:

- are autonomous, whole beings deserving of respect;
- are dynamic participants in developing their own skills;
- thrive when they feel safe and are acknowledged for their efforts and successes; and
- benefit from well-defined and achievable goals.

Most of all, sensitive teachers are aware that learners' needs shift and change over time, and we can—and should—adjust accordingly.

reflections from the field

Andrew Hale, founder of the Dog Centred Care group on Facebook, reminds us of what's important. He says:

> It's easy to get stuck in the task-based, operant world. In the operant world I can say, "Do this, this, and this, and you should get this result." But how often have we

ended up getting a behavior that we find more appropriate, but is still not giving a dog relief? Relief for me is the most important word.

Some dogs have been damaged through a heavy emphasis on training in adolescence. These dogs are trying to tell us, "I need to have that time out. This is too much for me. I'm pulling because you put me into an environment that I can't cope with. I'm jumping up right now because I really need your support, but you're pushing me back again."

We just have to learn to be a bit more humble, to give ourselves grace enough to get it wrong and to recognize that we're all growing and all learning. Some of the most powerful pieces in the Dog Centred Care online group are written by caregivers who have gone down the "train more, train more, train more" route and then realized, *You know what? I better start listening to my dog more because this just isn't working.* They may not be professionals or academics or scientists, but they are expert carers who got that damaged dog, that traumatized dog, and found that providing a return to safety for that dog, creating safe environments, letting the dog lead the way, has really helped.

Avoid Confrontational Discipline

Teaching and training methods that physically punish provoke excess stress in the learner. This poses substantial problems for long-term welfare and outcomes. Research confirms that corporal punishment worsens children's behavior whether applied at home or at school. For example, toddlers who get hit or beaten at home are twice as likely to assault their peers in nursery school.[92] Physical punishment by caregivers provokes children to become unruly, disruptive, depressed, withdrawn, and less able to learn and perform well in school.[93-95]

Despite the science linking these practices to poor outcomes, striking, spanking, and physically punishing a child remain unfortunately common worldwide.[96] You will also find dog training professionals who still use the equivalent of corporal punishment.[97, 98] Unfortunately, punitive and harsh methods increase behavioral and mental health problems for dogs too. For example, aversive training tools that deliver a shock or "stim" not only increase reactivity and aggressiveness, they can also cause significant injuries, including burns, wounds, and even brain damage.[99] Even when administered with great care, they often teach the wrong lesson, producing unwanted fear associations and increased anxiety.

Research finds a clear connection between training methods and dog learning. Dogs who are trained with positive reinforcement and rewards are more cooperative and obedient; those trained using punishment exhibit more problematic behaviors.[100-102] Smaller dogs are particularly vulnerable, as they are more prone to increased anxiety and fear from frequent use of punishment.[103] In one research study, dogs were videotaped before and after three different types of training: rewards based, low aversive, and high aversive. Researchers found that the more aversive the training and the more harsh punishments were applied, the more the dogs became stressed, tense, and anxious, and the more they made pessimistic choices.[104] Aversive, punitive, and confrontational methods of discipline do not get better results or greater obedience; instead, they are linked to problem behaviors and further aggression.[105]

Support the Individual

Supporting the individual isn't about giving a child or a dog freedom to run the show. Supporting the individual is about equipping and empowering them to live their best life.

Consider siblings. One is a sports lover without any interest or aptitude in music. When forced to study the violin and practice for hours a day, he struggles mightily and ultimately never achieves the virtuosity that his sibling achieves easily. Pushed into an ill-fitting pathway, he misses out on exploring his athletic potential.

Then think about a young rescue dog whose family returned him to the shelter, complaining that he is too rambunctious and destructive. A new adopter takes this same dog home and spends hours giving him exercise and training. This same dog is now a cherished companion, workout buddy, and proud holder of a canine triathlete competition ribbon.

Supporting the individual starts with seeing—really seeing—a little one's unique aptitudes and tendencies and guiding them along appropriate pathways.

Love Is Not Always Enough

Those of us with a caring heart want to believe that by providing the very best of care, we can engineer any dog's future for success in the modern human world.

Excellent care is of course important—if it weren't, this book would be moot. Yet the frustrating reality is that attentive nurturing and skilled caregiving can influence an individual's outcome only so far. A loving caregiver can diligently orchestrate every possible advantage at every stage of life yet still bump up against the boundary of innate capabilities.

Two pet Labrador retrievers that live down the road from me provide the perfect illustration. Both were carefully bred by a local service dog organization, raised with all the advantages of excellent care and resources, supported by donors and an enthusiastic community of skilled foster parents and trainers. Yet one, a small black female, proved too timid and shy for service dog challenges. The other, a large yellow female, proved too reactive and protective to circulate benignly in the community. On paper, both dogs have the same pedigree as many successful service dogs. In real life, their behavior is worlds apart.

That's why dog experts advise us to consider breed traits when we are considering a puppy, but after the puppy comes home, to focus on the individual animal who may or may not conform precisely to the ideal breed profile.

reflections from the field

Expert breeder Suzanne Clothier, developer of Relationship Centered Training and CARAT Assessment, puts it this way. She says:

Genetics gives us the template for temperament, and that includes the breed tendencies. There's a reason retriever owners call up trainers and say, "Oh, my Lord, this dog, he wants to put everything in his mouth!" And the trainer says, "Yes, ma'am. You have a golden, right? And they're retrievers, right?" That's why, as a breed tendency, collies want to supervise the children and herd them. But it's not a guarantee. If genetics were enough to make sure that every dog of every breed could do the job he was bred for, life would be simple. But it's not that simple.

There is considerable difference, even in the same litter. And if you doubt that, have a family dinner and just look around the table. Nothing like a family holiday dinner to remind you that genetics is a wild, wild little soup.

We tend to forget that every dog is not the same. So we say things like dogs have great noses. Well, some dogs do. It's hard to have a recipe that works for all dogs. It's like saying, "All my friends are the same." One individual dog is not a statistic. When we talk about dogs, remember that the S at the end stands for statistics.

Children and dogs are individuals with individual needs. The richest opportunity to improve a little one's outcome is during the days, weeks, and months before and after birth. It is during the prenatal and early life periods that quality nurturing plays an oversized role in unlocking the individual's potential. Harm or deficits that occur during these early periods can lead to lifelong disadvantages. Conditions such as maternal stress or exposure to toxics during incubation in the mother's womb can spark epigenetic changes that narrow the ability to heal or fully embrace one's potential.

Once a little one grows into an adult, with mature hormonal and neurological systems in place, change and healing and growth still remain possible through the wonders of neuroplasticity, but the range of potential is narrower. Conscientious dog breeders do their best to maximize the welfare of the animals they raise with these constraints in mind.

reflections from the field

Abigail Witthauer, founder of the Roverchase Foundation, which provides specialized medical assistance service dogs, encourages us to balance the needs of dogs and of people. She says:

> When I first started building the service dog program, I was very hopeful that I could feed two birds with one seed. I wanted to find shelter dogs that didn't have homes and train them to be service dogs. Then we could meet the needs of an individual with a disability and also provide a home for a dog that didn't have one. My main thought was, *How cool would that be?* But to be really transparent, it was wildly unsuccessful.
>
> We were able to look at adolescent dogs between six and nine months old and evaluate their temperaments and their current presenting health. We would do hip x-rays and cardiac exams, eye exams, things like that, and identify a candidate at that moment in time that was likely to be successful. But we were really unsuccessful with predicting long-term health and longevity. We ended up changing dogs late in the process after we had made a huge financial investment from our donors because we couldn't predict health because we didn't have multigenerational data.
>
> I do think it's important to note that the largest and most successful service dog organizations in the country, and in the world as a whole, produce the Big Three on purpose—meaning Labrador retrievers, golden retrievers, standard poodles, and mixes of the

three. There is a reason that those dogs are selected, and there's a reason that they have a higher rate of success. There are unicorns in other breeds—I know a working service husky that is truly a dream. But statistically we're looking at long-term waitlists for service dogs, and we need to be responsible with funding. We want to move everything in our favor, and this is what we found has been successful.

I love golden retrievers because my ideal service dog personality has two main features. First, their attitude is, "When in doubt, take a nap." And second, if they're doing something and you say, "Hey, how about you do this thing instead?" Their reaction is, "That sounds like a great idea! Let's do that!" They have very little original thought and very little drive for tasks outside of community tasks with their handler.

That was a huge piece for me as I started to really evaluate what we're asking these dogs to do and the quality of life it provides for that dog. Those two qualities in temperament and personality produce a much higher quality of life for the dog doing the work.

HEARTS Work Better Together

Using multiple slices of the HEARTS pie at the same time can make wonderful results possible.

I was first introduced to this phenomenon at the Hope Connection therapeutic day camp at Texas Christian University, where children struggled with behavioral challenges and developmental issues such as limited speech, motor skills deficits, and stunted growth.[106]

During each day of camp, the children were gently guided through a regular schedule of nurturing play, sensory games, rest, snacks, and interactions intended to promote secure relationships and a feeling of safety. After several days of this routine, parents remarked on unexpected improvements in their child's behavior and well-being at home, even physical growth spurts. Children were able to focus better and learn more easily, making dramatic advances in language ability. These improvements correlated with reduced stress levels, as measured by salivary cortisol tests, and were welcome side effects that flowed spontaneously from optimizing body, brain, environment, and relationships.

A multimodal full HEARTS approach is able to yield results that are greater than the sum of the parts. Together, multiple interventions tap into healing synergies that are unavailable using a single approach alone, whether for children or for dogs.[107-112]

parenting pearl

Too often, parents and experts look at behavioral disorders as if they existed separate from sensory impairments, separate from attention difficulties, separate from early childhood deprivation, neurological damage, attachment disorders, posttraumatic stress, and so on. We take a more holistic approach, because we know from a wealth of scientific research that a baby's neurological, physical, behavioral, and relational skills all develop and emerge together.

—The Connected Child[113]

When body, mind, and senses are supported at the same time, the healing is integrated and optimized spontaneously, often making it possible for a little one to make leaps in learning without direct or explicit step-by-step teaching or visible guidance.

Holistic and Progressive Dog Handling

Dog professionals whose work is HEARTS friendly have a deep knowledge of canine body language, are attentive and responsive to the individual animal, and are open to a team approach. They recognize the value of staying current with the latest research and collaborating with other professionals who could offer additional insights, including medical knowledge.

Notice also that in the HEARTS pie, teaching (or "training") is just one slice and not the entire solution. In fact, we often discover that by adequately addressing multiple HEARTS slices, less explicit teaching or training is actually required.

reflections from the field

Victoria Stilwell, founder of the Victoria Stilwell Academy for Dog Training & Behavior and host of the television program It's Me *or the* Dog, *shares an example of how a holistic, HEARTS-friendly approach can lead to amazing transformations. She says:*

> I met Marley the cockapoo for a recent episode of *It's Me or the Dog*. Marley didn't sleep well, and he kept turning his head around to stare at nothing. Worse, he humped his person nonstop.
>
> Marley had a caring, dedicated guardian. She took him to the park every morning to throw the Frisbee, then brought him home before dropping him at doggie daycare later. But the whole time they were at the park, Marley humped her, and he humped her constantly at home. This was the worst case of leg humping I've ever seen. This dog did not stop.

An old-style dog trainer would have assumed that Marley wanted to dominate her or to have sex with her and done everything possible to stop it. A more positive trainer might have taught an alternative behavior to humping. But I wanted to discover the true reason behind this behavior. Humping is a symptom. Don't just teach the dog not to hump, find out why he's humping.

After spending the day with them, I could see that Marley was trying to tell his guardian, "I'm so uncomfortable."

Marley's humping was saying, "I don't want you to throw that Frisbee again and again and again. I do not want to be here, surrounded by other dogs that I do not feel comfortable with. I do not want to play Frisbee in this place. I do not want to continually go and fetch this toy. And when I'm at home, it's too busy and I just need relief. I'm not sleeping at night because I don't feel comfortable. Please stop."

I suggested she take Marley for a walk in the woods instead of going to the park. No other dogs around, just Marley on a long line with him sniffing at his own pace in the woods. He'd never had the chance to do that before. I also suggested limiting doggie daycare to small groups, and finally, I encouraged her to visit the vet for imaging of Marley's right hip because he kept turning his head sharply in that direction as if something was bothering him.

This lovely guardian followed all my suggestions. She brought Marley to the woods so he could enjoy a new kind of enrichment. She cut down on busy environments with loads of other people and dogs. And she brought him to a veterinarian, where Marley was diagnosed with hip dysplasia, a painful condition, and prescribed medication to make him more comfortable.

In a few weeks, the change with that dog was profound. He was able to sleep through the night and he stopped humping altogether—and I had never actually taught him to stop humping. I just found the cause and, by addressing the root of the behavior, I was able to stop it. Marley was finally being listened to and his needs understood.

Marley and his guardian enjoy a better relationship than ever. She wrote to tell me, "He's sleeping through the night. He's not humping me anymore. It's a miracle."

CHAPTER 5:
Parenting Styles

SCIENTISTS HAVE DEVELOPED a useful and easy way to analyze different styles of parenting. They look at how the parent interacts with the child based on two dimensions: responsiveness and demandingness. Alternatively, these two dimensions can be thought of as nurture versus structure.

Responsiveness describes how sensitively and warmly the parent attends to and meets the little one's individual needs, preferences, and requests. Responsiveness includes providing affection and nurturing of all types, meeting needs, and accommodating the little one's wishes.

Demandingness describes how strictly and restrictively the parent sets and enforces rules and limits for the little one. This includes, for example, how much the parent structures and controls the little one's time and activities and how precisely they expect the little one to behave according to the parent's guidelines.[1]

Researchers chart these two dimensions on a graph, as shown on the next page. One axis represents the parent's level of responsiveness, ranging from low to high. The second axis reflects the parent's level of demandingness, from low to high.

The graph is divided into four quadrants to arrive at four basic parenting styles. Each style offers certain benefits to the child and to the parent.[2] But one parenting style, Authoritative, provides the most optimal long-term outcomes whether we're raising children or dogs. This style—which features higher levels of responsiveness and higher levels of demandingness—aligns with a HEARTS approach.[3-7]

We don't need to be perfect or consistently provide 100 percent responsiveness and demandingness to help children or dogs flourish. But understanding the pros and cons of the four styles will help us think through our parenting choices and the implications of care we deliver. As an added bonus, recognizing the parenting style employed by dog professionals can help us better predict the long-term impact their training and handling methods are likely to have on our dog's well-being. So let's look at each of the four in turn.

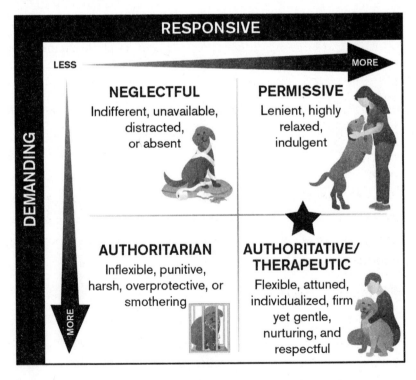

Neglectful

A neglectful parent shows little responsiveness to the child's needs and sets few demands on the child. A neglectful parent communicates these messages to the little one:

- you don't matter to me;
- I'm too busy to help you; and
- don't bother me.

The neglectful parent doesn't ask much and doesn't give much. They are essentially uninvolved and do not exert themselves for the child. This type of parent is not sufficiently physically or emotionally present to guide a little one to good choices or guide them away from dangers. This parent might ignore or forget their child, perhaps leaving them to wander unattended without food or adequate clothing. This style is associated with juvenile delinquency and depression in children.

In similar fashion, a neglectful dog parent might leave their dog unattended and without water, shade, food, or access to toileting for extended periods. Extreme examples of this style are animal hoarders and breeding operations that ignore animal welfare concerns. The animals are left to fend for themselves, even if they have no means of accessing the basics needed for survival, and in extreme situations they may perish in place.

The main benefit of this style is to the parent, who may be distracted with their own concerns or who may be unavailable for caregiving because of employment, substance abuse, or other competing priorities.

Authoritarian

The authoritarian parent pays little attention to the child's own wishes and insists on strict rules and dominates the child. An authoritarian parent communicates to the little one that:

- I know best, always;
- you're here to please me; and
- I don't care what you want; do it my way.

The authoritarian parent is most likely of all parenting styles to use aggression or violence to enforce their will. This parent will often correct unwanted behaviors in an aggressive manner, perhaps by shouting, slapping, or kicking.

On the surface, the authoritarian style may appear effective because it can produce short-term compliance, but it leads to significant long-term disadvantages because heavy punishment and harsh discipline are counterproductive to developing trusting and nurturing relationships, positive emotions, or voluntary cooperation.

Children raised in an authoritarian household develop unhealthy, chronic stress and suboptimum learning. And because they have been raised with little consideration of their individual needs and wishes, these children can become so frustrated and resentful that they act out and behave disruptively whenever they are away from the strict parent. Their ability to take care of themselves, become self-reliant, and develop social and academic competence suffers.

Authoritarian-style dog trainers prize immediate obedience above all. They use methods that provoke pain (known as "positive punishment" in a Skinnerian operant terminology), such as yanking on a dog's neck. They are also apt to use potentially injurious training tools such as prong collars and electronic collars, which have been linked to physical injury, chronic stress, reactivity, and reduced learning and performance on cognitive tasks.[8–10] In a crisis situation, when following commands becomes essential, this parenting style may achieve short-term goals, but consistent punishment poses serious long-term risks. Dogs raised this way have increased reactivity, anxiety, and aggression.[11, 12]

Permissive

The permissive parent is exceedingly responsive to a child's requests yet doesn't demand much. Their sensitivity and indulgence benefit the child up to a point, but the lack of guidance or boundaries can ultimately deprive the child of certain important skills.

A permissive parent communicates these messages to the little one:

- I'm here to make your life easier; and
- whatever you want is fine with me.

Permissive parents are not typically neglectful of a little one's physical welfare but are lenient and readily give in to requests, indulging their children without restraint. These little ones are likely to receive freedoms beyond their developmental ability to handle them and do not get important practice in respecting boundaries or self-restraint.[13] These children are likely to misbehave in school and engage in substance abuse.

Likewise, dogs that are raised permissively could feel free to snatch food off guests' plates, urinate throughout the house, or engage in other poor manners. One study shows that permissive parents are less likely to limit dog treats, making this parenting style linked to canine obesity.[14]

Permissiveness can reflect a parent's limited bandwidth and preference for the convenience this approach offers or their preference to avoid potential conflict around setting rules and limits.

Authoritative (Therapeutic)

The authoritative (not to be confused with authoritarian, which sounds similar) parent is highly responsive and also highly demanding. This parent combines kind nurturing with the predict-ability and structure of clear limits.

An authoritative parent communicates these messages to the little one:

- I'm here to help you become your best self; and
- let's figure out what you need to develop and thrive.

The benefits to a child raised this way are multiple: more secure relationships and attachment style, greater ability to learn and re-main emotionally balanced, and greater confidence and resilience. The authoritative parent likewise gains greater cooperation from the child and the satisfaction of seeing the little one blossom. The drawback is that this style of parenting can demand extra time and effort. And as the little one grows older, the parent needs to adjust and modify the specifics of their interaction to align with the child's developmental capacities and abilities.

The authoritative parent is sensitively attuned to a child's in-dividual needs, offering conscientious physical care with warm affection and clear guidance. This parent is willing to negotiate in re-sponse to a child's preferences, even while maintaining a position of authority in the family. Authoritative parents offer age-appropriate challenges, lots of positive encouragement, and consistent bound-aries. Discipline is limited and rarely punitive; instead, appropriate consequences may be allowed to play out.

This balance of parental control and parental warmth improve a child's behavioral and psychological adjustment.[15] Children raised with an authoritative parenting style are best positioned to make the most of their potential and to develop trust in other people as well as themselves. This parenting style is HEARTS friendly and beneficial for achieving therapeutic goals with at-risk children.

Similarly, dogs raised with an authoritative pet parenting style are treated with kindness, fairness, and expectations suited to their species.[16] They receive force-free physical and verbal cues that make it clear what is expected of them. They are encouraged to channel their canine aptitudes in appropriate ways and are not treated roughly for failing in a task or taking a misstep. They are guided humanely, with respect, according to their abilities, and nurtured without smothering or excessively intrusive handling. These dogs receive appropriate learning opportunities, sensory challenges to keep their brain active, and suitable physical care. Cooperation is rewarded, and unwelcome behavior is redirected in safe and gentle ways. Even when these dogs display behaviors labeled as "bad," they get handled and guided with respect and sensitivity.

Accordingly, this style is linked to better outcomes with dogs, including improved social behavior, learning, and other dimensions of dog welfare.[17] Raised in this manner, regardless of the animal's inherent aptitudes or challenges, this dog is empowered to grow into the most relaxed, confident, competent, and socially skilled version of itself. The Authoritative style is most likely to optimize a little one's well-being and cognitive development and is most aligned with HEARTS.

Looking at Our Own History

When I was twelve, my family adopted a docile little Shetland sheepdog from the local shelter. As the eldest child, it was my job to help walk and feed him. The dog was generally ignored by my father, except for one night, when the family returned from a holiday event to find our front door ajar and the house burglarized. My father grabbed a knife from the kitchen and stalked room to room, checking for intruders. Convinced the coast was clear, he turned to the dog.

"What good are you?" he bellowed, then kicked the dog square in the ribs.

That was my childhood. At any time and without warning, Dad could fly into a purple-faced rage that sent us whimpering to the corner. The blows we received were verbal but still landed in the gut.

When you think of "parent," what comes to mind for you? Do you think of someone who fed and cradled you? Someone who smiled and laughed when you smiled and laughed? Someone who soothed you in times of trouble? When we care for little ones, it's easiest to mimic what we saw and experienced with our own parents. If we rarely received the gifts of kindness or patience, we may struggle to offer those gifts to others. If we were discouraged from expressing needs in a healthy, direct fashion, or got punished for doing so, we are likely to have difficulty honoring the needs and requests of others.

Any adverse childhood experiences—such as neglect, loss, or witnessing or experiencing violence—can actually influence brain chemistry. Our early life traumas leave profound fingerprints and can interfere with our own emotional and cognitive responses. Even our mother's microbiome prior to pregnancy can influence our well-being. Our physiological systems, neurological circuits, and socio-emotional functioning can be preset at a deep level. This sets up a difficult cycle to break as reactive neurochemistry gets passed down from generation to generation.

No matter where we go and what we do, we bring along our "buttons" and "baggage." They reveal themselves in our relationships, including with dogs. Kim Brophey, applied ethologist and creator of the L.E.G.S. Model and Family Dog Mediation, observes that "Our dogs are our canaries in the coal mine. They are our indicator species. They show us, with one comfortable degree of separation, our own predicament."

Breaking Harmful Cycles

Perhaps you were lucky enough to have been raised by two well-adjusted and skilled parents.

Or maybe you weren't.

Until discovering the fields of child development and attachment research while helping write *The Connected Child*, I avoided examining my own formative years. Of course, I knew we tiptoed around my father's thunderous moods and threats of abandonment and that my mother wore mascara to remind her not to cry. But we had food to eat, clothes to wear, an education, a stable address, and periods of calm, so I figured we were okay.

Yet years later, with an out-of-control puppy, I turned to my father's example. Lashing out at little Hazel wasn't justified and it wasn't effective, but it was familiar. Seeing the puppy's distress woke me up and reminded me that I aspire to do better—I just needed to learn how.

Parenting style is communicated by words, and it is conveyed through body language, choices, actions, and inaction—often unconsciously. When you imagine your own parents' hands, what do you see? Can you describe them?

- Are those hands hanging limply to the side, negligent and uninvolved?
- Are the hands balled up into fists, demanding obedience?
- Are they outstretched, offering you anything your heart desires?

- Or are those hands loosely cradling—offering stable support and guidance when needed, yet enough space so you can explore the world safely at your own pace?

Do any of these gestures feel familiar? Can you identify which parenting style quadrant you were raised in?

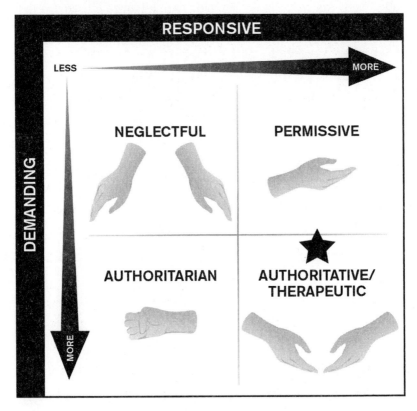

Harmful cycles take different shapes for each of us. They can lurk below the surface of our consciousness until a crisis demands we pay closer attention. If we can learn to interrupt these cycles before they escalate, we will be able to respond more thoughtfully to challenging situations.[18-20]

reflections from the field

Roman Gottfried of Holistic Dog Training shares his own experience of how trauma can impact our relationship with dogs. He says:

When I came to dog training, I had no clue that I had problems. As a child, I thought my parents got divorced because of me, that my mother didn't want me because I was a bad child, that my father sent me to live with my grandparents because he had to make money and that I was the problem in the family. And of course my grandparents put me in a Catholic boarding home with priests because that's what you do, right? And, of course, the priests would take advantage of me and become a little bit handsy. And of course, I couldn't talk about it because otherwise I wouldn't get home for Christmas and holidays.

After boarding school, my father sent me to engineering school, and I asked, "What is engineering?" And he's like "You'll see." Of course, I wasn't the best student there; I had no clue. And, of course, mathematics was a problem because I had trauma ADD.

At some point, I started becoming angry and frustrated. I started wearing leather jackets and roaming around with other guys. I thought it was cool to have tough friends. They had guns, they stole stuff, and I could be part of it. I could be part of a little community stealing stuff. Even stealing things from school until one day somebody knocked at the door and said, "You guys, up to the department."

That was my wakeup call that I was going in the wrong direction. Eventually, a friend says, "Hey, man, you have serious shit karma here." And I'm like, "My stuff is normal. I'm fine." "No, you're not." And back and forth, back and forth, until he says, "I'm giving you a name and a phone number, and you're going to talk to this person."

So I borrowed money and went to that person's workshop. All these nine people in there were so messed up. And I'm like, *Oh, my God, how are these people alive? How can these people actually function?* And then it was my turn. And everybody says, "Oh, my God, how can you survive? How can you function?" I recognized there was so much wrong that I wasn't aware of because I thought it was standard.

After that workshop, I started seeing patterns. I thought about the dog who just left the shelter and he's in a new home. That was like me when I left my mother and went to my first stepmother. I had no clue who she was. I called her "Mother" and she got offended. I was three years old. That mother was holding me out over the third-floor balcony by my T-shirt, trying to punish my father for going to work, and I thought that was normal. Like, we put the dog in the crate, close the crate while the dog is crying from separation anxiety, and we think that's the normal thing to do.

I started seeing all those patterns of my own trauma in the experience of dogs. The dog being moved from home to home and never feeling safe. He's always afraid, pretending to be sleeping but never does. The dog getting punished like I got punished when I made the mistake of playing in a pot of whitewash asbestos, like I pooped in the wrong place at the wrong time.

As a dog trainer, when I started, I was an aversive trainer. Not happy about it now, but that's all I knew: if a dog was wrong, it had to get punished. No questions asked. My philosophy was, "You'll figure it out. If you get punished enough, you figure it out yourself. You're smart, you should know better." Where was this thinking coming from, other than my own trauma brain?

When I got my first bite injury and the second bite injury and made a list of money that I paid for medical care—$16,000 there, $13,000 here—with serious injuries, I was like, *Maybe I'm doing something wrong.*

Why did the dog attack me? Isn't he supposed to love me? Dogs shouldn't have to be forced to love me because I'm giving them a home, I'm taking them out of the shelter. Many trainers are taught to use aversive tools; I did it because I saved the dog from the shelter. Like my father thought he was doing the right thing; he saved me from my mother. He put me somewhere else. Everything is justified one way or the other. I justified my actions based on my trauma brain.

We come to think abusive reactions are normal. We re-create our childhood of abusive, authoritarian parenting onto the dog because that's the only thing we know. I'm not a psychologist, but I have the feeling this is how it usually works. We just do what was done to us because we don't know anything better.

When I discovered Linda Michaels's hierarchy of dog needs based on Abraham Maslow's hierarchy of needs for people, I thought, *That makes sense.* Like meeting the foster dog's basic needs and my basic needs as a stepson, and if our emotional needs are never met, what problems that can cause.

We have knowledge about working with nonverbal children, and we have whole systems in place to help them communicate, right? Ways to help them understand and learn through their own experience. But thinking about dogs like children doesn't fit the concept, right? Because people are people and dogs are dogs, and we say the word "parenting" and people freak out. They say the dog is not a child. The dog is a dog, like a dog is something derogatory. What would you call a child who is not verbal? Is it not a child? What do you say about a species that has the same social structure? The same emotional needs, the same feeling—what would you call that? If dogs have emotional experiences just like children, why can't we help them just like we might help children?

CHAPTER 6:
HEARTS and Parenting Styles to Guide Us

BEFORE DIVING DEEPER into best practices of parenting and dog handling, let's step back and consider words and labels. It's important to remember that simple, common words can cause confusion when we navigate the human and canine divide.

For example, the word "correction" can have a dramatically different meaning depending on who is using it. In modern, positive parenting, a correction is typically gentle feedback that helps the child achieve a goal more appropriately. "Correction" is like coaching; it is not a slap upside the head or a whipping with a belt. Hurting or terrifying a child is no longer considered appropriate "correction."

But in the dog world, older meanings and newer meanings get mixed up. Some handlers "correct" a dog in a nonaggressive, gentle way. But the majority of professional dog trainers who talk about "corrections" are using a code word for physical punishment. They "correct" unwanted behavior by inflicting some level of pain or injury. To them, corrections can include a forceful yank on the neck, a knee to the chest, a repugnant spray, or an electric shock.

"Balance" is another term with wildly different meanings. For struggling children, a "balance of nurture and structure" is a science-supported, optimal therapeutic approach. This means treating children with equal parts nurture (warm and affectionate caregiving) and structure (rules, boundaries, and limits). In this context, discipline is not about physical punishment, it is about setting expectations and boundaries—gently and firmly. Structure is calm, consistent, and centered guidance that teaches appropriate social skills and manners. Balanced forms of positive parenting and similar best practices do *not* include physical discipline and punishment.

However, in the dog world, "balanced training" can and often does include physical discipline and punishment. Trainers who describe themselves as "balanced" are willing to use physical punishment methods, including devices and methods that cause pain, fear, physical injury, and potentially trauma.

reflections from the field

Justine Schuurmans of the Family Dog and developer of the Dial Method gives an example of how the aftermath of physical punishment can be heartbreaking. She says:

> A client of mine has two young children, one with special needs. Her family felt a dog would be good for the kids, but because they were short on time and energy, she decided to send the dog off for seven weeks of training at a board and training place.
>
> She thought this would help her get ahead of the game. She wanted to do it right. She wanted the dog to be well socialized with children and well behaved. She had a list of all these goals, she spent a ton of money,

and the dog came back after seven weeks completely traumatized, scared of everything. No socialization around children and almost no skills. This client had a horrendous experience, and now she's trying to unpick what has already been stitched into her very young dog's life so early on. That just crushes me. I mean, how did she get in this position? With so much misinformation floating around social media, people with the best of intentions get led down the wrong track.

What's more, different schools of dog training talk about the same exact tool using different words. For example, "shock collar" is the phrase employed by handlers who favor positive reinforcement methods while "electronic collar" is the phrase employed by handlers who use positive punishment methods. But they are both talking about the same device.[1]

A Framework for Making Evidence-Based Decisions for Our Dogs

We can use HEARTS and parenting styles as a framework that makes dog-rearing decisions easier and clearer. Here's an example. Let's say we are deciding whether to use pinch collars, prong collars, or electronic "e-collars" to train our dog.

First, we ask, "Does this choice work for or against each HEARTS goal?"

- **H—Heal the body**
  Metal pinch, prong, and choke collars were designed to squeeze and poke the throat. They restrict air flow and can easily injure delicate tissues around the throat and windpipe. Electronic e-collars are designed to administer a jolting

electric shock; additionally, the electrodes that deliver the shock can cause burns and skin lesions.[2] Conclusion: These collars harm the body, not heal.

- **E—Engage and optimize the brain**
  Surprise and fear caused by feeling choked or injured increases neurochemical stress reactions. Over time, chronic stress can impede learning and even permanently damage the brain.[3] In documented worst-case scenarios, choke and prong collars can cut off oxygen and contribute to neck injuries, either of which may result in permanent brain damage.[4] Conclusion: These collars work against brain health.

- **A—Appropriate environments with felt safety**
  Some e-collars deliver a warning beep or buzz, but that often serves to heighten fear, not reduce it. Treatment with an electronic collar has been documented to cause some dogs to tremble and panic at every smartphone buzz and ring.[5] When regular physical punishment can be delivered at any time, the environment feels unpredictable and unsafe. Conclusion: These collars work against this goal because they reduce felt safety.

- **R—Respectful and secure relationships**
  The more physical punishment is applied, the more trust fades and relationships deteriorate. Respect is not mutual if one member of the relationship can freely injure the other member of the relationship. Conclusion: These collars diminish feelings of security and trust.

- **T—Teach sensitively and positively**
  Devices such as electronic collars are exceedingly difficult to use with sensitivity and precision; the handler must have

split-second timing. Even in best-case scenarios, the learner easily and frequently learns the wrong lesson. Inflicting-then-removing-pain and rewarding-by-not-hurting meet the definition of abuse, not appropriate rewards-based, positive teaching. Conclusion: This equipment does not support sensitive and positive reinforcement, reward-based teaching.

- **S—Support the individual**
  Aversive tools and techniques that create traumatic fear associations are not supportive of the specific needs of high-strung breeds or dogs with backgrounds of harm, deprivation, medical issues, or other considerations. Conclusion: This equipment can interfere with specific individual needs.

Based on this analysis of HEARTS, we can conclude that these types of collars are not advised. This type of equipment would be counterproductive to HEARTS goals.

Next, consider these same collars by analyzing their parenting style. Look at each dimension of parenting individually.

- **Level of Responsiveness: How much does this choice nurture the little one and respond to their preferences, needs, and feelings?** This type of equipment is intentionally designed to cause pain, fear, and discomfort. These types of collars are not nurturing or responsive to the dog's emotional experience and preferences. Conclusion: These collars rank low on responsiveness.

- **Level of Demandingness: How much does this choice prioritize and enforce our rules and demands?** These tools were designed specifically to enforce rules and demands and to restrict behavior. These collars prioritize structure. Conclusion: These collars rank high on demandingness.

The combination of low responsiveness and high demanding-ness identifies this choice as Authoritarian. Authoritarian parenting is characterized by coercion, bullying, rigid expectations, and harsh punishment for noncompliance. Authoritarian parenting methods can produce short-term compliance by causing fear or harm. However, the more frequently that such harsh methods are used, the more they become abusive, heightening risk of physical and emotional injury, stress, and trauma. For dogs, as with children, a pattern of authoritarian parenting is likely to cause depressive behavior or progress to complete rebellion and even aggression. That is why an Authoritarian parenting style is associated with poorer long-term outcomes for dogs, including increased reactivity and aggressive behavior.[6-9]

Based on a parenting style analysis, these types of collars are not advisable, particularly because alternative equipment and positive reinforcement methods are available that provide equal or better compliance outcomes.[10, 11]

Identifying HEARTS-Friendly Practices and Practitioners

To get a sense of how to identify HEARTS-friendly practices across the parenting and dog training spheres, check the following table. Keep in mind that labels and buzzwords are just a starting point. Actual hands-on practice and style of implementation can vary widely. The professional dog world is not regulated, so when you consider labels, marketing, social media content, a program, or practitioners, look closely at what's actually being done.

⚠️ **CAUTION:** *It's tragically easy to find high-profile influencers and trainers promoting outdated and fundamentally cruel methods. One such influencer, for example, posts social media content and demonstrations that are widely shared, yet elicited a warning statement from the American College of Veterinary Behaviorists.*[12]

CHILDREN	DOGS
Supportive Practices ⟷	**Supportive Practices**
• Positive parenting	• Positive training
• Sensitive or responsive parenting	• Relationship-based training
• Gentle parenting	• Gentle parenting of dogs
• Trust-Based Relational Intervention (TBRI)	• Relationship Centered Training (RCT)
• Developmental Trauma and Attachment Program (DTAP)	• Animal Centred Education (ACE)
• Attachment and Biobehavioral Catch-up (ABC)	• Family Dog Mediation (FDM)
• Child-centered programs	• Holistic dog training
• Trauma-informed care	• Bond-based teaching
• Attachment-informed care	• Dog-centered care
• Affective touch	• Trauma-informed care
• Theraplay	• Attachment-informed care
• Ayres Sensory Integration (ASI)	• Low-stress animal handling
• Feldenkrais Method Awareness Through Movement	• Force-free training
• Anat Baniel Method NeuroMovement	• Canine sensory enrichment
• Intensive, Interactive, and Individual (3i) intervention	• Tellington TTouch (Tellington-Jones)
	• The Play Way (Cook)
	• Slow Thinking Is Lifesaving for Dogs (Donaldson)
	• ACE Free Work (Fisher)
	• Fear Free dog handling (Becker)
Supportive Models ⟷	**Supportive Models**
• Affective Neuroscience (Panksepp)	• Affective Neuroscience (Panksepp)
• Neurosequential Model of Therapeutics (Perry)	• Five Domains Model
• Hierarchy of Needs (Maslow)	• L.E.G.S. Applied Ethology (Brophey)
	• Harmony Model (Stilwell)
	• Hierarchy of Dogs' Needs (Michaels; Griffin et al.)

The wonderful news is that once we start digging into specific details of parenting and dog training, we find that a growing number of progressive dog professionals already employ parenting-compatible best practices.

They may not toss around terms like "parenting" or "mammalian attachment biology" or "trauma" or "developmental needs," but underneath, their core practices are essentially parallel. These professionals provide individualized nurturing, sensitive teaching, consistent limits, and a trusting relationship while addressing a dog's full range of welfare needs.

reflections from the field

Victoria Stilwell, founder of the Victoria Stilwell Academy for Dog Training & Behavior, describes how progressive dog training keeps pace with current science and today's lifestyles. She says:

> Positive trainers don't talk about "commands." We might talk about cues, but what I really want to teach the dog are life skills. We focus on flexible, simple life skills like "settle" and "touch."
>
> Settle, for example, is different from down. I don't teach down anymore because a down cue puts dogs into a rigid, vulnerable position where they don't feel comfortable. Settle gives the dog more choice and comfort about their physical position and has a reassuring emotional aspect.
>
> If I brought a dog to an outdoor café to "settle," I would make a safe space there so she can feel protected. I'm going to bring her favorite towel or small rug, and I'm going to give her an enrichment toy, like a chew, so

she's got something to do while I'm talking to my friend and drinking coffee. And I'm going to teach her that it's okay to settle there.

We try to move our students beyond the old, task-oriented idea of training. Instead of piling commands and cues and tasks on dogs—so the dog has to do this, do that, sit or stay or give a paw—we want to take the pressure off and make it an environment where the dog feels safe.

Today, progressive dog professionals talk about much more than using positive reinforcement to teach specific tasks. We talk about understanding a dog's needs, about enrichment, about giving choices, about attachment, about offering a sense of autonomy and empowerment. And yes, these are all things that people do with children.

Throughout the rest of this book, we'll explore specific practices that translate from the parenting realm to our dogs, then follow up with real-life case studies.

PART THREE

HEARTS-Friendly Practices

CHAPTER 7:
Consider Their Developmental Stage

IN THE BEST-CASE SCENARIO, all newborns—whether human or canine—emerge from a safe and nourishing womb to be welcomed by an adult who shelters, feeds, nurtures, and protects them.

Parental care and behavior have an oversized influence during early life, especially sensitive periods, when the growing brain requires specific inputs to develop optimally.[1] If all goes well, the brain develops properly. A secure attachment bond develops and brain chemistry is enhanced, providing a solid foundation for the child's development over the coming years.

At birth, the part of our nervous system that is responsible for calming us is immature. Experiences of stress that cause babies to be fussy require external calming until the child's own nervous system reaches greater maturity. Puppies follow a similar trajectory. They are born with eyes and ears shut, very much at the mercy of their environment. They rely on their mother, not just for milk, but also for the tongue bath that stimulates digestion and elimination. Later, as the litter interacts, the puppies get more sensory input and teach one another social skills, like how to play and inhibit their bite.

Puppies have a much better start on life if they remain with their mother and their littermates until eight to twelve weeks of age. Those early weeks with their family are critical for building social and developmental skills. Dog breeding operations that prioritize profit will instead remove puppies from their mother and siblings before the puppies are developmentally ready to leave.[2, 3] If the little one misses out on a critical stage of early life or faces trauma, they are at a disadvantage that can impair them for a lifetime.

reflections from the field

Suzanne Clothier, who has raised eleven generations of German shepherds and created the Enriched Puppy Protocol (EPP) used by guide dog organizations, service dog schools, and private breeders to maximize puppies' potential prior to eight weeks, shares some thoughts on the wonder of canine development. She says:

> The first eight weeks of early puppyhood is such a critical stage of development, and I hope in the years to come it gets a whole lot more notice about how critical this is. Because a nine-week-old puppy is roughly the equivalent, neurologically speaking and developmentally speaking, to a four-year-old human. Can you imagine having a baby and someone says, "Well, here's the baby, Mrs. Smith, and we'll be back in sixty-three days? By then he should be able to run and play and carry things, learn some games, toilet himself, feed himself. And oh, yeah, he's not going to be able to hear until

he's at least three weeks old. And his vision will be a little fuzzy most of that time but carry on." That's what happens to puppies. It's astonishing.

Welcome to the World, Little One

Conscientious breeders work hard to provide a warm and supportive welcome into the world for their litters. Hélène Marie Lawler of Kynic Stockdogs, for example, takes great care to give her puppies every genetic, relational, educational, and environmental advantage possible.

"My dogs are my family, so when I breed them, I am very involved from the get-go," says Lawler. She purposefully selects parent dogs that were raised in a positive reinforcement environment, believing this can impact the next generation, and ensures that both parents are in prime health.

She does her best to give the mother dog a low-stress, happy pregnancy. "For example, when I bred Raven, my main working dog on the farm, she got to continue her job," says Lawler. "I didn't ask her to do anything that could endanger her or be too hard as she went through her pregnancy, but working just brings her so much joy. She would have been more stressed if I had stopped her."

When a litter is due, Lawler moves out of her own bedroom and into her farm's guest area, where the whelping pen is kept, to stay close to the puppies. She covers the whelping pen to keep it dark, like a den.

"I'm lucky to have a breed that has very natural and strong mothering instincts and that whelp easily," she says. "This is not true for

all breeds and all dogs." Her border collies have never required a
Caesarean section, for example, unlike bulldogs, French bulldogs,
and Boston terriers, which require Caesareans in up to 80 percent
of births—a result of intentional breeding for oversized anatomical
proportions that make puppies' passage through the birth canal
problematic.[4]

"My job is to support the mother, and she takes care of the babies," says Lawler. "When they're first born, they're being licked and
kind of tossed around anyway, so I will put them on a little flat scale
for three seconds to get a weight and put them right back. That just
gives me a baseline."

Other than regular weighing, she isn't very hands-on during that
first week. She chooses not to use the early neurological stimulation
(ENS) protocol developed by the military, which starts at three days
old.[5] It involves briefly holding the puppy upside down, pinching a
toe, and placing the puppy on a cold, wet cloth. The idea is to purposely stress the young animal before returning it to its mother in
the hopes of promoting resilience.

"Maybe we consider these minor stressors, but I don't think that
the puppies find them particularly minor," Lawler says of the ENS
protocol. "That may work for some breeds, but I do not like it for
border collies. They would not experience this at this age in nature
unless there was some kind of an adverse event or an attack. I think
it was traumatizing them, and I quickly put an end to that practice."

When one of the border collie puppies is stressed, it squeaks,
cries, or screams and paddles fast, much like a distressed human infant.[6] "If I see very stressy behavior in a puppy, then I won't handle
that puppy a lot initially," she says. Lawler wants to give her puppies as much choice and agency as she reasonably can while keeping

everybody safe, even at this early age. "I found that if I just ease off a little bit, then that goes away. I let the puppies tell me. If the puppy says, 'Put me down,' and is obviously emotional about it, I'm certainly not going to push through that."

Instead of using a stress protocol, Lawler will gather up various items—a piece of cinnamon bark or herbs from the kitchen or a small stick or sheep's wool from the farm—for the puppies to sniff. This sensory experience is possible even when the puppies can't yet see or hear.

"I hold something in front of their nose. And it's fascinating. You can see them sniff. The puppies get very curious. Even some of the fussy puppies will immediately stop and orient their head toward it. I like to think it builds a more positive emotional response, and they get a new, interesting experience. Reactions vary throughout the litter about who likes what. It's really kind of fun. I first heard about it for dogs that are being trained for scent work."

When the puppies start crawling around, into the third week or so, she may briefly put textured items into the whelping pen, such as foil that crinkles under their feet when they go by, as an additional brief sensory exposure.

She is mindful about their early associations. "I try to make my touch very positive," she says, "because they are making associations and imprinting. I don't want them to associate my scent and my touch with something fearful. I think the puppies understand a whole lot more than we give them credit for at that age. Some people will take off dew claws and crop tails without anesthetic at that age because the puppies don't seem to show a response. But I believe they still do feel it, and the last thing I want is that association of my human scent and handling with pain, so I don't do any of that."

Around week three, if the weather permits, she begins to move the pups outside. She brings a blanket or mat from the whelping pen into the yard and invites the mother there for the puppies to nurse. That transitions the litter smoothly to the outdoors.

"I like them on natural surfaces because once they start moving around a lot, it's good for their joints. I have an organic farm, so they get all the good bacteria exposure while they're on grass." As the puppies grow and their vision improves, they start to become more active. Lawler will open the gate and give them the choice to follow her out into the farmyard.

Sixty acres await, complete with chickens, ducks, sheep, goats, and other dogs to visit. The puppies set the pace for when and how much they explore and leave the den. By week five, they might follow Lawler around the farm while she does chores. "Some will follow me right away while others will turn back to the puppy yard and stay there. I let them decide what they want to do."

Even short road trips are not rushed. Lawler says, "If I see puppies that are afraid to follow me out of the gate at five weeks of age, I know they're not ready to be put in the car and taken to PetSmart."

What about the protocols that recommend taking a puppy out to meet one hundred people in one hundred days or similar?

"That may work for some puppies, but I don't feel like it works for my puppies," says Lawler. "The working border collie was evolved to work for a single person on the side of a mountain with a bunch of sheep, not to be walking around downtown in a big city. They're just not naturally comfortable in those settings. Perhaps some are, but mine are all strictly working lines. These are not dogs who are naturally comfortable being social. Their default is to ignore other people and other dogs."

She is particularly attuned to the mental health of her specific breed. With high-performance border collie puppies, she says, "I worry about setting an overstimulated nervous system. My focus is to keep them stimulated and always experiencing new things, but at their own pace, so they're never in fight-or-flight mode. If they do get startled, they always have that secure base to go back to."

Developing at Their Own Pace

Development progresses on different timelines for different breeds and individuals. For example, Welsh terriers develop play behaviors later in puppyhood than do vizslas and standard poodles.[7]

By four or five weeks of age, puppies' sharp little teeth become so uncomfortable for the mother that it triggers weaning. Those sharp little teeth will continue to test everything and everyone for months—that's normal. Even so, we can still teach respectful house rules. This doesn't have to be confrontational or harsh. For example, if a puppy chews on her hands, trainer Sarah Whitehead lets her hands go limp to make them less exciting and redirects the little one to a more appropriate target.[8]

Early life is the perfect time for us to instill good habits while staying sensitive to a little one's developmental level, abilities, and needs. Teaching manners early is an investment in the puppy's safety and our own. Otherwise, that monster-sized adolescent dog could think grabbing your arm is fun because it's a way to keep you engaged with them, and when you flail around and try to scold, that seems like part of the game.

Soon enough, puppies grow into adolescents with all that that implies. Hormones kick in and they become bigger, stronger, and

more physically mature. They seek more independence, test boundaries, yet still need a safe base to return to for comfort and stability.[9]

We can enjoy playing with young dogs and laugh at their bold-
ness and at the same time set gentle, firm, consistent boundaries to
send them on the right path.

reflections from the field

*Jodie Forbes of Crazelpup, in the UK, reminds us to keep forgiveness
in our hearts, remembering that little ones are blasting off into a new,
exciting world that often befuddles them. She says:*

> As you spend more time with dogs, experience dif-
> ferent personalities and immerse yourself into their
> lives, it becomes easier and easier to understand what
> they're saying. But to somebody less experienced, a
> growl can only mean one thing: aggression.
>
> As I'm writing this, at 11 PM, Willow is growling at
> me. Her intentions aren't malicious; she's trying to get
> my attention. She's agitated, grouchy, and very, very
> sleepy. She thinks she's bored, she's fighting off sleep
> by squeaking her toys and rolling around the bed, but
> I know she's just overtired. She may be a year old, but
> she's still a baby.
>
> Sure enough, a minute later, she's curled up and fast
> asleep.
>
> Willow, feeling all antsy and full of sleep, doesn't
> need to be told who the boss is. She's a toddler on the
> brink of a tantrum, growling, "But I don't *want* to go
> to bed!" Meeting that grouchiness with aggression on
> my end will only end up in a full-blown palaver. I'm the

grown-up; I know better than to tell her off, pin her to the ground, or prod her in the ribs and hiss "tssh" at her. I'm the grown-up, she's the baby, so I need to cultivate a condition where she's more likely to succumb to her tiredness and go to sleep.

So I let her get all her grouchiness out. I let her squeak her toys and dig the bed in protest, offering her some calming strokes and a gentle "shh, night-night." Babies fight sleep. It's what they do. You can either be the grown-up and encourage them to relax, or you can "challenge" the baby in front of you until they're so pumped up on adrenaline and fear that sleep is no longer in the cards.

Willow growled because she was cross at being tired, not because she was mad at me. It wasn't personal, just a baby doing what babies do. This isn't to say that puppies cannot develop behavioral problems, and it certainly isn't to say that we should ignore all growls and grumbles, but sometimes it's just a baby being a baby.

CHAPTER 8:
Practice Attunement

CAN YOU IMAGINE RAISING A BABY without ever using diapers? Most of us in the West can't, but some cultures are so attuned to their infants that they never even diaper them. They sense when babies are about to evacuate and respond in the moment.[1,2]

This level of attunement in parenting requires great observation and visceral attention to small details. Attunement is a byproduct of noticing and sensing, moment to moment, what is truly happening. We can intentionally practice attunement by attending closely to nonverbal signs in others and ourselves.

Like babies who are not yet potty trained, dogs communicate their needs without verbal language. To become more attuned to a dog, we start by noticing their body position. Are they standing proud or hunched? How fast are they breathing? Where is their attention focused? And what about ourselves? What is our tone of voice? Nervous and quiet? Sharp and loud?[3-8]

By cultivating attunement and expanding our ability to notice, we can respond to a little one's needs more effectively and prevent problems from escalating. But that isn't always simple, especially when there's a species divide.

Who Has the Attunement Advantage?

Domesticated dogs have evolved to read us surprisingly well. They spot emotion in our body language and on our face, recognizing the difference between happy, neutral, angry, and even disgust, and can adjust their behavior accordingly.[9-11]

Wild wolves, even those raised near people, don't have the same repertoire of interspecies communication skills as domestic dogs. They won't turn to people for help solving a difficult problem-solving task, unlike dogs, who often do.[12] And if a wolf stares at you, you are likely to feel a prickle of concern shiver up your spine because canid species mostly use eye contact to signal threat.

When a domestic dog makes eye contact with you, you might feel that prickly shiver, depending on the hardness of their gaze and their intent. But there are a significant number of domestic dogs who, when they're feeling friendly and relaxed, use eye contact to communicate requests. They might use eye contact to request a walk, to play a game, or to remind us to that it's time to open the treat pantry and hand over the goods!

Raised and housed in close proximity to us, pet dogs become experts at reading us. They pick up on our emotions and respond accordingly.[13, 14] We, unfortunately, are less skilled at picking up and understanding their gestures. We often jump to conclusions based on how humans communicate. For example, when you look at another human to gauge their emotion, where do you look first? Research suggests that people visually scan another's face in a certain sequence, starting with eyes and mouth.

Have you ever scanned another person's face for ear movement?[10]

Well, you would if you were a dog. If we want to interpret dog emotions like dogs do, we need to pay a lot more attention to ear positions. Next, glance at the forehead and mouth.

Our ability to interpret dogs' messages—their invitations, pleas, and warnings—is actually rather hit-or-miss. This shouldn't be that much of a surprise considering how differently humans and dogs are constructed, even though we're both mammals. When it comes to interspecies communication, our underlying primate-canid divide leads to more miscues than we realize.

Humans use two limbs for walking and running and reserve our two other limbs, which conveniently end in long, flexible fingers with opposable thumbs, for other activities. Our compact jaws are helpful for chewing food but not for killing prey. Dogs have four limbs for walking and running, and each of those limbs ends in a stump-like foot with minimal flexibility. Their large, protruding jaws are effective for catching and killing prey.

These anatomical variations make dogs and people wonderful teammates because we bring complementary capabilities to the partnership, but these differences also likely contribute to miscommunication in body language.[15] For example, when reading others' intent, people tend to focus on head and facial expressions; dogs focus more on the body.[16]

Most of us see bared teeth from a dog as a threat of aggression. But how many of us recognize that sometimes a dog with lips pulled back to reveal teeth is actually waving the white flag of peace? This benign lip curling is what canine behaviorists refer to as a submissive grin[17]—a sign of deference and attempt at appeasement. There have been unfortunate dogs who actually faced euthanasia due to human misunderstanding of this gesture.

And think about what we consider a kiss. Like many primates, we extend puckered lips for an affectionate kiss. Dogs are more likely to pucker up when feeling ill or experiencing something distasteful.

To interpret canine licking, often assumed to be a kiss, we practically need a dictionary and thesaurus full of options. Dogs lick to pick up odors, to groom, to signal that they mean no harm and ward off aggression, and to release nervousness, among other things. Some appeasement licking (in response to human requests for "kisses," for example) can be done so begrudgingly that it veers into passive aggression with the dog's tongue darting out so hard and fast that it's almost like a strike.

Then there is the dog's tail, which has no direct human correlation and acts much like a semaphore flag. Gestures performed with the tail are messages best read in context. (Hint: a wagging tail is not always friendly.) And we may be surprised to discover that other behaviors that seem aggressive to us, such as growling or snapping, can have a peacemaking purpose. They serve as carefully calibrated warning messages designed to prevent real physical violence with all its attendant risks.[18]

These are signs that your dog is feeling relaxed around you:

- the dog approaches you voluntarily, without invitation, and presses up against your leg or body;
- the dog sleeps or lounges in varied contortions with legs poking up in the air in seemingly random directions; and
- the dog's movements are wiggly and fluid, and their facial muscles and bodies are loose and relaxed.

Tuning In

For most of us, reading the emotions and behavior of another, whether it's the fears and needs of children or dogs, takes practice.

Therapeutic parents cultivate and nurture that special talent and apply it daily to recognizing subtle signs of the moods and patterns of behavior in a child or dog in their care.

If you are a natural observer, you have a head start, but everyone can expand their observational skills and become skillful at picking up subtle aspects of behavior. Become alert to sights and sounds. Become alert to reactions—watch ear movement, lip movement, tongue movement, and tail movement. Watch for posture rigidity or looseness. Become alert to patterns as well as unique variations.

You'll particularly want to notice fine distinctions in body posture, muscular tension, and sequences of behaviors. Remember that dogs express themselves according to their own species. Sometimes innate human behavior will overlap and align neatly with dogs'; other times it will not.

A person might cheer and hoot in excitement while a dog might whine eagerly or bark in high, excited tones. Actual barking combined with wagging can be a sign of frustration and an attempt to communicate.[19] Dogs may also redirect frustration or anxiety through displacement behaviors such as looking away or sniffing their environment; this is similar to us checking the time or our phone when we're getting antsy or uncomfortable.[20]

To deliver effective HEARTS-based care to a dog, we need the ability to tune in and read their emotional reaction in real time. According to one small study,[21] people do a pretty good job of spotting happiness in dogs. But they're not nearly as good as picking up dogs' fear, and they're downright terrible at recognizing frustration in dogs. Here's the breakdown.

People accurately identified . . .	On other people's faces, approximately __ of the time	In dogs, approximately __ of the time
Happiness	95%	93%
Fear	84%	41%
Frustration	21%	2%
Neutral	58%	42%
Positive anticipation	9%	22%

Because we're less familiar with dogs' signs of fear and frustration, we can miss the signals that how we're touching and handling them is perceived as unpleasant. Petting and holding a dog around the head, for example, is not as welcome as we assume.[22] Think of how a child feels when a distant relative squeezes their cheek or slaps them on the head in greeting, and you'll get an idea.

Notice Fear

You might be surprised to learn that children who appear to be sitting quietly are sometimes experiencing extreme distress; their immobility is a sign of a paralyzing fear reaction. Child welfare specialists are attuned to these subtle signs of trauma. They note the rigid posture, rapidly beating heart, and unnaturally focused eyes, which can all signal a serious fear reaction.

Dogs can also show dissociative signs when deeply nervous, becoming immobile and seemingly unresponsive. We can become adept at noticing signs like this, along with other subtle signs of stress in dogs. For example, have you ever spent time in a crowded dog shelter? The first time I ventured behind the scenes as a shelter volunteer, I was thrown by a pungent, acrid odor in the air. It permeated every kennel and hallway. The shelter was well tended and cleaned daily, but by the time I returned home, I couldn't wait to sprint for the shower and change my clothing. That bitter, musky smell remained stubbornly lodged inside my nasal cavities even hours later.

That funky odor is a tip-off that a dog is feeling deeply upset. During moments of panic, their glands can release a powerful musk. No wonder many boarding kennels and veterinary offices burn cloyingly scented candles—they vainly hope to mask the telltale smell.[23]

How well do you recognize stress or fear in your dog? For example, can you identify which of these behaviors can indicate that a dog is feeling worried or scared to some degree?

Dogs that are worried or scared may	YES	NO
Pant	O	O
Shed excessively	O	O
Snore	O	O
Bark	O	O
Bite	O	O
Lick their lips	O	O
Tremble	O	O
Turn their head away	O	O
Hide	O	O
Lower tail between legs	O	O
Spin in circles	O	O
Pee	O	O

How many of these behaviors did you check off with a yes? How many with no? Here's how 114 dog owners responded to that question via my own informal online survey:[24]

Worried or scared dogs may
(114 responses)

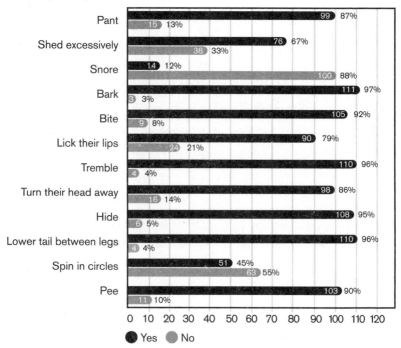

Would it surprise you to learn that only one entry on this list merits a no answer? That's snoring. Depending on the context, all the other behaviors listed can signal a spectrum of distress from discomfort and anxiety to fear and panic.

Unless you've made a study of dog behavior, it's easy to overlook the more subtle signs that a dog is worried and fearful. Perhaps you recognized that a tail between the legs means a dog is afraid, but were you surprised to learn that stressed-out dogs may shed hair in copious quantities, spin in circles, or pant excessively?

I think back to the day I met Bernie, our current rescue—a short-legged, long-bodied, silky-haired, thirty-pound mixed breed—at the shelter. His tongue was hanging to the ground, and he was panting. The weather was on the warm side, so I assumed he was thirsty. But when we offered him a bowl of water, the dog declined. The problem, I understood later, was not heat, but fear.

Externalizing and Internalizing: Opposite Sides of the Same Coin

When stressed or terrified, some children and dogs will freeze or seem to shut down while others lash out or flee. How can we make sense of these seemingly contradictory ways of expressing fear and distress?

Experts have a useful way of talking about these seeming discrepancies in children's behavior. They talk about "externalizing" and "internalizing." An externalizing child shows emotions in visible, overt behaviors. They may show anger, rage, aggression, and antisocial behaviors such as kicking, screaming, hitting, or flailing.

Children who are internalizing are much quieter. On close inspection they may appear withdrawn, dissociated, sad, or depressed. They keep stress bottled up inside, even when experiencing raised blood pressure or a spike in stress hormones that is not obvious to the casual observer.[25, 26]

In very much the same way, dogs and puppies can reveal their discomfort and fear in seemingly contradictory ways.[27] We see this in dog rescue and shelter settings where some dogs become hyperreactive at the sight of visitors. Others shrink and look away, curl into themselves to appear small, and try desperately not to engage with visitors. At times dogs even alternate between these reactions.

EXTERNALIZING   **INTERNALIZING**

Is an externalizing animal innately more confident or potentially aggressive than an internalizing one? There is no clear rule. Sometimes animals that "act out" are innately more confident than those that "act in," but not always. A reactive, externalizing dog may actually be dramatically more fearful and feel desperate to protect themselves. This can be especially true of toy breeds, such as Chihuahuas, who live in a world full of what look like giants compared to their tiny stature. They may bark incessantly and lash out in warning. A typically mild-mannered dog, who appears to be an internalizer, might also suddenly strike out with a snappy warning when his personal boundary gets crossed.

Body language and behaviors correspond to a dog's emotional state, from relaxed to increasing levels of stress and fear all the way up to crisis mode.[28] As fear heightens or becomes chronic, the stakes increase. Depending on circumstances, a dog's fear reaction can become externalized and escalate all the way up to dangerous bites that break skin.

Both externalizing and internalizing are common in children and dogs with backgrounds of harm or neglect. Fear and distress exist along a continuum, as shown in the table "Is Your Dog Getting Stressed Out?"

Is Your Dog Getting Stressed Out?

POSITIVE ◄———— NEUTRAL ————————————————► NEGATIVE

Comfortable and relaxed	Becoming stressed/ uncomfortable	Increasing stress/fear	Fear/ panic	Extreme stress/ crisis mode
• Leaning toward or against your body	• Yawning	INTERNALIZING		
	• Blinking	• Tail tucked under	• Trembling[A]	• Freezing
• Initiating touch	• Tongue flicks	• Pawing or seeking attention/ assistance	• Pee accident[A]	• Dissociation
	• Licking own nose		• Lying on back stiffly, feet in air	
• Relaxed posture	• Offering placating lick			
• Loose, fluid movements	• Heavy panting (not heat related)	• Displacement behaviors[B]	• Pancaking	
• Settling calmly nearby	• Turning head away	• Excessive shedding[A]	• Cowering	
	• Lifting paw	• Dander kicking up[A]	• Body odor/anal glands release[A]	
• Relaxed wiggling	• Avoiding contact			
• Engaging in friendly play	• Purposely focusing elsewhere	EXTERNALIZING*		
• Playful growl	• Pawing or seeking attention/ assistance	• Ears flattened back	• Hard stare	• Biting
• Head down/ haunches up ("play bow")	• Displacement behaviors[B]	• Barking to alert/warn	• Menacing growl	• Attacking
	• Tightening facial expression	• Snarling	• Air snapping[A]	• Fleeing
• Certain wags (e.g., relaxed tail swung below horizon of back), but not all wags	• Whites of eye extra visible ("whale eye")	• Moving away	• Lunging	

A– This behavior sometimes has an unrelated medical cause
B– Examples: chewing paw, humping, snapping at tail, seeking a toy to chew, pacing
* This is different from the predatory sequence (searching, orienting, stalking, chasing, catching, killing, carrying, dissecting, and eating)

parenting pearl

Chronic fear is like a schoolyard bully that scares children into behaving poorly. Parents might easily confuse fear-based outbursts with willful disobedience, but they are not the same thing at all.

—*The Connected Child*[26]

A calm and comfortable dog has a loose posture and relaxed muscles and willingly approaches. But just like a nervous child may bite their fingernails or cling to a favorite toy, dogs also have subtle ways to express fear and anxiety. Depending on the situation, they may lick their lips, pant, slink away, get their own toy, lose control of their bodily functions, or give other clues that reveal their discomfort, fear, anxiety, or distress.

These behaviors can be subtle and fleeting, as when a nervous dog turns its head away from a perceived stressor and licks its lips. But when a dog feels it cannot escape from a serious stressor, it may develop repetitive or compulsive behaviors.

Attunement helps us distinguish the reason behind a given behavior. For example, a dog might chew its tail for any number of reasons. It might want to groom or relieve a fleeting itch, it might feel irritated by a pervasive food or environmental allergy, or it might be displacing frustration related to isolation, boredom, fear, or confinement until the tail becomes raw, red, and weepy.

Animal behaviorists and zookeepers call the most profound and seemingly dysfunctional repetitive behaviors "stereotypies." When taken to the extreme, these behaviors may signal "zoochosis," a profound mental imbalance that is caused by institutionalization or captivity with poor attention to the animal's welfare. An animal's repetitive, compulsive behaviors are akin to the continual hair pulling and rocking sometimes seen in deeply traumatized children or the learned helplessness of children raised in an environment where the caregivers are unresponsive to their needs.

Looking and Listening

Dog training can be used as an opportunity for building reciprocal attunement with a dog. We begin by learning to give cues and rewards. Some dog training classes even include exercises that prompt us to "imagine you are a dog."[29] Seeing the world through our dog's eyes by getting down to their level and experiencing sounds, smells, and movements from that perspective is invaluable.

The more attuned we become to our dog's experience, motivations, and symptoms of distress, the sooner and more effectively we can take steps to improve their well-being. Easing distress before it becomes full-blown panic or misery goes far toward earning a little one's trust, improving their comfort, and building a relationship.

It's tantalizingly easy to describe a dog's behavior in terms of the problem it poses to our human lifestyle. But simple labels can distract us from taking the time to probe and identify what's behind a behavior. Rushing to assign labels, judgments, or an alphabet soup of medical jargon can limit our attunement and sometimes prevent us from seeing the true, bigger picture.

reflections from the field

Victoria Stilwell of the Victoria Stilwell Academy for Dog Training &
Behavior reminds us to approach with an open mind. She says:

Humans label behavior all the time. We use labels like stubborn, guilty, aggressive. Labels are very suited to our human perspective.

But when it comes to dogs, I tell my students, there's no "bad" behavior—it's just behavior. We label behavior "bad" when it's something we don't want and "good" when it's a behavior we do want, but it's important to value "bad" behavior as much as "good" behavior because that is how a dog is feeling whether you like how those emotions are being expressed or not.

To understand a dog, you have to literally look at what you're seeing right in front of you. What's the head doing? What are the ears doing? What is the body doing? What is the tail doing? What's the environment around this dog? This dog is responding emotionally to a situation and to its learned experience. Dogs are communicating all the time; we just need to listen.

Let's say our dog is barking. Instead of fixating on getting them to stop, we could consider what the dog is trying to communicate. A bark could carry a variety of messages:

- This is so exciting!
- I can't wait to see my friend!
- Stop right there!
- Danger! Danger!
- Look at me!
- Hello, is anyone there?
- Come on, I'm waiting!
- Where's my dinner?

Just as attentive parents learn to recognize when their young one's cry means serious distress, we can get a sense of the message behind our dog's sounds through pitch, intensity, and frequency. A crisp, clipped staccato bark can mean something very different from a melodic, crooning bark. Researchers describe three types of barking: disturbance alert, isolation distress, and play.[30, 31]

Disturbance alert—These barks are loud, urgent, repetitive, and full force. They can occur in long clusters that are harsh and low in tone, with less modulation and less harmonic nuance than other types of barking (similar to, "Hey, you, what's going on there?" or "Look sharp! Check this out!" or "Stop right there! I said stop!").

Isolation distress—These barks can occur with longer pauses between sounds and with greater tonal variety (similar to us calling "Hello?" Pause. "Anybody there?").

Play—These barks vary in tones, tending to be higher and more harmonically nuanced than disturbance alerts.

Those of us who live with dogs might propose another category of dog vocalizations called "delight." At times, these happy sounds can be urgent, as in "Let's get to the park, quick!" and "I can't wait to start!" Our dog Bernie produces a tenor yodel, often on returning from a great walk. When he is overjoyed to reunite with someone, he makes a whiny squeal (as in "Oh, boy, oh, boy, oh, boy! I'm so happy you're here!" accompanied by overwrought wiggling).

Admittedly, barking can be inconvenient to us humans. At the same time, suppressing or punishing barking penalizes the dog for attempting to communicate. It's like slapping a child who is crying from fear and saying, "I'll give you something to cry about." If we're attuned to a dog's bark, sometimes the best response is simple reassurance: "Yes, I see that; that's okay."

Dismissing a behavior as "being stupid" or "bad" can blind us to important information. Punishing growling, for example, is similar to removing the yellow light at an intersection. Without the yellow light, the red light occurs without warning, leaving no time to avoid a collision. If we can't hear polite warnings like growls, dogs may raise their voices and "shout" by biting.

Attunement Is Dynamic and Daily

Bernie and I are returning home after a walk through our quiet, shady neighborhood. I stop in front of the garage, and he stops too. I loosen his martingale collar and he wriggles out, flapping his ears side to side with a quick shake. He trots into the garage, but instead of staying with me, he veers to the right toward a side door. He looks back at me to make eye contact, purposefully glancing toward the side door and back at me again. I shake my head and quietly say, "Not now." In response, he abandons the effort and trots after me into the house.

This simple interaction is an example of nonverbal attunement, a behavioral volley and response. I invited him to have his collar and leash removed; he agreed. He asked for extra playtime in the grassy yard adjacent to the house; I declined. Bernie understands that sometimes I accommodate his requests but not always. Besides, good things also happen inside the house—so he can still look forward to the possibility of bits of food falling unexpectedly from the counter.

Here, in this familiar setting, Bernie is attuned to me and I to him. He cooperates willingly. We are both calm and relaxed.

Attunement is a dynamic biochemical process, a shared, subconscious responsiveness to each other and the environment. Research shows that between parents and children, attunement happens at an unconscious level. It involves the hypothalamic-pituitary-adrenal axis, which regulates cortisol, a key stress hormone, plus other aspects of central nervous system functioning. Attunement is so important that many parenting interventions teach attunement to improve the parent–child relationship. Teenagers, too, benefit from greater parental attunement, engaging in fewer risky behaviors as a result.[32, 33]

Now that we've lived together for a few years, I've become attuned to Bernie's reactions and needs. I try to create win-win situations so his needs are met appropriately for our household. Bernie has blossomed, but due to a combination of innate genetics and previous trauma, he remains a sensitive guy who struggles in certain situations.

Right before Bernie joined us at age two, he had been surrendered to a rural shelter from the only home he'd ever known, transported to a distant rescue, surgically neutered, and put up for adoption. By the time he landed in our living room, he was a trembling, nervous wreck, healing from surgery, battling violent stomach upset, and struggling to understand his new surroundings.

It was months before tension fully left his face. At home with us, years later, he is an effervescent, enthusiastic family member. He eagerly jumps into the car for an adventure, but at the vet's office, he becomes so desperate and pants so violently that calming medication barely makes a difference. Practicing attunement means I try to support Bernie as his needs shift. Tossing a small, savory treat on the ground for him to nose around and find when we're walking can be a great way to avoid poor manners—sometimes overeagerness, sometimes defensiveness—but if a nearby dog is reactive, I put as much distance between us as possible. And any time we must go somewhere deeply unfamiliar or potentially overwhelming to him, like a busy downtown street, I try to choose routes that offer escape from stressors and carry treats for distraction and reassurance.

Attunement means being alert to another's body language, affect, and needs. It's an ongoing, dynamic practice.

reflections from the field

Andrew Hale of Dog Centred Care and Train Positive in the UK is frank about what's involved. He says:

We have all these models out there in the dog industry and in human psychology circles and they can
all be great, and they can help inform us. But regardless
of all the dog training models and stuff that's out there,
regardless of all the techniques we might learn, the child
or dog or puppy in front of us is a unique sentient being
on this planet.

No other being will have the same genetics, trauma
experience, life experiences, life learning, all these kinds
of things in the moment.

A care-orientated approach is always about starting
from learning from the other first, about being humble
enough to put my ego at the door and let you be whatever you need to be.

To truly be available to the emotional experience of
another, we have to be in a well-regulated state. That's
one of the golden rules of therapy from my days of
working with humans. There's no point in me turning
up all hot, flustered, angry, upset, and tired because then
I'm not listening to you, I'm not available now. Our own
trauma, our own belief systems, our own unconscious
biases can also be barriers to acknowledging a dog's care
and support needs.

So when we're striving to be available to the truth of
another, how do we do that?

It starts from recognizing that we come with our
own baggage, which affects our value systems, our belief systems, our safe worldview, the things that we think
about, the unconscious biases. There may be voices in

our head that come from that schoolteacher or our parents or whatever it is. It's okay to have all the baggage that we bring. It shouldn't be seen as a negative as far as I'm concerned. The only emotional experience that I can validate is my own, period. And we may need help ourselves navigating that. There's a lot for us to work out. So actually, being available to the care needs of another can be quite challenging.

CHAPTER 9:
Help Little Ones Feel Safe

PART OF RESPONSIBLE CAREGIVING is providing physical safety. But after we stash electrical cords and sharp objects out of reach and secure a solid roof over their head, our job isn't finished. We also need to provide the *emotional experience of safety*. Not because we're soft and indulgent and spoiling the child but because a feeling of safety is the only way to turn on vital nervous system functions.

The neurochemistry of fear disrupts and prevents complete wellness. By helping a little one feel safe, we're supporting their parasympathetic nervous system and all the related internal mechanisms the body uses to restore and repair well-being. We're reassuring their nervous system that it's okay to "rest and digest." Without a feeling of safety, the body diverts energy and resources to escape and survival. This is why, for example, high stress is associated with gastrointestinal disorders.

Children from a background of trauma and dogs that experienced early life adversity are likely to have a heightened stress response.[1, 2] When a little one is experiencing distress, we can take any number of steps to address and support their emotional experience.

Once we are attuned and alert to when they need help and comfort, we can begin to take corrective action. And remember, even when their fears seem silly to us, their fear reactions are legitimate, instinctive survival impulses that deserve our respect.

parenting pearl

What scares a child can often seem inconsequential to adults. For example, fear of rainstorms is very common in children who have been brought up in an orphanage or other institution. Being sent alone to a room can trigger panic in a child terrified of and used to being abandoned. A simple touch or hug can be overwhelmingly scary to a child who was never held or rocked as a baby. . . . Without having lived these children's lives, it is hard for us to comprehend what they endured, and what fears remain.

—*The Connected Child*[3]

Fear Drives Problem Behaviors

Denise Fenzi, founder of Fenzi Dog Sports Academy, points out that a barking and lunging dog is yelling, "Stay away from me!" Often, though, we tune out the signs because we're absorbed in our own concerns.

Fenzi recalls visiting a bustling street fair and noticing a tiny Yorkie spinning on its leash. "The dog was freaking out, and the owner wasn't seeing it," she said. "They weren't paying attention to the fear."

Her solution is to distance a scared dog from the perceived threat so it doesn't protect itself by acting out. "Your dog sees that support, and it makes them feel better. They start to rely on you, which is safer."[4]

Be Cautious with Eye Contact

Eye contact makes many of us feel socially and emotionally connected to other people.[5] However, this is not a universal experience, and it's important to avoid assuming that if we want eye contact, everyone else welcomes it too. The same goes for dogs.

There are cultural, neurological, developmental, and experiential reasons for variations in eye contact preferences. For example, Eastern and Western cultures have different eye contact expectations. Averting gaze can signal respect in some cultures.[6, 7] Children on the autism spectrum and other non-neurotypicals can experience oversensitivity to eye contact that makes them feel uncomfortable, just as being denied eye contact feels uncomfortable to neurotypicals.[8, 9] Youth with developmental delays and social anxiety disorder tend to avoid eye contact, and so may children with dysfunctional attachment or certain types of traumatic history.[10-12]

Comfort with eye contact also varies among breeds and individual dogs. Some dogs perceive direct eye contact as comfortable or socially informative while many others find it confrontational. Aversion to eye contact can reflect dogs' underlying genetics, especially those bred to detect movement and potential predators. Other genetic profiles, specifically those linked to more confident and less fearful behavior, show more willingness to follow the human gaze.[13]

Child welfare experts who work with frightened and traumatized children often choose therapeutic interventions that involve side-by-side activities and wait to introduce eye contact over time as trust develops. We would do well to follow their lead and avoid making eye contact when working with unfamiliar, sensitive, and potentially aggressive dogs.[14]

Attune to Signs of Stress

In traumatized children, what may appear to be symptoms of ADHD can actually be traced to chronic hypervigilance rooted in fear. Once the child feels safe, these types of ADHD symptoms recede. A similar phenomenon can happen in dogs whose fear manifests itself in nervous activities and reactivity, a condition that dog trainers often describe as "overarousal."

Because of the highly individualized nature of fear, even common and well-intentioned gestures can easily be misinterpreted and make a traumatized child or dog feel unsafe. Think about it like a veteran with posttraumatic stress disorder (PTSD). Deep in their minds is a foxhole with enemy shelling filling the skies. Even after the war is over, if a car backfires in the garage, they are transported to that foxhole.

One veterinary case study describes a Shiba Inu brought in for behavioral consultation because any time a cellphone buzzed, the dog freaked out. They traced the problem back to training with an electronic "e-collar," which delivers electrical shock or "stim" to the dog just seconds after a warning buzz. Although use of the shock collar was discontinued, the dog remained in a constant state of high alarm. It took months of positive behavioral techniques, hiding the phone and changing its signal tones, and medication to help the dog cope better, but it never fully recovered.[15]

If dogs are left kenneled, isolated, or confined in small spaces for extended times, their social comfort and skills can completely break down. In fact, they can experience a type of psychosis. It can be scary to walk the halls of certain no-kill rescues where dogs spend extended periods of time in very tiny kennels without any social interaction or sensory stimulation. At the sight of a visitor, some of these dogs explode in a mouth-frothing ferocious meltdown, flinging themselves high against the walls of their kennel.

In general, to help a dog feel safe:

- never use training methods that prioritize harsh, fear-based physical punishment; and
- don't leave a puppy or dog socially isolated or physically confined for extended periods.

Address Individual Fears

For many dogs, fireworks, thunder, and loud noises are deeply frightening.[16, 17] Common, nonmedical coping strategies include the following:

- managing the environment by giving the dog a safe hiding place, closing windows and blinds, and playing soothing music;
- treatment with calming products such as CBD, pheromones, neutraceuticals, homeopathic products, or essential oils;
- giving dogs a weighted blanket to get under or a weighted pressure jacket ("thunder shirt") to wear;[18] and
- interacting with the dog in a friendly way, such as petting, body contact, and talking to them while giving treats and chews and playing together to distract the dog.

Research suggests that the last option above is most reliably helpful. In one survey of 1,225 respondents, more had meaningful improvement by feeding and playing together with the dog during fireworks than by using other techniques.[19]

reflections from the field

Veterinary behaviorist Christopher Pachel, DVM, DACVB, CABC, gives an example of how individualistic dogs' fears can be. He says:

A case that sticks with me was a case from years and years and years ago, back when I was practicing as a house-call veterinarian in Minnesota.

This dog was aggressing toward unfamiliar people, which is not an uncommon problem. When certain individuals would come into the home or into the dog's proximity, this dog would show what looked to be a fear response, and for those individuals he would lunge forward and make contact, breaking skin with bites.

The tricky piece was that it was really difficult to pinpoint who the dog would aggress to. Now, usually, just by getting a detailed history, we're able to get a better sense of, oh, it's men, it's women, it's somebody wearing a hat or some weird clothing. It's the parka guy in the middle of winter, or it's kids who are screaming, or there's some identifiable trigger that we can pinpoint, usually pretty easily.

For this particular dog, we were going down all of the normal pathways to try to figure it out, calling out all the usual suspects, watching the dog in these different situations to try to figure out what the trigger was. I could not for the life of me figure out what that particular trigger was, at least based on the investigation, and we try never to provoke the dog into aggressing in any way. Nobody needs that. But by just observing the dog in different situations, we can usually get some subtle indications of where they're more comfortable or less comfortable. And we can lean into that.

It wasn't until there were a couple of additional incidents with folks that the owners knew that they were then able to dig in a little bit deeper and say, "Hey, wait a minute. What's different?" Turns out when all was said and done, the difference was that every single individual who had ever been aggressed toward by that dog was a smoker of menthol cigarettes.

I don't know why. I don't know if there was something particularly offensive from a sensory standpoint or if it correlated with actual trauma memory. I don't know. But it was such a relief when we were able to go back and go, there it is. That's what it was.

Now we had a way to manage this dog. Before visitors were coming over, we could tell them, "Okay, just ignore him and don't smoke menthol, and you should be fine." And we had no more issues.

That always stuck with me. It was a reminder very early on that just because I can't pinpoint the trigger, it doesn't mean that there isn't one, it may be something that's coming through for that animal. Dogs have a different sensory perception than I do. They may be hearing, they may be smelling, they may be seeing something in terms of their ability—or lack of ability—to see certain colors. They live in a different sensory world. So I have to always be curious: What do you know that I don't? What do you see? What do you hear? What do you feel that I just don't have visibility of?

I could look at that animal and say, "Well, that shouldn't trigger a reaction. That was no big deal." But it's not up to me to determine whether it's a big deal for you, you know? Big feelings are valid, and little feelings are valid, too. The animal is having an emotional response. And the more of an emotional response they're having, the more challenging it is for almost all of us to think our way through those situations.

Emotion essentially clouds judgment. It's supposed to. It keeps us safe in times of danger. We're supposed to short-circuit until we're safe again. Then our brain can come back online, and we can start to think about things like our grocery lists and two plus two equals four and all those things that we're supposed to do. But in the fight-flight moment, in that panicky moment, we're supposed to short-circuit.

So if the animal is having a significant reaction, I may not understand why, but from an empathy standpoint, I can acknowledge this is tough for you right now. Is there a way I could make it easier, right here, right now? Is there a way I could make this easier in the long term? And what might that look like?

More Ways to Help Them Feel Safe

Try these additional strategies to reduce fear in a dog:

- Offer to touch or hug the dog with just one hand—not two—and allow them to decline touch entirely. This is the same way that therapists avoid triggering deep-seated fears in formerly abused individuals. They invite consent and use one hand for hugging instead of two to avoid triggering fear of being trapped.

- When greeting a dog, turn to the side and avoid eye contact. Even though many dogs may come to accept eye contact and use it to read people, avoiding it is an easy way to dial down a dog's anxiety.

- Gently toss treats on the floor nearby, and do not force the dog to come to your hand to get them.

- If a dog shows willingness to be touched, you might rub their chest or stroke their shoulder or flank. Avoid patting the top of the head, and avoid using short and jerky movements, such as scratches with fingertips, as those add to excitement and are not calming.

- Greet and speak to them quietly. It can be helpful to use words to "explain" and reassure them quietly about what is happening, in simple language, as the sound of these words can become a familiar signal that increases predictability.

- Allow them to move away to a comfortable distance from whatever object, person, or situation is causing distress. If they are reacting to you, let the dog back away, and allow them space.

- Offer a voluntary escape or hideaway, particularly a space that is dimly lit and covered on multiple sides. This should provide a safe haven and getaway retreat that the dog can use voluntarily. (Be aware that closing them in a crate may trigger more fear.)

- Dogs sometimes calm themselves by pushing into small spaces and pushing up against things to stimulate the nerves from beneath their fur that respond to pressure. It's an instinctive, calming option, much like weighted blankets are used for children.

- A tiny toy dog might feel safer in a dog bed with raised edges that has a towel thrown above it that they can burrow under and peek out of at will. A walking stroller can provide similar feelings of safety while out on a walk.

- For shaggy dogs with a lot of hair, groom them so that their eyes are free of obstructions. Being able to see the world around them helps them anticipate when they will be touched and reduces their being constantly startled and scared.

And general reminders:

If you wake or disturb sleeping dogs, you could startle and provoke them into a fear reaction. And be aware that common household chemicals like disinfectants and scented products can offend dogs' heightened olfactory sensitivities.

parenting pearl

When your child sees that you are responsive to his concerns, his trust grows and wonderful progress can be made.

—The Connected Child[20]

CHAPTER 10:
Nurture at Every Opportunity

TRUST MUST BE EARNED; it is not given automatically, especially by traumatized individuals. The more we intentionally take the time to build a relationship of kindness, predictability, and connection, the more we fill a metaphoric "trust bank." We make deposits in the trust bank by being responsive, consistent, and kind. We withdraw trust by being aggressive, volatile, or unkind. The trust bank is like a relational bank account that pays dividends in cooperation and companionable connection.[1, 2]

As we build a relationship, it's important to invite a dog to be an active participant in whatever is going on as often as possible. We need patience, though, because an insecure dog will not magically forget its past trauma and embrace us. The dog could even struggle to accept any comfort from us at all.[3] In attachment terms, we are encouraging the dog to experience us as a secure base, but we have to let the dog arrive there at their own pace.

We can use nurturing to connect with dogs that internalize their distress and shut down, as well as those that externalize it by biting.

Nurturing can be as simple as feeding them with no strings attached and not crowding their physical space. Although most of us shy away from aggressive animals and instinctively recoil at the idea of treating them kindly, therapeutic parents know that nurturing (while maintaining safety for ourselves) can hold the key to unlocking a little one's potential.

reflections from the field

Roman Gottfried of Holistic Dog Training learned from a pitbull mix named Siggi that overcoming our own inner resistance to nurturing is the first step. He says:

> Siggi was the last dog left at a Long Island animal shelter after a big adoption event. The shelter got stuck with him because he was so aggressive. Siggi actually lived in the red kennel, behind the red door, and was fed through a drawer. Nobody could take him out. Siggi came to the shelter with a severe injury to his front leg and had to have two surgeries, and one leg was totally amputated up to the shoulders. Between physical trauma and medical trauma, he was not a happy puppy.
>
> He was so miserable that I didn't know how to get him in the car. I was not expecting that kind of aggression. Fortunately, I had a bite suit with me and put it on to get him in the car and get him home. The first time I put the food bowl down for him to eat, I stood about ten feet away. When I shifted my leg less than an inch, he attacked me.
>
> Back then I was still an aversive "balanced" trainer. I still used punishment to correct behavior. So I thought,

Oh, I'm gonna fix that guy. Gonna show who's the boss. But this dog wouldn't have that. No matter how high I turned the shock collar, it made no difference. He was a different case; he had a different sense of justice. It became kind of a standard procedure; I would open the kennel, and Siggi would attack me.

Every time, just before he attacked, I felt a real cold breeze coming, like the sensation when you sit in a restaurant and feel a cold breeze coming down your shoulder and you turn around and see a guy staring at you. That kind of thing.

I was so frustrated with this dog, even to the point of crying at home. People in public were watching how I would do with this dog from behind the red door. If I didn't succeed, I might need to close my dog training business.

There had to be a way out of this problem. Maybe that cold breeze feeling was a clue. Don't ask me why, I just thought, *I will give him a treat for that and see if I can make more of it.* The next time I felt that cold breeze, I tossed him a treat. That was the first time he didn't attack. He sat down and actually looked at me differently.

And I was like, *Oh, hold on a second. That cold feeling was him telling me something is wrong.* So I kept giving a treat whenever I got a certain feeling. In the first week after implementing this new approach, I was able to open the crate without a bite.

I thought, *Wait a minute, that's different than what I had been taught to do. There is no punishment involved.*

Then I started thinking back to my own trauma experience. If he feels the same way I feel, and punishment doesn't work for me, what would work? Communication. Well, I feel like he's sending me a message. A nonverbal, emotional, energetic message.

So I started implementing that. Now beyond the dog training and classical conditioning, there's empathy, sympathy, telepathic communication? Whoa, that's a lot. And then there's parenting? That's not what I was taught in school, right? That's not what I graduated with. But the more I focused on the energy aspect of it and looked away from the rewarding, I could see the dog actually had a purpose. We had a relationship that was rewarding in itself. The dog would do things for that relationship and not for the treat.

Then I remembered the incident at the church when the priests were very handsy with me. Every week I would get an extra bonus for staying over the weekend. I took the money, but I didn't like the relationship. So the dog may take the treat, but you don't have a relationship. I realized a dog is not just a black box, where you lure him into position and you click. Because I wouldn't sit with that priest if you gave me $1,000, now that I know what happened. So classical conditioning doesn't work. Luring me to sit on the same table with that guy? Not even if he asked me for forgiveness. I can't do that. He ruined too much back then.

But if I come from the angle of how can I make my dog feel better? Then I have to reach out with the food.

Then I start thinking about, *What food makes my dog feel better? What water makes my dog feel better? Which bed does he prefer?* I let him have choices: "Do you want to stay home at night, or do you want to go potty? It's fine with me, just let me know when you want to go to the bathroom."

Letting go of control made me feel better. And Siggi was better. I got more control in return because my dog wanted to keep the relationship alive. And he wanted to do things that make me feel better, which is having control.

So we had fun. We did things that a dog likes to do. "Do you want to do more of that? Let's do that." The dog responded, "This is okay. What do you want me to do?" In this way, a reciprocal exchange developed. I didn't need to lure or push the dog to sit. I could offer a treat to the dog and ask, "What would you do for that?" If he responded with sitting, he would get a treat for sitting. If he responded with lying down, he would get it for lying down.

By working with Siggi, I was also working with my inner self. In him, I saw a reflection of my childhood trauma and the need for secure attachment and healing. The more I learned from Siggi, the more I adjusted my own temper and emotions. I learned to master my emotions and convey to Siggi he was free to make mistakes, so he did not need to be afraid of getting hurt or punished. That improved our relationship and the way he responded to environmental triggers.

I learned to say yes instead of no. He offered more behaviors that gave him joy, and I was able to acknowledge him for making right choices.

Siggi taught me about the complexity of human–dog relationships and incorporating techniques from cognitive behavior therapy, classical conditioning, desensitization, and free shaping. He taught me to challenge misconceptions around dog training and dog parenting.

Soon, I was able to introduce Siggi into individual playgroups and to other dogs in a controlled environment. I was able to bring him with me to public places without having him physically interact with people.

Siggi was the first dog that led me to practice the holistic dog training I do today. Before, I only thought about obedience and training behaviors. Now, I look at everything, literally: food, sleeping, water, work, energy, exercise, emotions, environment, trauma, and attachment relationship. Everything's considered, including my lifestyle, because that affects my dog's environment too.

Siggi did not become a social butterfly, but he became a safe dog to be around. I learned to read his signals and keep him safe, and he learned to communicate his needs to me and ask for help. Siggi became a great teacher to me and helped save other dogs from the euthanasia list.

Touch: Another Way to Nurture

The way we touch has biochemical, neurological, and emotional implications. When we slowly and warmly stroke areas of the skin that contain "C-tactile nerve fibers" (typically areas with hairs) by using a full hand and gentle pressure, we stimulate "feel-good" neurochemicals. This nurturing touch produces a soothing, oxytocin calm that contributes to secure attachment in people, and there is evidence to suggest that the same effect happens in dogs too.[4] Herky-jerky, fast, and fingertip tickling touches, in contrast, have an irritating, energizing, opposite effect. I made the mistake of handling Hazel in this irritating way when she was a nippy puppy.

Some dog professionals practice a hands-on system of touch and movement for animals called Tellington TTouch,[5] which features gentle, attuned massage with circular movements on various areas of the animal's body, such as the chest, shoulders, and ears. People who use TTouch with dogs report it can have a deeply soothing and therapeutic effect.[6, 7]

According to its creator, Linda Tellington Jones, certain aspects of TTouch were informed by the work of Moshé Feldenkrais, originator of a neuromuscular modality that bears his name.[8] Both the Feldenkrais Method and the Anat Baniel Method (ABM) it inspired are touch- and movement-based modalities for promoting learning that are used with children as well as adults.[9-11] ABM is used with a range of children who have special needs, from those with cerebral palsy to those on the autism spectrum.[12, 13]

But touch doesn't have to be fancy or highly skillful to benefit dogs. Simple, kind petting is valuable. One study found that dogs spend quite a bit more time near an experimenter who pets them rather than verbally praises them.[14] Friendly, warm touch is also an effective reward in the positive reinforcement dog training technique known as constructional affection.[15, 16]

CHAPTER 11:

Show Respect, Expect Respect

WHEN WE BRING A PUPPY or dog into our life, we often become so focused on our goals and wishes for it that we forget this little one is on its own journey. Just as an adopted or foster child might have endured deprivation, neglect, or harm before arriving in their new home, this new dog's past may have been less than ideal. When we welcome puppies and dogs to our home, especially those from rescue situations, wisdom from adoption specialists rings true:

- We cannot understand the environments or relationships a little one may have endured in the past. When you are raised in harsh or dysfunctional circumstances, it's normal to become a survivalist.

- Our home and family are a new world for the little one. They cannot be expected to understand the advantages, house rules, or expectations of our own family life.

With this in mind, we can admire their resilience and introduce them to the basics of living together as a family. The Golden Rule is a good starting point. We offer the same courtesies that we expect; we treat others how we'd like to be treated. Most importantly, we treat one another with respect.

What Does Respect Look Like?

Imagine you are watching a parent and their little one from a slight distance, perhaps through a window. You see them interact with each other and see their actions and body movements. Perhaps you detect a murmur of sound, but you cannot distinguish actual words.

As you watch this near-silent movie, how would you describe the relationship between the two? Is it antagonistic or friendly? Respectful or disrespectful? Could you recognize respectful behavior through body language alone?

Most of us can pinpoint the basics if only by thinking about how we'd treat someone we look up to and hold in great esteem. In mutually respectful relationships, each individual is able to set and observe boundaries.

So how would a respectful interaction look? To begin with, there would be no physical assault or striking each other. No screaming or flailing arms, no cowering. In the scene through the window, the adult's movements would be calm and measured and friendly. Both individuals would have sufficient personal space. The adult might offer helpful gestures or guidance on a task. Perhaps the two would complete a chore together in synchrony.

Next, consider this potential scene viewed through the window:

The little one becomes excited and shouts and runs around boisterously, perhaps bumping into the adult—appearing "disrespectful" as little ones sometimes do—and the adult reacts by jamming a knee into the little one's chest or reaching out and whacking them with an arm. Or perhaps the adult grabs the little one's collar and yanks it so tight and hard that the little one's head snaps up, her eyes bulge out, and the oxygen supply to her brain is cut off. If this was the adult's idea of showing respect, hopefully that individual would find themself in a serious discussion with a public safety officer or family court judge.

Unfortunately, each of the disturbing adult behaviors in the second example reflects recommendations that are still popular in certain dog training communities. While it's understandable—and advisable—that an adult actively stop and redirect a little one's unwelcome behavior, the method also matters because the relationship matters. Instead of lashing out in the moment, a therapeutic parent safely and gently interrupts the unwanted behavior and redirects the little one to an appropriate alternative. In this way, we show respect while maintaining clear boundaries and gaining respect for ourselves.

Skilled parents make it very clear—in a kind, calm, deliberate way—what behaviors are welcome and expected while living in the family. Giving and expecting respect means communicating clearly about boundaries and following through. When boundaries are clear, the feeling of security increases for everyone involved.

A mutually respectful relationship builds trust and feelings of safety that promote optimal outcomes.[1] Therefore, a therapeutic parent always considers, *Is this respectful to both parties?*

reflections from the field

Sherry Steinlein of Paws for Success shares some thoughts about expectations. She says:

> In the beginning of my professional career working with dogs, you couldn't talk about animals being like children in the home. I had an early mentor say to me,

"We never talk about that with clients. You can never say that dogs have feelings. You can never discuss this stuff, even with positive trainers. You always just talk about science."

I felt, *But why?* I've had dogs in my home since I was two years old, and even though I had kind of a dysfunctional family life as a child, I have great memories of animals that I saw as very equal, like siblings. I knew in my gut that dogs were very clearly showing emotions, they were very clearly acting similarly to children.

After a while, in my own practice, I started changing. I would say things like, "Yeah, your dog has some jealousy going on with the other dog in the home." Then I would put into place protocols in the home and behavior things that would address those, and I would do it quietly.

Now I talk about this all the time. When I go into a home and find chaos, I say, "You guys really have to set house rules. Don't you have house rules for the children? Do your kids stand on the table during dinner and throw food?" I'm not using shock collars or prong collars or anything like that, but I'm still setting rules about what is acceptable.

Seven Ways to Show Respect to a Dog

1. Respect their boundaries. Allow them the option of not greeting strangers.
2. Don't force a cuddle. Watch what the dog requests through their body language. Are they turning their head away when

you reach out your hand to them? This suggests they are declining contact. Are they leaning toward you or nosing your hand for petting? This means they are eager for contact.

3. Make your requests in a clear and simple way through your body posture, sounds, touch, and rewards. Vocal cues should be short and easily distinguished from random, normal chatter.

4. Give signals, not surprises.

5. Just like we'd find it rude and unsettling to have someone grab food off our fork, don't take food from a dog who is eating.

6. Assume that dogs would cooperate if they could understand the request, had the requisite skills and aptitude, and were in the right frame of mind to comply. Assume they are doing the best they can.

7. Assume dogs are entitled to have a voice and to ask for what they want and need.

Examples of Dogs Showing Respect to Us

- Adhering to house rules, such as waiting while the food bowl is put down
- Taking an assigned seat, if requested, when the family is resting or relaxing
- Not using teeth to break our skin
- Chewing and playing with their own designated toys and not our designated items
- Cooperating when it's time to get ready to go outside

I recall a beautiful large husky mix at the shelter who ignored the gentle encouragements that usually worked to get dogs moving in the right direction on a walk. Instead, this dog just flopped down and stayed put. He wouldn't go forward or backward. I was out of treats to use as a lure, so I tried crouching down and urging him forward, but no dice. I finally just stood up straight and tall and essentially barked a short command at him. Not a deep growl or a chirpy puppy sound, but more like a confident instruction among dog companions. That got this dog's attention and cooperation. In this case, behaving with clear and confident assertiveness made a difference.

As the family leader, it's up to us to set house rules and follow through with consistency. We always have the option to share control—for example, by providing free time to run around off leash within a safe area or loosening up the leash to allow a "sniffy walk." Kids and pups will test limits; it's up to adults to communicate what's expected and uphold limits in a kind, firm, and occasionally flexible way.

parenting pearl

Early in my career I was trying to help a family deal with an aggressive twelve-year-old boy. I spoke to him in the usual sweet, singsong manner reserved for young kids. No matter what I said or did, he continued to act out and oppose any adult instruction. We finally brought the family to a group of specialists. The minute the boy arrived, he tried to smack the lead therapist and run out of the room. The therapist was a small woman in her seventies. Without any fuss, she approached him, put a hand on each of his shoulders, looked up into his eyes, and said firmly, "We're not going to have that here. You're not going to do that here." We all felt the air in the room immediately change and everyone's anxiety drain away. The boy gave a sigh of relief, because he had finally found someone stronger than him. That directness made him feel safe, and he calmed down. I learned how important it is to be direct and come from a place of strength and firmness, even when a child is making you feel anything but strong and firm.

—Raising the Challenging Child[2]

We can't solve all our dog's problems by staying calm, but we do set the right tone by keeping ourselves centered and grounded. Often, once a dog understands that a calm and competent adult is in charge, it is less likely to feel an urgent need to protect itself. It is more apt to mirror our serene assurance and may feel less defensive toward visitors. Signaling that we are capable of managing the situation and ensuring safety is sometimes as simple as stepping in front to address a novel situation first.

parenting pearl

For safety and a host of other reasons, you need to make rules, set and enforce limits, and make decisions about family life. A child's world is more predictable and less stressful when parents provide consistent structure and authority.

—The Connected Child[3]

CHAPTER 12:
Water the Seeds You Want to Grow

THE MORE WE point out and reward a specific behavior, the more likely it is that the behavior will be repeated. This is a double-edged sword. It makes gaining cooperation from a child or dog relatively easy as long as we focus on appropriate positive associations and celebrate the right wins. But we don't always realize what we're rewarding, especially during ordinary casual interactions.

Take Bernie. He and I often take a leisurely walk in the afternoon. But recently, during an oppressively hot spell, I dragged my feet about going outside. Then, realizing he needed a chance to relieve himself, I put him outside into our side yard right before giving him his dinner.

This happened a couple of times with an unintended consequence. Bernie has begun bugging me to be let out to the side yard more often and yodeling with joy when I let him back in. I inadvertently created a positive association between the side yard and being fed. Bernie has become like a glassy-eyed player working the casino slot machine, hoping that rubbing his lucky shirt will help him hit the jackpot again. Oops!

That doesn't mean we shouldn't do nice things for little ones. It just helps to be intentional.

reflections from the field

Christina Waggoner, former operations manager of Victoria Stilwell Academy for Dog Training & Behavior, describes how she learned to create positive associations for a struggling rescue dog. She says:

> My third Siberian husky rescue was Dante. The morning after we got him home, he woke up very sick from a virus picked up in the shelter. For about a week, I slept beside him in the living room, waking up every few hours to spoon chicken broth into his mouth. When you do that, that's it, you're done for. That dog is yours and you are theirs, forever.
>
> After he recovered, we soon discovered that Dante couldn't even see another dog without losing his mind. He would start pawing the ground and frothing at the mouth. His eyes would turn bright red, and he would essentially scream. We kept asking ourselves, *What did we get ourselves into? This dog is a nightmare.*
>
> A local trainer suggested we yank him by a choke collar, and television suggested we throw him on the ground and pin him. I hate to admit it now, but we were desperate, and we tried those methods. It was a disaster and made things worse, so I went online and found the book *Don't Shoot the Dog* by Karen Pryor. It explained how to change behavior by using the science of learning.

The idea was to change Dante's reaction to other dogs by pairing their presence with something he liked (and I knew he liked hot dogs), rather than something unpleasant, like a tightened collar. I set out with Dante and a bag of chopped hot dogs, admittedly not knowing what the hell I was doing.

Every time we saw another dog—it could have been a football field away and he'd still react—I gave him a bit of hot dog. Lucky for me, he was young, and he had an appetite! Eventually, it got to the point where there'd be some space before his reaction to the approaching dog. So I would use that space. And slowly, over time, Dante began to associate the sight of the approaching dog with something good. He would sit quietly and look to me and not so much at the other dog. He learned to trust that I would never close the distance between us and the trigger until he was ready.

He turned out to be the gentlest dog I would ever know. He became the dog that I would put our new dogs with and our puppies with when we took them in, because he was so gentle.

Dante changed my life. He sparked my interest in how dogs learn and helped me use that knowledge effectively, in a way that's fair to the learner.

Create Positive Associations

Creating positive associations is a powerful way to shift a dog's behavioral and emotional reactions. We can use this technique intentionally to help dogs feel confident in situations that might otherwise cause stress, as discussed in the example on the previous page. This approach can also be helpful in reducing dogs' fear of fireworks and thunderstorms. Studies suggest that playing with dogs and offering special treats during these noisy events can significantly reduce and prevent their phobic responses to these situations.[1]

We can also use positive associations to make it easier for kids and dogs to cope with medical treatment. Visiting the vet for a fun visit, just to get a treat, rather than only going when a vaccine or exam is needed, is a start. Many trainers employ protocols that use positive reinforcement and consent procedures to facilitate easier handling and grooming.

In "cooperative care" husbandry, dogs choose to opt in or opt out of activities such as getting brushed or having their nails trimmed. Some trainers teach the dog that stepping off the mat makes the activity stop while stepping on the mat is like saying, "Okay, I'm ready for more." Either way, the dog gets a reward. Another approach to consensual husbandry is Chirag Patel's "bucket game," in which a dog signals its willingness to proceed with grooming by turning its head toward a bucket that contains treats.[2]

Catch Them Doing Something Right

Specialists who work with at-risk kids make a point of "catching" kids doing things correctly. They might say, "Good job asking with respect!" or "Nice job taking turns!" or "Thank you for speaking quietly!"

We can do the same thing with dogs. The tricky part is remembering to do it.

Without realizing it, parents often fall into the trap of believing they are praising their kids more frequently and criticizing them less often than they actually are. In one study of 128 families seeking behavioral health services for preschoolers, the parents criticized their children almost three times as often as they offered positive feedback during a brief parent–child play session. Yet when asked to self-report, these parents dramatically underestimated the amount of negative feedback they had been giving.[3] When parental communication and feedback given to children is weighted toward the negative in this way, it contributes to insecure attachment.

Game designers understand the importance of celebrating preferred behavior. That's why they design games that reward us with bells, shooting stars, and points for achieving specific goals. These rewards trigger the neurochemistry that motivates us to repeat the process. This is the power of positive reinforcement.

In dog training terms, we "capture" behavior when we reward something that occurs naturally. In this way, we can capitalize on the dog's natural inclinations and celebrate when they've made us happy.

Celebrate Lots of Wins

"In the dog world, we talk about splitting versus lumping," says Denise Fenzi. "Splitting means to take a behavior you want to teach and break it down to its tiny, small parts so that no one gets overwhelmed."

Animals and humans struggle more when tasks are lumped together and do better when tiny successes are strung together. Each of those tiny parts gets praised and rewarded with positive reinforcement. Fenzi puts this into relatable terms. For example, if we're feeling blue and having a bad day, we might split tasks into separate steps that can each be checked off when completed. Take "do the laundry." That splits into gather the clothes, run the washer, transfer clothes into the dryer, fold them. "Splitting gives confidence," she says, "because you'll win, you'll win a lot. Lumping is going to trash you."

Splitting gives you lots of wins to celebrate—plenty of spoonfuls of sugar to help the medicine go down.

The Power of Positive Reinforcement

Like many people who play games on electronic devices, I feel a wave of satisfaction when I see a cascade of stars in multiple colors shimmering across the screen to let me know I've won. Imagine if instead that game flashed red comment bubbles on the screen, criticizing every time I made a poor strategic choice. Who would want to play that game? It would be awfully depressing. That's what happens when we don't give a dog any clear direction and just wait in ambush to chastise and critique and play "gotcha."

We can help a dog experience a "win" in a variety of ways. Positive reinforcement isn't solely about colors bursting on a digital screen. It can be something as simple as a pleasant feeling or enjoyable sound. Notice what motivates your particular dog. Perhaps she has a passion for playing fetch. Tossing a ball can be her reward for cooperation. Or maybe she loves getting a neck rub, so you can ask her for cooperation and thank her by rubbing her neck.

Watering seeds we want to grow just requires a little creativity and understanding of the richness of a dog's experience and the kind of associations that they are likely to make. As an added benefit, if we are a dependable, trustworthy source of kindness, food, and games they love, dogs will become more receptive and cooperative with our requests in general.

Be a Coach, Not a Cop

It's human to feel the urge to strike back and punish when we feel frustrated or threatened, but punishment is not the most effective approach for raising kids or dogs. Instead, we can kindly redirect them to correct behavior and then praise compliance. Remember:

- approach each interaction as a new opportunity;
- stop learning sessions on a positive note (if something goes off track, offer a do-over to reinforce the correct response into muscle memory); and
- restart interactions from a place of neutral calm.

Also remember that parenting style comes through in nonverbal messages. Our body language and handling methods toward dogs are all parenting choices.

You don't need a close attachment relationship with your dog for positive reinforcement methods to work or for this framework to hold true or to be useful. Each day, we can set aside difficulties of the past and strive for more optimal interactions going forward.

CHAPTER 13:
Use Play Creatively

FOR CHILDREN AND PUPPIES, play is important developmental business. During play, children learn to use their bodies with increasing precision and dexterity. They practice walking, running, jumping, touching, and manipulating objects. They gain practice in social relationships and behaviors that will serve them in adulthood.[1]

Puppies, too, gain enormous benefits from play. They get to practice pouncing, chasing, biting, reading body language, and interacting with other dogs. They discover how far they can provoke one another and what the consequences might be. They learn give and take, how to wrestle using body and mouth, and when to inhibit the strength of their bite. Playtime benefits their brains, lighting up the developing nervous system with sensory input, improving physical coordination, and balancing neurochemistry.

Many people instinctively invite puppies and dogs to play with balls, ropes, and other toys. Research suggests that the enjoyment is mutual; dogs at play are energized by having an attentive human audience.[2]

Play, a pillar of childhood, can be a rich and versatile tool for improving outcomes, but using it therapeutically isn't always as simple as it may sound. In some circumstances it's not even an option. Children and dogs with a history of harm are often not able to play because they do not feel safe enough. Those who have been mistreated, neglected, or grew up with unpredictable and insecure attachment struggle the most.[3] For these individuals, simply showing signs of playfulness is a sign of recovery.

reflections from the field

Sherry Steinlein of Paws for Success celebrates small successes, especially with one of her rescue dogs. She says:

> One of my own dogs is a rescue named Freya, and she has some physical and mental signs of abuse. I took her to a veterinary dermatology specialist, a lovely older woman who asked me if this dog came from a certain southern state. I said yes. The specialist told me that in very rural areas of that state, people believe that if you pour hot motor oil on mange, it will fix the skin condition.
>
> That explained so much about why Freya was fearful around people and why her torso is black, scarred skin and the hair only grew back around her face, her tail, and her legs. Now she always wears pajamas so her skin is protected. She's much better, but she's still a little uncomfortable with being touched in certain places.
>
> Freya really needed help getting over her fear of people. She loves other dogs, but part of working through that fear of people was she needed to come to you. She needed to be able to feel safe. She gravitated

towards me because I would just sit and I would allow her to come sit next to me. I would turn my head away so she would not feel threatened.

It took more than a year for Freya to get enough feeling of safety to come running up with her tail wagging and really be engaging and playful with me. When Freya looks at me with those big brown eyes with love in them, I really feel like it's me, Freya, and a higher power. It's beautiful.

Play has the advantage of combining movement with learning, stimulating the brain, and promoting healthy development. Play and the use of toys are also a pathway for children and dogs to communicate with adults. The challenge to adults who want to use play with very young children is that it can require "delicately calibrated participation through leading, following, and leading by following."[4]

When used to its full potential, play supports multiple HEARTS that strengthen attachment, enrich the senses, optimize the brain, build motor skills, and teach collaboration and cooperation. Let's look at how play can be used.

Playing Together to Strengthen Attachment and Social Skills

Handled with sensitivity, social play is therapeutic because of its relational focus. Kids, for example, show significantly less problem behavior following child-centered play therapy (CCPT).[5, 6] During CCPT, a child is free to explore, make choices, and express themselves in an accepting environment with a play therapist; the only limits are appropriate safety. In one study of five- to seven-year-old children with oppositional defiance disorder, CCPT not only significantly reduced symptoms, the children who received it for twelve weeks continued to show improvements at a six-month follow-up.[7]

Another play-based intervention for at-risk children with developmental trauma, called Theraplay, engages an adult and child in responsive interactions that are designed to strengthen attachment bonds.[8-10] A therapist can use this method directly with children or guide family members in the method. A centerpiece of Theraplay is shared playful activities, even as simple as helping each other blow bubbles. The idea is to get the adult and child engaged in carefully titrated, give-and-take interactions of trust and reciprocity. Theraplay helps parents develop skills in nurturing and attachment-sensitive interactions.[11]

A comparable intervention for dogs is called the Play Way, developed by Amy Cook, PhD.[12] She teaches people how to use "piano hands" to gently invite their dog into unstructured, improvisational playful exchanges in an unpressured way that keeps each participant feeling safe. Dogs with a tendency to get wild with their mouth can still participate with a small plush toy held in their teeth during the interaction. Edible treats are not part of this method. Instead, the focus is on building attunement, attachment, engagement, and mutual fun.

Many dogs welcome play with their people. In one study, Labrador retrievers responded playfully when their owner performed a "bow," and the dogs responded with extra vigor to a playful "lunge" posture.[13] Like kids, dogs respond positively to relational play with people,[14] appearing to relish the physical contact, level of movement, and physical closeness.

Games for Cooperation and Self-Control

Young kids are taught to play a game called Simon Says, which requires them to stop and start bursts of physical activity based on instructions from a leader. Players try to keep up with instructions such as "Take two steps forward." When they successfully comply, they continue playing. "Losing" occurs when they cannot accurately keep up with the instructions, and they are "knocked out" of the game. Simon Says gives kids practice in cooperation, motor skills, and impulse control.

Comparable self-control games are widely used by dog trainers and dog sport enthusiasts, and they can be used in home environments. For example, consider an ordinary game like Tug. Tug can be set up so that the game continues if the dog follows established "rules." If the dog doesn't follow the rules—for example, by grabbing the toy prematurely or putting teeth on skin—play stops. More varied and extensive protocols are seen in methods such as Laura Donaldson's Slow Thinking Is Lifesaving for Dogs.[15]

Less-structured play with peers can also build self-control. Wrestling and rough-and-tumble play offer important developmental benefits for children as well as for dogs.[16, 17, 31] Such vigorous play provides valuable practice in physical self-control and being responsive to social cues, and it is especially important for certain breeds and dogs. These dogs may love slamming into one another with intense physical body contact or wrestling with one another. Other breeds or individual dogs prefer chasing or playing tug with one another.

Peer-to-peer play has the benefit of helping dogs learn to control their bite strength, read social cues, and develop motor skills. When choosing a playmate for your dog, be sure that all playmates have the same play style. A bully breed that loves muzzle punching and hard play would be a poor choice for a mild-mannered breed or a fragile sight hound, for example. The wrong matchups can be deeply frustrating to the participants (like forcing a punk rocker to listen to opera) or worse yet, truly dangerous or even lethal.

Interrupt Bullying!

When one player chases, attacks, or provokes the other without a break or reciprocity, that is not playing, that is bullying. Healthy play is mutual and features give-and-take. This is true whether the play is human-to-dog or dog-to-dog.

When dogs are playing together, we can check whether we're witnessing healthy play or bullying by interrupting the play and then giving the vulnerable dog the option to resume or quit. If the dog chooses to quit, honor that choice.

To prevent bullying and violence among dogs, exercise caution when considering dog play groups and dog parks. Be sure playmates are well matched. Learn to become attuned to body language that signals escalating fear and predation behaviors.

CAUTION: *Supervise dog-to-dog play! Do not let dogs "sort out their disagreements among themselves." That choice can encourage later serious aggression or prove fatal.*[18]

Play to Meet Other Developmental Needs

Being playful and mischievous is inherently fun for young social animals. It also provides important developmental learning.[19, 31] Dogs will playfully provoke reactions for entertainment and to gather information about the social landscape.

So when a dog steals our shoe, it's not necessarily because they are bored and seizing an opportunity; they may be attempting to initiate play and test outcomes. When they try to get up a game of chase in this way, we can choose how to react. If the item is something we truly care about, we should pretend to be uninterested and unresponsive. By appearing bored and not taking the bait, we make the game less fun and reduce the odds that they will grab that item again in the future.

But we also have the opportunity to use this natural impulse to our advantage. We can purposely allow them to "steal" something we don't care about, like a toy or an empty carton, and then give chase in a lighthearted way, pretending that they're being "naughty" and we're going to get them. The dog gets to enjoy the dynamic social interaction and attention and feels agency in their world. This satisfies their urge for playful mischief and also helps us gently teach and reward socially acceptable behaviors. Kim Brophey likes to call this strategy the "naughty dog hack."

When to Ignore the Bait

It's fine to ignore attention-getting behaviors when a dog is trying to goad you into a fun game of chase with a valuable object. But if a dog requests attention at other times, we should give them the benefit of the doubt and find out what they need. Their pestering may feel irritating to us, but they have no other way to communicate pain, frustration, fear, or other serious need. Once we validate the underlying need and do what we can to meet it appropriately, the issue generally resolves itself.

Family therapists who practice Parent-Child Interaction Therapy give similar advice about ignoring kids. When a child engages in inappropriate ways of trying to get an adult's attention, that particular behavior can and should be ignored (unless it is urgently dangerous). Appropriate requests for attention, by contrast, should be rewarded with a positive reaction.[20]

reflections from the field

Michelle Stern of Pooch Parenting, a former schoolteacher, finds that by incorporating playfulness with creativity, fun and easier solutions are often available. She says:

> When I first became a schoolteacher, I was strict and had very little tolerance for shenanigans because I didn't want to lose control. Over time, that shifted. I found that using playfulness and humor helped with classroom management. For example, I would reward students by letting them play an educational game they loved. We gave points, and I would throw candy at them. It was great fun, and we had the best time.
>
> Later, I used playfulness in parenting my children when I was able, and now I use it with dogs. Dogs understand playfulness, and they appreciate less rigidity.
>
> For example, if my puppy takes a child's toy or a personal item of mine, like a sock, that I want back, I don't chase my puppy to get it. If I did, this would encourage him to run away from me with the item in a grand game of keep away. But if I turn the tables and run the other way, saying, "Oh, no, you can't catch me," in a fun voice, sometimes, the puppy will chase me instead. Then I can easily reward him for engaging with me, trading in the sock for a treat instead!

Dolls to the Rescue

Dogs, playing with dolls? Yes! Just as young children gain developmental benefits from playing with stuffed dolls and action figures,[21] so can dogs. For kids, research suggests a neurological value from pretend doll play.[22] Using near-infrared spectroscopy on children ages four to eight years old, researchers looked to see which parts of a child's brain became activated during play. They compared kids engaging with other kids, solo children engaging in doll play, and solo children engaging in play with a tablet. They found that the same brain regions lit up during play between two children as during solo play with a doll. The tablet, however, did not activate this social circuitry. Pretend doll play offers unique social and developmental benefits.

Family counselors incorporate dolls as part of play therapy for children. Dog professionals, such as Kim Brophey and others, use a life-sized plush dog to address a variety of behavioral issues.

A plush dog designed in the standing position can serve as a valuable substitute playmate for puppies and energetic dogs. This type of pretend playmate is especially beneficial for solo or high-drive puppies who would otherwise take out their bitey urges on hands and ankles or torment other dogs in the household. The technique is simple: Introduce the pretend dog to your real one and let them interact freely. If necessary, attract your dog's interest by moving and animating the pretend dog by hand or leash.

Some dogs respond with joyful abandon, jumping on the doll and wrestling with it immediately. Others only show interest at certain times of day, such as in the evening when they are brimming with excess energy and launching into "zoomies."

Supervision is important, at least at first, to ensure that the dog doesn't swallow or choke on a piece of the doll. When first introduced, the dog may sniff the doll's rump and belly and greet it much as they would a real dog.

A dog will understand that the make-believe friend is an approved outlet for roughhousing and may even begin to voluntarily redirect mischief onto the doll.

- Shy or very small dogs can find make-believe a more relaxed opportunity for exercise and social-style play than doggy daycare, where they can face real-life harassment from peers or worse. Small dogs, in particular, have high-pitched and squeaky barks that can potentially trigger dangerous predatory instincts in certain dogs, even when the dogs are similar in size.

- To find an appropriate dog doll, search online for "lifelike stuffed animal dog" and then browse for one suited to your animal's size and breed. Individual animals respond differently, so it can be worth experimenting with different dog dolls.

Social Learning Buddy, Even for House Training

The dog doll, which from the dog's perspective appears to behave reliably or calmly, can have a soothing effect. In such cases, it may be useful as a kind of security blanket or safe friend. This safe pretend friend can also join you on a trip to the vet or be useful for teaching life skills. For example, dogs from a traumatic background often resist handling and leashing, even if they need to be taken outside for toileting. Creative trainers put a collar and leash on a plush dog doll, then pretend to walk it outside to toilet. After a few demonstrations like this, a fearful dog often relaxes and follows the doll's example.

Reserve Time for Free Play

Free play—those periods when young kids are allowed to enjoy autonomy and control over their specific activities free from adult direction—offers young children unique benefits. It helps them gain physical coordination, sensory development, and social skills, particularly if the child is operating from a base of secure emotional attachment.

During free play, kids might pretend with toys or costumes, engage over a simple or elaborate game, make up their own secret language, explore a park or playground, chase one another in a game of tag, or do any number of other activities. Free play has benefits whether it is quiet or physically active and adventurous as long as the play allows a substantial degree of self-direction and enables children to follow their curiosity, explore their world, and experiment with outcomes. Immersive free play in nature can improve brain activity, mental health, physical activity, and sleep.[23, 24]

Free play is linked to fewer unwelcome behaviors in kids, possibly because it provides what's called "positive stress"—the type that challenges the mind and promotes resiliency without crossing over into toxicity or trauma.[25, 26] Paradoxically, the same free-play activities that adults describe as "chaotic, nonsensical, and disruptive" are also the ones that promote later adaptability, flexibility, and resilience.[27]

Research suggests that the more free play a child engages in, the greater their ability to self-regulate years later.[28] Toddlers and preschoolers who engaged in quiet free play or physically active free play were significantly more able to manage their mood and self-regulate two years later than a control group that didn't. Some scholars point out that the decline in early childhood free play corresponds to the current rise in psychopathology and a growing mental health crisis in children.[29, 30]

Free Play and Enrichment for Dogs

Dogs can benefit from the equivalent of free play too. This relaxed and self-directed activity promotes a dog's social skills, sensory development, and motor skills. It allows for curiosity and exploration, which are among the needs identified by Panksepp.[31] Dogs that are bred and raised in high-density urban or agribusiness settings or strictly kenneled captivity, such as for laboratory use, sale through pet stores, or designated as certain types of working dogs, receive little opportunity for free play.

Doggy daycare may meet the need for free play, but some facilities are so high density and high energy that the dogs do not get to proceed at their own pace. Another concern is that they may not get relaxed outdoor access. Unfortunately, in some cases, the daycare environment actually serves to stress and overwhelm a dog instead of happily engage them.

If we can give a dog unfettered access to a spacious yard with natural elements, we're essentially providing free play. Ideally, in this space, the dog is allowed to engage in typical dog behaviors, such as observing, finding, or chasing wildlife; digging; chewing sticks or toys; possibly playing with another friendly dog; and simply smelling air currents. Fortunately for those without a yard, suitable "private dog parks" are available for rent by the hour in certain regions. Note that some dogs develop unhealthy behaviors when left alone in the yard for extended periods, though, so even a yard is not a perfect analog to the natural environment.

A therapeutic application of free play for dogs is seen in Sarah Fisher's animal-centered education (ACE) Free Work.[32] This dog-centered protocol allows dogs the time, space, and freedom they need to process new surroundings and gain confidence through control over their environment. During an ACE free work session, a dog is brought into a gymnasium-sized building. People may sit around the perimeter to observe, but the balance of the space is arranged like a doggie gym. It contains a water station as well as activity stations, some of which feature durable equipment that can be climbed or entered and others containing toys or edible treats hidden in different surfaces. The dog is released to explore freely. He can choose to step up onto different levels, nose at various objects, drink water as needed, and forage for treats. Sometimes a dog will walk and sniff around the entire perimeter to gauge and assess the environment before working on the treat puzzles. A session lasts about twenty minutes, but the dog sets the pace. When the dog has had enough exploration, he or she is free to lie down and relax.[33]

At home, we can think about offering similar, informal free play for our dogs as unstructured "enrichment." Enrichment can be as simple as adjusting our daily walks to allow our dog more freedom to sniff and inspect their world. We can also repurpose ordinary items for enrichment at home. Some people give their dog empty cartons to play in or shred. I fold up an old quilt and place it on the floor, where my terrier-shepherd mix Bernie makes his own party. He leaps on it, digs in it, burrows under it, squirms on his back, flings it playfully around with his snout, rearranges it multiple times, and finally emerges tired, happy, and grinning. Experiment with simple choices like this to see what your dog enjoys.

CHAPTER 14:
Avoid a Head-On Collision

SOMETIMES IT'S NECESSARY to tell a little one "no." Unfortunately, for children and dogs who are easily dysregulated, that message is often triggering and difficult to accept.

The last thing we want is to provoke further reactivity or trauma. Instead, we can find ways to help them accept a no without catapulting them into deeper reactivity. We achieve this through strategies that focus on delivering a win-win situation with the least amount of confrontation. When it comes to discipline and behavior correction, experts advise us not to reach for a hammer when a tweezer will do the job. Whenever possible, choose a sideswipe over a head-on collision.

Turn Off the Fun

Remember that monster-sized adolescent dog who thinks grabbing your arm is fun because it's a good strategy to keep you engaged with them? When you flail around and try to scold, that seems like part of the game, right? In such moments, the easiest way to disengage is often to freeze, stop engaging, and remain still so the dog sees that their provocations don't yield the results they want. Instead of shouting, "Stop," or trying to physically force compliance, we simply make the undesired activity boring.

Redirect and Distract

Shifting the focus off an undesirable behavior and on to a preferable alternative is what's called "redirection," and it's a valuable strategy for reducing confrontation. A UNICEF survey of 218,824 respondents across sixty-three countries[1] found that children who were gently redirected and reasoned with had better discipline outcomes than those who got shouted at or spanked.

Parents use redirection when they distract fussy toddlers by pointing out something in the environment, starting a new activity, or doing something surprising. This strategy works for older children too. For example, a staff member at a residential facility saw a group of adolescent boys becoming unruly and physically confrontational. They appeared to be on the verge of a fistfight. Instead of throwing himself into the middle of the group and speaking sternly to them, the staff member did something surprising and fun to shift their attention. Without saying a word, he lay down on the floor with a straw and a ping pong ball and used the straw to blow the ball around. The kids got curious, stopped what they were doing, and came over to investigate. Soon, everyone wanted to get in on the game.[2]

Positive dog trainers routinely redirect puppies and dogs away from holding something valuable or teething where they ought not by trading the unapproved item with an acceptable alternative, such as a dog toy or chew or by starting a fun game. Then they praise and pet the animal for focusing on the better choice.

reflections from the field

Irith Bloom, a certified dog professional and faculty member at Victoria Stilwell Academy for Dog Training & Behavior, uses redirection for dogs who put teeth on furniture and objects around the house. She says:

> We can help the dog by temporarily blocking access to the things she likes to chew on, so that it's harder for her to do the wrong thing accidentally.
>
> Next, we put chew toys in the area she's in, and when we see her interacting with one of those chew toys, we praise her for engaging with it. In other words, we first reduce the odds that she'll make a "mistake" and then reward her for chewing on objects that are meant for her.

Redirection and distraction also come in handy when we and our dogs are out walking together. Many trainers teach the dog to give attention when requested, typically by making eye contact. The trainers use this skill to capture the dog's focus when there's a provocation in the environment that needs to be avoided. I have used distraction with Bernie by holding a nice smelly bit of treat in my hand, a foot from his nose, while we walked briskly through a downtown area. In more leisurely situations, I might distract him by tossing a few treats for him to hunt in the grass while another dog walks on the other side of the road.

Three Times to Proceed with Care

Redirection and distraction can be quite effective if we use them in combination with careful observation and sensitive responsiveness.

But sometimes redirection acts more like a dismissal of the dog's true needs or becomes downright dangerous. Here are three situations in which to proceed with care.

1. **Fear and anxiety**—Sometimes an excited or noisy dog simply craves reassurance and will settle once she receives soothing validation. Offering her a bit of calm stroking and a few soft words may be more effective than redirecting with treats or toys and serves to put deposits in the trust bank.

2. **Medical issue**—When a dog is acting out or struggling because they feel physical distress, such as pain, then the ideal approach is to fix that underlying problem if at all feasible. Redirection would, at best, mask the underlying problem.

3. **Predatory or aggressive behaviors**—Redirection has clear limits when a dog's impulses kick in. I was reminded of this recently when our garage door happened to be open at a moment when Bernie was unleashed and uncollared. I didn't realize that wildlife was foraging nearby until Bernie took off. Within seconds he had treed a raccoon (which looked pretty silly trying to hide its bulky self among slim palm fronds just above my eye level!). Fortunately, Bernie's predatory sequence favors stalking and chasing, and once the raccoon stopped moving and was out of his view, it became less interesting. I was able to gently break the spell and urge Bernie back inside with promises of fun there. But we should always proceed with care.

⚠️ **CAUTION:** *It is dangerous to touch or get too close when dogs have kicked into the most active and violent phases of the predatory sequence or into the most active externalized fear behaviors. Do not try distraction or redirection unless it can be done from a safe distance. The definition of "safe distance" varies based on breed and circumstances. Consult a professional if you have questions. High-energy breeds especially require expert handling in these situations.*

Orchestrating Win-Win Solutions

One effective approach to avoiding head-on collisions is to co-opt natural behavioral tendencies and let instincts work for us.

reflections from the field

Linda Keehn of Positive Canine Training and Services shares how a bit of creativity can meet everyone's needs safely and kindly. She says:

> I worked with a dog who was chasing and grabbing the kids. I explained to the parents that it's unrealistic for your one-and-a-half-year-old cattle dog to be in the center of kids running circles around him and have him sit there and stare. This dog has got a lot of genetics that say chase moving things. But in a busy household with three young kids of school age and other friends in and out at any moment, we couldn't tell the kids not to run.
>
> In this environment there were kids shrieking and running in different directions and the mom coming in yelling at everybody to stop the chaos. That was just revving the dog up more. I taught them to play a game of freeze tag with toys they always had laying around their yard and house. Each kid took a toy, and we started

having the kids move around in a controlled run. As soon as the dog started chasing and getting ramped up, we'd yell, "Freeze." Immediately, the kids stopped right where they were and threw toys for the dog. They had fun and it was a way to get the dog's attention off the kids and onto the toys.

When the mother shouted, "Freeze!" all action would stop, toys would fly, and the dog would go pick up a toy. It got to the point where when the dog hears, "Freeze," he goes straight to pick up a toy. They tell him, "Good job! Go get your toy! Good boy!" Now he doesn't even want to chase the kids the same way.

So instead of teaching the dog to stay, we taught the kids to help the dog stay calm and deal with the situation. We did other things, too, like teach "come" because that gets you out of a lot of trouble. The mother could call the dog and reward it well for showing up with whatever works in that moment—she could feed him, play with him, or offer a toy. We taught the mom to be proactive and not wait until the dog was on top of the kids.

One smaller child in particular would be playing on the floor, and the dog would tackle him for fun. There was no aggression, but the kid would be crying at this point because this was a fairly large dog. I told the mother, "Don't let that happen. He shouldn't be on the floor playing with the dog. It's just too close for comfort." So we taught the child, as soon as the dog comes over, just stand up.

We also put in management so that when the kids go down to the basement to play together, we close the doors, and the dog isn't allowed down there. Mom's not there and nobody's there to control the dog while the kids are shrieking and roughhousing and playing with toys, so the dog can't be there. We also upped the dog's exercise and enrichment. Now, instead of a once-a-week playdate with another dog, he gets three to four play-dates a week. We put in other enrichment, too, and we taught everybody how to live with this dog.

It's really satisfying to help people live better with their dogs. And once you think about the whys, you are generally steered to a lighter hand. Then you understand it's not the dog being disobedient or unruly or domi-nant or whatever words you want to use. There's a way of looking at each situation that is dog and people friendly.

Now it's a breeze for this family. And the kids are literally doing it. Before, this dog usually wound up getting slammed in the crate or yelled at. Now it's just this harmony because the kids have tools, the mom has tools, and the dog has tools.

More Options to Reduce Confrontations

- For dogs that have become attuned to our guidance, a gentle reminder is sometimes sufficient. We can use a mild "oops!" or "unh-unh" to remind a dog to avoid something. We can calmly remind them to "leave it" as a way to interrupt cer-tain behavior. Better yet, set up a pattern that reinforces the desired behavior so they are eager to do what's preferred.

- Teach loose-leash or slack-lead walking to help avoid confrontations on walks. We can also be courteous and alert dogs to what's coming up, making our behavior predictable, such as giving a friendly "Okay, let's go" and patting our leg as a signal.

- Wait for the desired behavior before proceeding with something the dog wants. This doesn't require any commands or cues. For example, we can wait for the dog to settle quietly, perhaps in a sitting position or with "four paws on the floor," before putting down the dinner bowl or delivering a treat.

- If you take, also give. This is similar to redirection and increases trust.

- Proactively meet enrichment and exercise needs and arrange the environment so confrontation is unnecessary.

CHAPTER 15:
Honor Their Talents

Imagine walking a bloodhound and a miniature schnauzer together. Not an easy task. The hound wants to slowly sniff every blade of grass while the schnauzer wants to get moving.

Knowing a dog's breed can often help us predict their preferences and aptitudes, which also makes it easier to anticipate potential issues that may arise when we live together.[1] Researchers analyzed the genome and behavior of 4,261 purebred, mixed-breed, near-feral, and wild dogs and found these statistically significant correlations:[2]

- the most energetic dogs are herders, terriers, and retrievers;
- herders are the most trainable, but they are also the most fearful and anxious about their surroundings;
- retrievers and terriers are most likely to seek attachment and attention;
- terriers show the highest level of predatory chasing, excitability, and aggression toward other dogs; and
- breeds least interested in close interactions with strangers are sight hounds, Asian Spitz, and sled dogs, followed by herding dogs.

These correlations rise to the level of statistical significance, but we need to remember that breed is not a precise guarantee of behavior. One study noted that breed accounts for just 9 percent of behavioral variability.[3]

See Who They Really Are

The most compassionate option is to lean into your particular dog's innate tendencies and find ways to help them channel those tendencies into appropriate outlets. A helpful starting point is recognizing which part of the predatory sequence they instinctively prefer. Predatory behaviors include seeking, orienting, chasing, catching, biting, holding, shaking/killing, and eating.

Predatory behaviors are generally triggered by the environment. The bloodhound enjoying a sniffy walk is in the seeking phase. Dogs that dash off in hot pursuit of a squirrel are enjoying the chase phase. Dogs that enjoy biting and shredding games favor the shake/kill phase. Fortunately, not all predatory behaviors are potentially lethal.

reflections from the field

Oliver Ringrose of Dog Smart Training and Behaviour (UK) sees value in recognizing a predatory sequence and using that insight to our advantage. He says:

> You can tell when a dog is in predatory mode because their social side is completely gone. They are in a different mode of operation. In predatory mode, they can have an incredible level of concentration.
>
> One little puppy spaniel came into my training field where the grass was quite low. She came into the field and just kept running in her circular spaniel patterns.

To me, they were beautiful patterns because I know what I'm looking at. But the owner was really frustrated and said, "When she gets like this, she can't even respond to a recall cue. It's like I'm not even in the field with her. I can go and step in front of her and wave and she'll carry on doing it."

All I did was go out and drop a ball in the grass, but I didn't let her see. I just hid the ball in the grass, and she went round and round until she found this ball. Once she got hold of the ball, she carried it around in her mouth and became really responsive.

Finding that ball shut down the predatory sequence; it was like she completed her mission. Once we can end that predatory sequence for her, all of a sudden, she's like, "Right, I've done that now." The environment had its role to play in that story because the environment creates affordances for those behaviors and also holds the motivators.

We've got to try and get inside her head and think, *What is she looking for? How can I fulfill that need?* She was hunting and hunting and hunting, and the seeking system arousal and dopamine levels were going up and up and up, and she was getting faster and faster. She wanted to hold-bite. With retrieving dogs like spaniels, they bite the thing, hold it in their mouth, and carry it around. It's a prominent behavior we have selected in these breeds because it serves us well.

Working dogs are very stimulated by the environment. For a lot of them, you don't need to teach hunt patterns or anything—they're in them genetically. If you can allow those dogs to access those genetic behaviors, all of a sudden, they listen to you. Because all of a sudden, you're really valuable, and more importantly, you are useful and make sense to them. For this little spaniel, just one ball closed that loop. It was never going to be a treat.

A dog's prey sequence is hardwired and needs to be respected. If we pay close attention to our dog's natural inclinations, we can channel those talents appropriately.

- Offer work or play that fulfills the predatory sequence or phase that appeals to your dog. For example, a sight hound will enjoy chasing a fast-moving lure along a course, like greyhound racing. Energetic "bitey" breeds may enjoy leaping to grab a knotted rope. Retrievers are likely to enjoy chasing and returning a tennis ball.

- Motivate your dog during training or management activities by using the predatory sequence or phase that appeals to them.

Once we truly recognize who our dog is—not just their size or shape but their inner drives and motivations and aptitudes—it's easier to accept them and find accommodations that make it possible to live together more harmoniously.

reflections from the field

Justine Schuurmans of the Family Dog describes one of her own light-bulb moments. She says:

I took my difficult, tricky little five-year-old dog to a training camp on Suzanne Clothier's farm. He's tiny, just eleven pounds, half terrier, half toy breed. When he is in toy dog mode, he loves to just sit in my lap like a cat, but when he's in full-blown terrier mode outside, he doesn't care about me at all. He wants to do what he wants to do. As a trainer who felt like I always needed to be in control, I was having a really hard time with that.

Suzanne told me I hadn't accepted who this dog was—and she was totally right. My first two dogs were biddable and easy to work with. They were gun dogs, bred for connection. My previous dogs would always look at me to find out, "What are we doing? Doesn't matter what it is, as long as we're doing it together." But this little dog just had a mind of his own.

I realized I was trying to make my little terrier mix into a gun dog—and slamming my own head up against a brick wall simply because I was in denial of who he was. As soon as I changed that, I started to really enjoy him. It changed my relationship with him overnight because I saw him for who he really was. Then I was like, *Wow! He's awesome at his job.*

Dogs that have a high prey drive can be extremely energetic. They require appropriate and controlled outlets. If your lifestyle, environment, and expectations don't match your dog's innate talents, skills, needs, and temperament, life together can become difficult for you both.[4]

reflections from the field

Oliver Ringrose of Dog Smart Training and Behaviour (UK) reflects on how dogs' innate talents reveal themselves. He says:

A dog with a strong predatory drive has to be able to pick up subtle little changes around them. It may sound corny, but a dog is not going to be good at hunting or herding if it can't understand what a shape in the environment is going to do next.

I work with a lot of smooth vizslas, and they're very good at that. They're alert to all the signs, really tuned in. Even when these dogs are hunting or tracking out in front of you, they still understand what you're up to behind them.

They are also very empathetic. They understand all of your emotional responses, and they will reflect them straight back at you again. If you're really excited, they're going to get really excited. So, they are not always an easy breed to deal with.

It helps to be emotionally resilient. If you can calm down and become cool, calm, and collected, they generally will calm down with you. Sometimes people aren't emotionally in the right place themselves to have a dog like that.

CHAPTER 16:
Help Them Self-Regulate

WHEN KIDS OR DOGS are overcome with excitement or fear (what's often called "arousal" in dog circles), we can help them dial down the intensity to a more manageable level.

Some little ones have difficulty finding the off switch. This problem is pronounced in high-energy working breeds such as Malinois that are "do-ers" and constantly need a job. Guidance and structured, predictable patterns and protocols can help them relax.

Dr. Karen Overall, for example, is among the many experts who teach dogs how to relax. Relaxation routines usually involve practicing a carefully calibrated ritual and can include giving positive reinforcement for responding to a cue. Some trainers combine verbal cues with a physical or visual element. For example, a fabric mat can be placed on the ground when it's time to rest and taken away when it's time to work, or vice versa. A specific location, such as a raised platform, can also be designated as the spot where the dog is sent only when it's time to chill out.

Establishing habits and patterns sets up expectations in the dog's mind about what comes next and promotes a feeling of security. For example, we might sandwich high-excitement fun between calmer activities so the dog can anticipate and self-regulate. In practice this could involve beginning an outing with simple walking or a pattern game, boosting the excitement through big energetic games or sports, then gearing down to a cool-off walk, and potentially finishing by giving the dog a chew or food discovery toy on a mat.

For ultra-athletic dogs whose endurance skyrockets the more exercise they receive, increasing the cognitive challenge can actually help them dial down the physical frenzy. For example, during the high-energy activity, rather than throwing a ball until your arm falls off, throw the ball as a reward for following a cue. This might be the dog touching your other hand with their nose, weaving through your legs, or waiting for a release from a sit cue. All these behaviors require thinking and self-control.

Use Time-Outs and Time-Ins

A time-out—which involves brief isolation, but not too far out of sight—can make it easier for a child to hit pause on wild behavior. Dogs, too, benefit from the opportunity to settle down in a safe and quiet space. These short periods of quiet separation can be a useful tool. One nine-month-old cattle dog, Bucky, was driving his busy suburban family crazy with hyperactivity, barking, and nipping.[1] A big part of the solution was more exercise and what amounted to time-outs. Whenever the dog showed signs of becoming agitated, the family brought him into a quiet bedroom where he could lie down by himself for a little while. This proved so helpful that the dog began going into the bedroom to relax on his own, which reduced the problematic behavior dramatically.

Research into canine separation anxiety underscores how nuanced and fraught alone time can be for some dogs. During the

COVID-19 lockdown, getting to spend extra time in human company reduced dogs' separation behaviors, such as barking, pacing, destruction, and unwanted toileting, by 5 percent. But once ordinary work schedules resumed and dogs had less human company, those gains were lost and there was a net increase in separation-related behavioral issues.[2] Interestingly, many dog professionals anticipated this possible outcome and during the lockdown purposely left their dog at home while they walked or drove somewhere else for fifteen to thirty minutes at a time, hoping to prevent the dog from having too many readjustment problems after the lockdown lifted.

Dogs that suffer from serious cases of separation anxiety often require highly individualized professional help. However, sometimes their distress can be eased simply by changing the environment and conditions of their time-out. One young dachshund finally calmed down and quit his continual separation barking and howling after his family gave him a soft and snug, cave-like little dog bed in which to hide when he was left alone.[3]

Attachment-Friendly Time-Ins

Adopted children with a history of harm are not well served by being sent away even for brief periods of time in a standard time-out. Isolation reinforces their insecure attachment and further alienates them from people. It encourages them to withdraw into electronic games and dissociative worlds, making attachment disorders more entrenched.

For these children, specialists prefer a "time-in" instead. In this gentle disciplinary approach, the adult invites the child to a "think-it-over-place" that is close by and under gentle supervision. A time-in for a child might mean sitting quietly on a chair near the parent or accompanying the parent during household chores. If appropriate, the child may be led through a "do-over" that corrects the earlier error and earns praise. The child does not suffer further rejection; they are reassured that they remain part of the family and matter enough to receive adult time within appropriate parameters.[4]

A time-in strengthens attachment and social connectedness while offering casual teachable moments in context. This approach can likewise benefit dogs, particularly those who are new to the environment and need extra guidance or practice in good manners. For example, a time-in can help a new dog learn "house rules" before they are allowed more access and privileges.

Some foster dog volunteers use this approach, although they do not explicitly call this a time-in. They keep a new foster dog leashed or tethered to their belt while going about life at home for a few weeks. There are no formal lessons. The dog trails around with them and becomes part of the household's flow. Since the foster is always close at hand, they can gently steer the dog away from missteps while offering low-key positive social connection. This relaxed and consistent supervision helps ensure that each dog succeeds at assimilating into the home.

Note that a time-in doesn't require a tether. Young puppies getting into mischief or needing a rest can be strategically placed behind a baby gate or inside an X-pen near the family in the house. There, the puppy can enjoy a chew and a soft spot suitable for resting yet remain within easy sight and access. This helps them learn that they are part of the family.

In all cases, we need to be sensitive to individual needs. Too-close tethering will distress certain dogs, such as those recovering from abuse or recently removed from an institutional setting. Dogs like this may lack secure attachment, but they often cannot tolerate too much remediation at once. They require more distance and possibly a minimal visual boundary from which they can emerge when ready. That's why the ASPCA, as part of its successful rehabilitation program for highly fearful shelter dogs, provides those animals' kennels with an object that the dog can hide behind.[5]

reflections from the field

Sherry Steinlein of Paws for Success finds that some dogs are able to give themselves a time-out, while others—particularly young ones— need a helping hand. She says:

> When my husband and I had two boxers, we also had Zoey, a pitbull mix. The boxers would bounce and make a big ruckus greeting us when we came home, and Zoey just couldn't get near us with all their boisterousness. Instead, she would go grab herself a Nylabone and take it on one of the dog beds and chew until she could come over and greet. We never taught her to do this. She just figured out how to self-soothe until she could come do her own greetings.
>
> Our new puppy, Elijah, is from a local rescue group called Pit of our Souls. When he gets overaroused or overexcited, he gets a little loopy. If I come in the front door, he runs to me, and he will do the big, excited jumping, which is fine. I can deal with that, but he was doing that puppy biting and going for my forearms. No puncturing, but he's a big dog with a big head and a big mouth and I'm little. I'm 4'11" and 110 pounds. Elijah's 70 pounds now; even when he was 60 or 50 pounds

he was hurting me physically. I also had a big problem when I would load the dishwasher because he is very food motivated. Elijah would stand on the dishwasher door to try and get in. I was concerned that he was going to break the dishwasher.

I borrowed techniques from Kim Brophey's Family Dog Mediation "hacks" and from Laura Donaldson's Slow Thinking and worked on being very consistent and giving Elijah much more structure and predictability. In my kitchen, Elijah now knows where he needs to go. He automatically goes to a big mat that's foamy and soft. This is his safe, happy place, like his anchor.

In the beginning, I tossed a treat on the mat every time, but as he learned, I would drag the time out a little bit more. This happened over weeks until he just associated that mat with good things. Very often now, he'll just go sit on the mat. He'll look at the corner of my counter where I keep dog treats, but because the mat is associated with calmness, he doesn't jump on the counter area. He knows if he just goes and sits on that mat and looks at me, I'll say, "Okay, you can have something," and I'll treat on the mat. What's important is that I don't hand it to him, I toss it on the mat, so the association is the mat equals the treat.

When I load the dishwasher now, even when there is food on the counter, he still goes to that mat. I don't have to constantly be treating him anymore. He'll pick up one of his toys or a Nylabone and go lay on the mat and just play with this toy quietly. If he looks at me or looks at the treat counter, I can also acknowledge that and give him a cookie. So we have that nice communication of "Okay, you want something? You can have something. You're a good boy."

The other part that Kim and I discussed is the freedom harness, which is good quality and lined with velvet. If Elijah starts getting too excited and can't be redirected easily, I can move him with the back of the harness. I don't have to physically grab or hold him directly, which would make him more excited. I just want to be able to communicate, "Okay, this is not acceptable." I gently take the back strap and move him away a little bit, and then I talk to him and explain I'm going to remove him for a little while to behind a baby gate where he can have toys or a Kong and a timeout to decompress.

It's like a timeout with a kid. It says, "You need to decompress for a little bit. You're overwhelmed at the moment. You might be having a tantrum, your mind might be kind of exploding, and the chemicals in your brain are just going boom, boom, boom. When you're hysterical, I can't talk to you at that moment. You can't hear me at that moment in time. I still want to help you, but I have to have other options." What kind of options? Even in positive training there used to be all these pat answers: use this protocol, use that protocol. But really, it depends. It's important for us when working with behavior to be flexible.

Become a Good Example

Just as a parent is a role model for a child, we serve as a role model for our dog.

During the back-and-forth interactions of earliest caregiving, when the biology of attachment springs into action, children naturally synchronize with their mother. They may mimic each other's eye contact, emotional expressions, sounds, and physical touch. Even heart rate, stress response, hormonal coordination, and alpha and gamma brain waves naturally align.[6] As children get older, they naturally copy what they see others around them do.[7]

In a similar way, dogs synchronize with our stress levels and mirror our emotions (whether those emotions are positive or negative), as revealed through facial expression, body posture, or voice.[8, 9] Dogs and their people tend to match stress levels during dog sporting events as well as over the long term in ordinary life.[10, 11] In one comparative study, puppies spontaneously watched and matched human actions in an unfamiliar situation more than did wolf pups and kittens.[12]

Dogs tend to move when their people do, stand when their people do, and gaze in the same direction as their people do, much as children do with their mothers.[13, 14] Even when a dog is generally indifferent to other dogs, it will stop and sniff another dog if their person engages in conversation with that other dog's handler.[15]

We will set a better example for our dog if we remember that anytime we get physically excited, perhaps gesticulating wildly or shouting or becoming angry, our dog's agitation will also ratchet up. When we display calm, we model the desired behavior.[16] If we purposefully manage our own stress, we are less likely to transmit it "down the leash" to our dogs. This can work for puppies too. Oliver

Ringrose of Dog Smart Training & Behaviour (UK) says that's why he never struggles to get puppies to go to sleep. He says, "All I do is just lay on the sofa and even pretend to be asleep or go to sleep with them. I show them how to chill. Once they realize nothing else is happening, then they'll start to mirror that behavior."

Give Practice in Self-Regulation

Like a professional athlete getting amped up to start their workout, some dogs know that a rewarding game or activity is coming. Their tail stands up like a barometer of excitement. Dogs that find certain activities or treats so fantastically appealing that they get compulsive about them can benefit from practice shifting from high excitement to low excitement until they learn to go back and forth with ease.

- What's high excitement? Playing a vigorous game of tug or fetch or chasing a piece of real meat.
- What's low excitement? Chewing a long-lasting treat, licking a smear of peanut butter, or sniffing around for kibble bits scattered in the grass.

We can deliberately guide our dogs between high-excitement and low-excitement activities as needed. We can also empower our dogs to self-regulate by keeping a selection of toys and enrichment options within easy reach for them at home. With more options available, our dogs might go to a bucket and grab a toy themselves instead of jumping up and grabbing at us.

CHAPTER 17:
Set Everyone Up for Success

JUST AS PARENTS of toddlers carry diapers, bottles, snacks, drinks, and wipes along for outings, we can equip ourselves when we walk or travel with our dog. Carrying "cookies," small dog treats, in a fanny pack or pocket can be useful for on-the-road training, distraction, or getting a dog's attention in a pinch. Also helpful are poop bags for courteous cleanups, a bottle of water so the dog can have a cooling drink, and perhaps an air horn to use in an emergency if there's risk of a dog fight.

If we plan on staying out a while, we can also bring activities to keep dogs busy, such as a long-lasting chew[1] or a favorite toy. We can even bring a designated safe place like a mat where they can rest and calm down. I sometimes carry a small sun umbrella that pops open quickly and can be used as a visual block when set on the ground.

Get Outfitted

Collars put direct physical force on a dog's neck. The amount of force depends on the type of collar used and the direction the dog is moving relative to the handler. In one comparative study of four nylon and canvas collars, peak force occurred while the dog moved in a counterclockwise direction wearing a double-layered nylon collar. The lowest pressure occurred when the dog traveled straight ahead in a single layer canvas or nylon collar.[2] In another study comparing seven styles of collars and a slip lead, the difference in force exerted on the neck varied between 40 and 141 Newtons, or between 83 and 832 kilopascals. None of the collars had low enough pressure to avoid risk of injury during pulling on the lead.[3]

Wide nylon collars are an improvement over choke collars, which pose a great risk to delicate structures in the throat, including the thyroid gland, salivary glands, and lymph nodes. Prong and pinch collars pose all the same injury risks as choke collars and can also cause puncture wounds, become embedded in the skin, contribute to brain damage, and actually worsen dog aggression.[4, 5] Electronic collars, or "e-collars," which deliver electric shocks or other aversive punishments, are also problematic. They have been shown to cause burns, wounds, and trauma and to increase reactivity and aggressive behaviors.[6]

Other Choices

Small and light dogs pull more often while big, heavy dogs exert more leash tension.[7] Chest harnesses can be a great choice to distribute force away from dogs' delicate neck and throat areas. Harnesses may cause chafing and skin irritation from repetitive wear, and some designs impede a natural and comfortable gait, leading to orthopedic pain. So careful fitting is crucial, and rotating styles can be helpful.

With chest harnesses, we have options about where to connect the leash. A model that connects at the front of the chest, rather than on top between the shoulders, can make it easier to teach loose leash walking or control a dog who pulls often. Some models have multiple connection points plus a handle, for extra control options.

A harness doesn't work for every dog, however. In the case of our thirty-pound mixed breed, Bernie, his short, stumpy legs, narrow chest, and silky hair made harness fitting a bust. Instead, I settled on a wide nylon martingale collar, which can be preset so that it only tightens to a limited degree when he pulls.

The martingale has a few benefits. First, it is easy to put on (Bernie voluntarily pokes his head through the loose collar area anytime he is given the opportunity for an outdoor adventure) and easy to remove (when I loosen the collar, Bernie assists by wriggling free, so he can be unencumbered at home).

Second, the martingale allows for a harness hack that I learned at a local shelter. After hooking the leash to the martingale collar, you can slide the leash behind one front leg, under the belly, and back up behind the other front leg and then thread it upward through the collar's extra loop on top. This creates a temporary harness "wrap" that offers more control than a simple collar and also redistributes pressure points if the dog pulls. If the leash happens to go slack and the wrap slips off, the martingale collar still remains in place as a backup.

Head halters, such as the Gentle Leader, are another option for controlling strong dogs who pull fiercely; however, these are often difficult for dogs to accept.[8] Care and sensitivity are required with head halters and head harnesses since their misuse can create the equivalent of whiplash and all the physical harm that entails.

⚠️ **CAUTION:** *Because of the innate physical risks of neckwear, headwear, and harnesses, "loose leash" or "slack lead" walking is an important safety skill to teach a dog. It helps prevent injury both to the dog and to the person holding the line.*[9]

Considering Longer Leads

In theory, long leads are the next best thing to a dog being off leash, but there are safety considerations.

Retractable leashes automatically extend and rewind back into their plastic-cased handle. On the plus side, they can be unlocked to allow a dog to roam freely within a wider range, and locked to a shorter length when more control is needed. Dogs get to enjoy more choice and exploration of the world while on a walk this way. On the negative side, dogs must pull against their harness or collar to some degree to feed out the lead. Some professionals believe this encourages pulling.

A bigger problem is that when the leash is unlocked, the dog can dash into the road or toward other danger, leaving the handler with little time to respond. When the mechanism is unlocked, all bets are off if your strong and fast dog bolts after a squirrel. The momentum created due to the length of the line increases the jolt when your dog hits the limit of the line. I've been knocked off my feet and nearly had my shoulder dislocated due to an episode like this.

Another challenge with some retractable leashes is that the very narrow cord can cause a nasty abrasion burn if it gets wrapped around your leg or someone else's. Also, other people may fail to notice the cord and trip over it. A somewhat less-risky alternative is the wider tape version, but that does not eliminate all the risks.

Many progressive trainers use a long line that is not retractable.

This type of lead is good for leisurely "sniffy" walks and hikes or practice of a recall cue. Certain materials, such as biothane, clean up more easily. A newer long-line option for people with adventurous dogs is the "belay leash," inspired by rock-climbing equipment. It has a roller carabiner, allowing more deft handling on long lines.[10]

Invisible Fences

"Fenceless" systems pose multiple dangers. These systems won't stop another dog from entering the area to attack. They won't stop a dog thief from coming onto the property to steal the dog. Worst of all, these systems work via sensors and an electronic collar to deliver an unpleasant stimulus, such as a noxious spray or a painful electric charge. Containment systems like these can provoke defensive aggression in dogs who don't have a history of biting, as attested by multiple lawsuits.[11]

Make Your Dog's World Predictable

Predictable schedules are reassuring, especially to reactive individuals and those with a background of harm. The sense of security schedules provide is a valuable part of rehabilitation after trauma. Consistent schedules are also comforting to dogs and are routinely used with working dogs and rescue rehabilitation.[12, 13]

Another way to make a little one's world predictable is to explain it to them in real time. Just like kids benefit when we reassure them while introducing them to new experiences, dogs can benefit when we can act as a "tour guide" and narrate the world for our dog. Yes, I am suggesting we actually speak aloud, in simple words, explaining the actions we're taking or pointing out something in the environment. Many dogs respond when we calmly acknowledge what they're experiencing or give warnings about potential triggers.

Our commentary gives the dog an opportunity to react more calmly and even remove themselves from a situation. And before you say, "That's ridiculous, my dog doesn't understand any of that," try it a few times and see. Many trainers speak to dogs to ease their way through challenges such as grooming. Narrating the world can be particularly helpful for reactive and high-strung dogs. Just keep in mind that there are breed differences in auditory sensitivity and the ability to detect the naturalness of speech, with the advantage going to longer-headed dogs.[14]

Set Consistent Expectations

Let's say we want to call a dog back indoors after outdoor play. To increase success, we have a few options:

- Practice having him come inside and go outside frequently and repeatedly, perhaps rewarding a trained recall cue, so that he's not afraid that coming in means he'll never get to go out again.
- Establish a predictable pattern of a five-minute warning with a phrase like "Finish up!" before the final call of "It's time to go inside."
- Establish a predictable pattern of giving your dog a treat or dinner right after they come back inside.

We can also proactively set expectations by arranging the environment so there are fewer opportunities for problems. Dog trainers describe this as "management."

reflections from the field

Michelle Stern of Pooch Parenting emphasizes the importance of straight talk about management and being honest and realistic about a little one's developmental stage and needs. She says:

When families have kids and a dog, I talk to them about safety because all kids get dysregulated, and that can look different at different times. A dysregulated kid might scream, run, play, or have tantrums. Toddlers, in particular, simply cannot use self-restraint or follow complex directions. There's nothing wrong with these children—they just can't do it developmentally. It's like asking a one-year-old to drive a car.

Any time that kids' behavior becomes unpredictable, dogs also get unpredictable, especially anxious dogs. Dogs react in the moment, and if they get scared or need to communicate their frustration, that's when injuries and bites happen. A lot of my work is around safety and preventing the child from having access to that dog.

I talk to parents about finding safe and natural outlets and managing the environment to prevent anyone from making a mistake—just like we put knives away so a toddler can't grab a knife. If a child needs to run and scream and play, where can they do that away from the dog, so that the dog feels safe? What's a natural, safe outlet? Can they run and scream and play outside, while the dog stays inside? We want to look out for everyone's best interest.

The best strategy is not to give kids or dogs access to situations they cannot manage. Parents don't need eyes in the back of their head to constantly monitor situations —we can use tools, like a baby gate. When there's a gate, the baby can't surprise or irritate the dog, the dog has a safe harbor, and you can breathe, check your phone, fold laundry. With the right structure in place, you can take care of yourself and cope better, and everybody in the household benefits.

Ideas for Easy Enrichment

When we set everyone up for success, we think about the dog's needs, such as providing one of these types of enrichments.

- Give pieces of crunchy vegetables to your dog to clean their teeth and improve their diet. Consider a few sticks of raw carrot, raw sweet potato, or raw cauliflower florets.

- Freeze meat broth into "pupsicles" that can be enjoyed on warm days, outside where it's less messy.

- Wrap a small towel around slices of vegetable or cheese or raw peanuts to create a "taco" that your dog can nose open to discover what's inside.

- Create a food puzzle by hiding an edible treat in an old cupcake baking pan and covering all the openings with tennis balls.

reflections from the field

Debbie Sheridan of Debbie's 4 Dogs, LLC, knows that setting everyone up for success also means preparing the humans. She says:

> When my daughter and I agreed to adopt an eighteen-week old rescue puppy, we already had a seven-year-old rescue dog at home. We arrived to meet eight puppies—six that were normal size and two that were a third of the normal size. The small ones had been separated out to protect them because the bigger puppies had been bullying and attacking them.

When I met the two undersized ones, the female growled and was standoffish. The male seemed very friendly and came over, but he was covered in blisters. They both just looked so sad. I used to counsel humans with substance abuse and issues around adolescence. I had a problem with the relationship with my own mom, you know, and I was just so interested in trying to help others. I've always wanted to help dogs too.

This litter had been born to a malnourished stray mom, and I discovered that these two smaller puppies had an autoimmune skin problem called strangles. The dogs were so malnourished in utero that their immune system had turned on itself. I looked at my daughter and I said, "Wow, this is not what we signed up for." And she said, "Right, but there must be a reason why we're here." I agreed. Of course, how could I turn my back and walk out? But how could I leave the second puppy alone?

So we took both. I hadn't heard about littermate syndrome at the time, where everyone tells you how it's such a bad idea to bring home littermates, but if they're male and female, you may have better luck.

Fitzy, the male, was a husky pit mix. Stella, the female, was a husky Anatolian shepherd. (With dogs, you can have different dads in the same pregnancy.) My daughter Samantha sent a photo of the puppies to my daughter Eva, who posted it on Facebook. Then my husband called and said, "Do you have something that you need to tell me?"

I took the puppies to my vet right away. She said that without treatment these puppies would have been dead in one or two days. They were completely dehydrated. She lifted their skin and started giving them saline solution. Their bellies were full of worms; they weren't getting any nutrition from anything they were eating. They were emaciated, and their little tummies were distended. When they finally pooped out the worms, it was like a huge bowl of spaghetti. The vet put the puppies on steroids and antibiotics.

Luckily our dog at home was welcoming. Two days later, when the male puppy, Fitzy, was out in the backyard, he fell over, and his eyes rolled back in his head. He had parvo. He had to stay in the hospital for a full week. Before, Fitzy seemed like a free spirit. After parvo, something changed in him. He became afraid of the world. When people came to the house he would bark and run away, bark and run away. He was very conflicted.

My house had been the one where everybody would just pop in and say, "Hey Deb, what's going on?" All that stopped. Now people were afraid to come in, rightfully so.

Fitzy is a husky pit, so he's very vocal with many different octaves. When he's happy and excited, he makes a sound so high that it hurts your ears. His upset bark is very scary and deep.

People don't realize that most dogs find it rude and confrontational for you to look straight at them. And that dogs naturally have a very ritualistic way of greeting each other. They start from a distance, moving their bodies in an arc and circling around. They lose the ability to do that when they're on a leash. So to keep guests safe, we kept all three dogs behind a gate inside the house and followed a protocol with every visitor.

One day, I scheduled a new handyman to come do a lot of work around the house. I said, "Tony, my dog Fitzy is really uncomfortable with strangers coming in. For safety, we have this protocol that we follow to help him to see that you don't mean him any harm. But I need you to be comfortable with it."

He said, "Oh, I'm fine, I'm fine. I've had dogs, I've had scary dogs, I've had all kinds of dogs all my life, and I'll listen to whatever you say. It'll be fine."

I explained, "When you come in, you'll see a gate up with the dogs behind it. I want you to just stand sideways toward Fitzy and toss him some treats behind the gate because when we toss treats, the dog can see that good things happen when somebody comes over. But he doesn't have to come near the person who's tossing the treats."

This is hugely important. Often, people hand a new dog a treat, and while the dog eats the treat, they put their face right up to the dog, making the dog come face to face with the scary human. We needed to avoid that.

Tony arrived, stood outside the gate, and tossed treats inside as I had instructed. Then he looked directly at Fitzy from afar. Fitzy responded with his deep, serious barking. Suddenly, Tony stuck his face close to the gate and shouted in a loud and deep confrontational voice, "I'm not afraid of you. I'm not afraid of you."

Fitzy immediately reacted by barking in a huge way. Tony is a big guy, over six feet tall, but I took him by the arm and pushed him out the door. I said, "What was that? That's not anything that we talked about."

Tony said, "He's not what I expected. I had to show him that I wasn't afraid."

My mind was spinning. Tony heard what I said during the phone call, and he understood all the instructions. But in that moment, his mind went right back to fight or flight; it was a fear reaction.

Outside I talked to him and said, "I can't have you come back in today because now Fitzy's already triggered and there's a thing called trigger stacking that could put him over the top. But if you want to try it again, we'll have you come back in a few days—if you can hear what I'm telling you now. We'll see how it goes."

Tony was open to learning new things, and he came back three days later. I said, "We have to try hard to do it the right way this time because seeing you will most likely trigger him. That first visit was really scary for him."

Tony laughed and said, "Well, it was scary for me."

I said, "I know. So I'm doing a redo for both of you. Let's have a clean slate."

This time I upped the treats. Fitzy's favorite food is salmon, but I wasn't going to throw salmon all over the floor, so I got chicken. As soon as Fitzy saw Tony, he started his deep barking right away. Tony looked at me.

I said, "Just stay sideways and talk calmly to me because if you talk calmly to me, he can see that you and I are having a nice conversation. Then he gets to think, 'Wow, Mom seems really comfortable with this guy. She's not upset. Maybe it's not as bad as I thought it was last time.'"

Tony started saying things like, "Okay, Deb, how's your day going today?" He had a big smile on his face. Fitzy was still barking and then backing up and barking and backing up. He was conflicted. Tony started tossing chicken, not making eye contact with Fitzy, just standing sideways toward him.

All three dogs were behind the gate, and they all began eating the chicken. Fitzy was like, "Wow, this guy has chicken. This is awesome."

Everything was going well, so I said to Tony, "All right, everybody's eating the chicken. This is great. You can walk in but keep yourself sideways. He's still checking you out. If he's feeling comfortable, he's going to come up and sniff you. But if you're not comfortable with that, we can go back behind the gate."

Tony said, "No, I've got it this time, but I'm trusting you."

I said, "I've got your back." But I also had Fitzy's back.

We walked inside the gate and Fitzy came up. I told Tony to just keep talking to me. Fitzy sniffed him, and Tony tossed some more chicken. Now Fitzy was eating the chicken and walking by Tony to eat the chicken.

Fitzy had watched us talk. He had watched the calm. And now he was feeling comfortable. Of course, if Tony had turned around and started shouting at him again, that would have ruined everything.

"How are you feeling?" I asked Tony.

He said, "I'm amazed."

I said, "Well, I hope you're amazed in a good way."

He said yes, and we laughed. At that point, I told him all the dog's names, and had him toss a treat to each dog, using their name first, starting with the other two, so that Fitzy could see the nice interaction.

Tony began to say, "This is fun. I'm having fun with this." He called Fitzy's name and tossed chicken and from there we walked out into the backyard and sat on lawn chairs while the dogs did their thing and hung out. Fitzy was checking it out, checking it out, getting a little closer, until finally he was comfortable enough to lay down on the ground.

Tony and Fitzy went on to become great friends. It got to the point where Tony would come down the road in his white truck and Fitzy would look out the window and start to make a high-pitched happy cry because it was his friend Tony, and it was going to be a beautiful day.

PART FOUR

HEARTS to the Rescue— Three Case Studies

CHAPTER 18:

Case Study 1—Duke and Dr. Rudy De Meester

DUKE WAS EIGHT WEEKS OLD when Katrien De Clercq and her wife, Carine, took him home from the breeder.

While other families were lifting and cuddling their new puppies at the breeder, Duke refused to be held or touched. He wouldn't even sit on Katrien's lap for the ride home; he insisted on wriggling to the floor by her feet.

Duke was an English cocker spaniel and Katrien's first puppy. She was eager to train him, compete together, and win prizes. And when not competing or training, she expected Duke to be as delightful as any animated movie dog. "I wanted what I saw on television and what I saw at dog shows," she says. "I wanted a Walt Disney dog."

By the second day home, Duke was able to sit on command. By three months, he was mastering obedience skills at a rewards-based clicker training school. "I am a very driven person," she says. "The training at this school had a very competitive focus, just like me. It was all about the length of time he could sit, the length of time he could lay down, how well he could hold positions, how quick his recall was."

Duke and Katrien trained together, striving for the highest levels of obedience competition, levels that required great precision. For example, to perform a recall, Duke would have to stop exactly on the line and not before and not after.

The school told Katrien she should not pay attention to Duke except during training and to ignore him if he tried to interact. She was advised not to greet him first thing in the morning, or when she came in the front door, or at any reunion at all. The trainers said it would make the dog respect her more and work harder to earn her rewards. Katrien took the school's advice to heart, earnestly wanting to do the best job possible.

"If they told me in dog school, 'You need to train this twice a day,' I was the kind of person who would train six times a day," she says. Even though the school was rewards based, teachers there did not approve of prompting behaviors by encouraging a dog to do something; Duke was only rewarded by a click if he happened to do the correct action by himself.

"He needed to figure out on his own what I wanted from him, with freeshaping, so he had to think very hard," she says. "For example, when I wanted him to weave between agility poles."

At first, Duke was energetic and eager to learn. "He loved doing all kinds of stuff with me, but it was very hard for him to rest," she says. "For him, sleeping was a very hard thing to do. I read all the trainers' books about how to become a winner, and Duke was very good in obedience. He was a star, but when we left the field, he was a nightmare."

Like a high-performance race car, Duke entered a high state of arousal in a split second. He reacted even before anyone else noticed the trigger. "He saw everything before we saw it—flies and bees and mosquitoes. He was very alert, very persistent visually, olfactorily, auditorily," Katrien says. "This made him difficult to handle sometimes because if there was a trigger that I did not see coming, he was already a Maserati at the end of my lead."

At six months old, Duke began whining. "High-pitched whining from the time we left the house and during the entire forty-minute drive to the school. At the school, they said that the whining would stop if we trained more." Katrien followed their advice, but Duke would not relax. He paced at home in a figure-eight pattern. "He circled around our living room table and then back around a little table, and he didn't stop pacing unless I told him to lie down.

"When I left the scene, he immediately fell asleep. When I got home from work, he switched on, and he followed me everywhere. It drove me absolutely nuts, and at the worst point, we went to bed at 7 PM just so he would sleep," she says. "We bought a television for the bedroom just to be able to go to bed early so he would settle down. When we went to bed, that was the end of his working day."

Duke had also stopped playing with toys. Instead, he began behaving more and more like a grumpy old man. Katrien brought home agility poles and set them up in the backyard for extra practice time. Duke reacted by growling. On a couple of occasions, he bit hard enough to bruise her but stopped short of breaking skin. His performance also deteriorated.

"Exercises he could do in 12.2 seconds, he now was doing in 16.7 seconds. They told me in dog school, 'You need to train harder.'" She did, but Duke kept whining harder. "His times decreased even more, and I got more cross with him and disappointed with him. I took it very personally."

When Duke was three, Katrien shared her concerns with a classmate, an older woman who recommended a book titled *If a Dog's*

Prayers Were Answered, Bones Would Rain from the Sky, by Suzanne Clothier. Katrien read the book, contacted the author, and was referred to Dr. Rudy De Meester, a behavioral veterinarian and researcher who lived nearby in Belgium.

"After three years, this was a very hard decision for me to make because the dog trainers had become my friends. I babysat their first kid. We hung out a lot together," she says. "I actually went against their advice to see Rudy."

The consultation lasted for one hour and fifty minutes. For the entire one hour and fifty minutes, Duke whined and howled and barked and paced.

That afternoon, Rudy told her, "You have to stop all training with him immediately, and you cannot ask anything of your dog anymore, anything. You can't ask him to go in, to go out, to go to bed, nothing. You don't ask him anything."

"For me, that was 'Wow, okay. How am I going to handle this?'"

Rudy told her Duke was overtrained. "Actually, he said Duke didn't like training. Duke would love to do other stuff but not the training. Rudy explained Duke's emotions, about how silly the exercises we did at the dog school were, how stupid it was to ask for obedience on a dog walk, like telling Duke to go lie on his leash six times during the walk just because I wanted to see if he could still do it.

"Rudy talked to Duke like you would talk to a boy. Just a grown man, talking to a boy. Rudy taught me that instead of ignoring Duke's whining, I should comfort him when he was stressed. Tell him what was going on. This was a shock to me. I was taught not to talk to Duke when he whined.

"Now I recognize that the Skinnerian, operant approach that the training school used is often the opposite of the biological and emotional approach. But at that moment, I did not have a clue."

Katrien worried, "Is this my fault? How Duke became, is it my fault?" Rudy answered, "First of all, as long as you struggle with the guilt question, you are not going to be able to help him because you are too self-involved if the guilt question is still there. It's not your fault that Duke had the potential of becoming a problem dog. But you did everything you had in you to make sure he did become this problem dog as an adult."

Katrien paid close attention. "The good thing is that immediately after Rudy told me all that, I wanted to become the best in not training him."

Rudy warned that Duke's behavior would get worse before it got better, and it did. "Duke completely did not understand why I didn't train with him anymore. He was very sad in the beginning." But less than two months later, the dog surprised her. She says, "He came running into the living room, playing with a silly stuffed toy. It was a frog, I remember, and the frog stuck out of his mouth, and he looked so happy. Both my wife and I said, 'Oh, my God, it's been so long since he has been so happy.'"

Katrien e-mailed Rudy a steady stream of happy photos: Duke sleeping in the grass outside. Duke sleeping in the living room. Duke sleeping late in the morning. "Duke slept a lot more, and for me, that was the best," she says. "He became an expert in settling down."

Duke still didn't like to be picked up and was quick to react, but he sought out more physical proximity. "I remember laying my hand on the car seat where Duke was also sitting. He lay down and very deliberately placed his paw next to my hand. That was a milestone."

In place of obedience training and competitions, Katrien tried "man-trailing" with him, a noncompetitive scent work activity that involves tracking a person. "It wasn't easy for Duke because he had to trust his own nose. It was him guiding me, and that was very good for our relationship," she says.

Man-trailing was by consent only. "He had a special harness he had to wear, so we would show him the harness. If he walked away, we knew he didn't feel like it. If we showed him the harness and he got all excited like 'Yes, let's do this,' then we did it."

Katrien stayed in touch with Rudy and enrolled in a postgraduate course in Companion Animal Behavior and Welfare. Rudy invited her to help with puppy socialization classes in Hamme, East Flanders, where she assisted Rudy and Laura Statius for three years.

"One of the first times that Rudy allowed me to teach his classes," Katrien says, "there were four puppies. One of the puppies was whining and yelping. I was afraid to give that pup attention because I was afraid that would teach it to whine and yelp more. Rudy was supervising my class. He walked up to the whining puppy and sat down. The puppy crawled in his lap, and that was that. From that moment on, I never let a puppy drown anymore if it is so stressed that it whines and yelps."

She came to realize that Duke's earlier whining was an attempt to tell her, "I'm too excited. I can't handle this. Let's do something else," or "I'm too motivated for this food. The reward is too high for me. I'm losing my self-control," or "Stop asking this of me. I'm not that clever."

"When I got Duke, I thought I had a very clear idea of how I was going to raise this puppy, but in hindsight, I didn't have any idea about how to raise him," Katrien says. "I had an idea how to train him." Now she understands the distinction between the two.

"I grew up on a farm where all kinds of animals' emotions were denied. I left home when I was nineteen with a whole lot of luggage from my parents in my head about how we cannot be friends with animals, about being competitive, and about being the best.

"I have completely shifted my focus and actually went on a mission to prevent this from happening to other people because I had no idea that I was doing something wrong. I had no idea. Nobody told me. The only thing they told me was that I needed to train more and be a better leader for my dog.

"Now I see being a leader more as offering safety and teaching skills, so society doesn't see dogs as a threat or so society just sees them as the social beings that they are. Dogs actually don't need a lot of training to be able to thrive in our community. They don't need a lot. If they are able to look at their handler when they are asked to look, that's a huge skill, just to be able to look at the handler and seek information and communicate."

Today Katrien helps people with private puppy coaching. "People need to understand that the minute a puppy is awake, it has landed in a world of choices. A puppy makes a million choices a day. Our responsibility is to create a world of 100 million correct choices . . . and cheer them on.

"Shy puppies need encouragement and empowerment. Bold puppies need impulse control lessons. The minute a puppy figures out what makes the owner happy, the world becomes predictable for the dog. And structure and predictability are the only things we need to reduce stress levels!"

She wants people to understand that "dogs just want to be a family member. Our dog is seeking to be our friend, and so we need to be the best friend we possibly can. We need to guide them through this human environment as safely as we can for them."

In the years since she brought Duke home, Katrien also noticed something else. "Somehow, somewhere along the road, I began noticing that I didn't need to be the best. That my personality and my identity were no longer defined by my results at competitions, but by how I am as a person, by how I am in relationships. Duke and Rudy and Suzanne opened that up for me. They opened me up to a whole different way of being."

CHAPTER 19:
Case Study 2— High-Performance Sports and Mr. Grin

DOG SPORTS COACH Hélène Marie Lawler breeds and raises high-performance border collies on her working farm in Ontario, Canada. She is careful to give her litters every advantage, but that doesn't mean outcomes are always predictable. Sometimes, to achieve the best outcome for each puppy, she veers a little off the original game plan.

Mr. Grin was one such case. By three weeks old, he stood out from his litter. A handsome tricolor border collie with beautiful structure and movement, he showed potential for speed—and a flair for drama.

"Grinny would get very upset about stuff that none of the other puppies were stressed about," Hélène says. "He'd vocalize and let you know, 'I'm too hot, I'm too cold, I'm bored, I'm too far away, I'm too close'—he had a lot to say. He was a summer puppy, and he would scream if they were outside and it was getting warm, just letting us know he was too hot. So I'd bring everybody into the air conditioning, and he would calm right down. Anytime he would get upset, I would soothe him and settle him, and then he would relax."

Mr. Grin was shaping up true to breed. "He is very much the profile of a puppy sought by people who do competitive dog sports, especially agility," says Hélène. "But he's also the type of puppy who can quickly end up with a lot of problems when not raised and trained in a way that keeps his brain calm and thinking."

Mr. Grin was the polar opposite of Hawk, a littermate. "When Hawk is unsure of something, he immediately freezes," she explains.

That's not Mr. Grin. "A couple of days ago, I put oil into a pan on the stovetop and it caught fire. Flames shot up two and a half feet. I shouted, and Grin came flying into the kitchen and jumped onto the stove. I had to catch him and explain that no, we don't jump into fires. He doesn't have any impulse control. He throws himself into everything; his reaction is to simply dive into stuff."

All that exuberance can lead a pup into trouble, and Hélène saw potential for issues on the horizon.

Meeting Puppies Where They Are

With every litter, a specific pool of people is on standby to purchase Hélène's puppies. "These are wonderful people with big hearts and really focused on positive reinforcement," she says. "I'm always so grateful for the people who come into my life looking for puppies, but I still look for a very specific match for each one."

Hélène was concerned about finding the right placement for Mr. Grin. "This puppy was showing me that he needed a little bit of something different and extra."

People buy her dogs with the goal of competing with them. "When you buy a puppy to go off and do competitive dog sports and your puppy can't function in puppy class, you start thinking, *Oh my goodness, I've made a mistake. We're never going to achieve our goals. What do I do now?* You think, *I'm stuck for fifteen years with a dog that is going to be an extra dog.* You know, our brains go to all sorts of drama when our puppy alarm barks at the other puppies in puppy class."

Hélène knew Mr. Grin needed a special home. "Someone who believes this is just a puppy being a puppy," she says. "Someone who understands Mr. Grin just needs to feel safe and take his own pace. Someone who doesn't have an agenda for where this is taking us. They're here for the ride. And not everyone is in that place."

"No matter how wonderful the person is," she says, "there are enough challenges in raising a puppy. When you add in high-drive, intense, working border collies, if you don't get the right match, it can be so frustrating and heartbreaking for everybody involved."

When no one in the current puppy pool seemed like a fit, Hélène thought, *Okay, then I guess that means he's supposed to stay here, at least for now. I'm going to be his person who takes that approach with him. Because I don't have an agenda for him. I have hopes, but that's very different.*

Others in his litter went to their new homes at three months, but Mr. Grin got an open stay on the farm. And he was not the first.

"I had a puppy from my litter last winter who was very shy and withdrawn and wouldn't come near anybody who came to visit. She clung to me like a little shadow. So I thought, *Okay, maybe you're meant to stay here.* When she was about six months old, I had somebody visit and she climbed into their lap. I thought, *Oh, okay, you're ready for your own person now.* Then, all of a sudden, the perfect home showed up for her. And she's doing so well. She's about fourteen months old and just had her first rally obedience competition."

Adjusting to Mr. Grin's Needs

Hélène did not want to send Mr. Grin home with someone who would bring him all over town and make him interact with a multitude of strangers in unfamiliar environments. She knows that Mr. Grin—true to his breed's working line—is not a social puppy. Instead he is genetically wired to detect subtle changes in the environment and bond closely with one individual handler. What's more, his own excitable nature means he can go from zero to one hundred in a blink. Hélène is purposefully helping him take it slow and learn to self-regulate.

"The concept of high arousal versus overarousal can confuse some people," she explains. "Competitive dogs need to be in a very high arousal state to perform at the speed that people are now running agility courses. There's a fine line before we cross into a fight-or-flight state. These dogs need a high level of energy but also need to remain focused and in the zone so they can function and perform really well.

"I help my dogs practice by using arousal manipulations where they get worked up and I show them how to calm down. For example, I do pattern feeding or pattern movement. With a puppy like Mr. Grin, I might take cookies in both hands, and have him just eat back and forth between my hands. Then I'll slow my hands down and move them farther and farther apart. That will get the dog moving back and forth and that pattern settles them. Another way is to have them do figure-eight patterns around my legs. We will also move away from something that's scary."

These practices are especially important for an excitable fellow like Mr. Grin.

"I want to teach him how to calm down because arousal responses become habitual," she says. "This is something that I have done intuitively, but lately I'm learning about the biology of trauma and the nervous system and found there's science behind what I have done intuitively. This is giving me new ideas about how I could work further with it."

Taking It Slow

The farm has over a dozen resident dogs, and Mr. Grin gets plenty of practice socializing with them. What he needs most is the ability to remain calm and focused on his person in new situations and settings.

It took months before Mr. Grin coped well on short excursions, such as to pet stores. When he reached eight months, Hélène felt he was ready for his first puppy class, a foundational agility class, provided it was the right environment.

"I really love how this teacher runs the class," she says. "The puppies never interact. So it's very safe. Grin doesn't have to worry about other dogs or people coming up to him. He is just doing the things we do at home in a setting where there are other people and other dogs. It's a big space and a small number of other people and other dogs."

On the first day, Mr. Grin barked a few times but was able to settle in a crate with treats when needed. By the second class, there was no barking, pulling, or lunging—just watching.

Hélène served as his anchor, bringing Mr. Grin to various training stations for brief visits. He received treats for putting his paws on something wobbly, heeling around cones, or hopping over a bar on the ground. Then they took a break for a walk outside, before trying again.

During the second class session, his behavior shifted. "I noticed that he was getting sharky—biting, taking the treats hard, and I was getting teeth on skin, which told me that he was no longer in a learning state," Hélène says. She stopped training immediately and sat on the ground, tossing treats for him to chase and letting him practice getting treats quietly from her hand.

"I just wanted to return him to a calmer state," she says. The strategy worked, and overall, she was pleased. "He made it about forty-five minutes without going into that state of overarousal. That was pretty good for just our second class.

"If, on class one, we'd walked in and all he was doing was alarm barking the whole time, I would have hit pause on this. If he had shown me that the class was overwhelming, I would have not come back, or maybe we would have spent the whole class walking around the fields outside." Her priority was keeping him under threshold and creating comfortable associations.

"With Grin, his default response to most things is to charge up and bark," she says. "I didn't want him to practice that more than necessary." By moving at a slower pace, Hélène keeps him in learning mode and prevents his tipping into overdrive. "Grin showed me that he was capable of doing more, so we've done more.

"At this point Grin is blossoming and doing so well," she says. "He still has a long way to go before he's solid and comfortable in a lot of different settings. But he's got such good focus with me and joy of working with me. It's trust in me, which is, I think, really important.

"He is learning and exploring and experiencing new things in a very titrated way, just a little bit at a time," she says. "I'm always making sure where that edge is and not going up to it or over it—if I do, then we back off really fast—and letting him lead the pace. Now, he's telling me, 'I can handle more. Let's do more. This is fun.' And we'll just keep going from there.

"I have a lot of dogs, so Grinny can be himself. He doesn't need to be anybody else. I have dogs that can breed, I have dogs that can do agility, I have dogs that can do herding. So Grinny can do whatever Grinny wants. I'm here for the journey together, and it's a really nice place to be. I haven't always been in this place, but it feels really good. I feel very grateful that I have the ability to just let puppies find their own path."

CHAPTER 20:
Case Study 3—Changing the Lens on Cooper

MARLENE O'NEILL LABERGE and her family adopted a large shepherd mix from a local rescue, and despite some training challenges with him, they agreed to take on a new rescue pup two years later.

The new puppy, who they named Cooper, won everyone's hearts, but life turned into an emotional roller coaster. Conventional training did not improve Cooper's behavior in a meaningful way, and a specialist advised they give him one final six-month window of opportunity before considering the last resort, behavioral euthanasia.

Here's their journey.

Not What They Were Expecting

By the time the Laberge family adopted their first rescue dog, Marlene had been working for almost twenty years as a registered social worker specializing in internationally and domestically adopted children. Certified as a Circle of Security Parenting facilitator and trained in Trust-Based Relational Intervention (TBRI), she assisted children's services by serving kids in care and foster parents.

"I was proud to be among the top colleagues in my area who you went to if you had a complex adopted child. With children and families, I could see all the developmental challenges and early life dynamics at play. In relation to dogs, I could see none of it. I didn't make that connection until our second rescue dog, Cooper, set that on fire for me."

Their first rescue, Conway, had arrived during a period when social media was exploding with talk of the "Go Anywhere" dog, the "Adventure Dog," the dog you can take anywhere. "I thought, *Wouldn't that be fun?*" says Marlene.

At four months, young Conway was a handful. Marlene describes him as "challenging on the leash—overaroused by other animals, scents, environmental contrasts. He went bananas, bucking on the leash when we tried to walk him along a nearby park corridor where it's common to see deer, bobcats, rabbits, porcupines, and other wildlife."

Marlene decided the solution was classes: puppy classes, adolescent dog classes, urban adventure class, dog camping class, hiking with your dog class. She enrolled Conway in class after class. "As a naive dog owner who was seeing all this stuff on Instagram and other places saying you can make a dog anything you want, I ended up treating him like he was a constant fixer-upper project."

Marlene consulted a trainer who competed at a high level in police dog sports. "Sometimes she would say to me, 'If you can't get a handle on him, we're going to have to put him on a prong collar.' And I'd say, 'No, I could never do that,'" says Marlene. "There were moments of things not resonating, but I couldn't make the leap that this dog was a sentient being that had the same wants and needs that a small child does. Instead, I felt the social pressure of 'Don't anthropomorphize your dog,' of memes making fun of people treating their dogs as children in the extreme wrong way—all indulgence, no structure."

Marlene was disappointed in Conway and disappointed in herself. "I ended up in this place where I felt, *Oh my gosh, I'm a teacher, but I'm useless at dog training. My mechanics are terrible. If I just had better mechanics around clicking and treating, he wouldn't struggle so much.* I loved him, but I was chronically disappointed that he couldn't do all these things. I felt, *My goodness, what a lemon of a dog.* We had what I would describe professionally as a relational rupture."

Today she observes, "Poor Conway fell victim to my assumption that you can shape a dog into anything you want them to be." DNA test results helped explain Conway's challenges: He was a free-roaming puppy surrendered from an under-resourced community where pregnant dogs are generally underfed and under threat from other dogs regarding scarce resources.

"Our expectation that he would walk nicely beside me on a six-foot leash and just look at wildlife, not chase it or get overaroused by it, was very foreign to him," she says.

The New Puppy

When Conway was about two, the family agreed to take a puppy from a community located hundreds of miles away. The litter of eight-week-olds would be separated from their mother and transported by car for more than eight hours to arrive at the local rescue. After a mandatory five-day disease quarantine, each would go to a home. Marlene's family agreed to step up and take one of the puppies.

Because the local rescue facility was brand-new, the incoming litter was all by itself during those days in quarantine. Each morning, the puppies were taken out to a pen for feeding while someone cleaned their kennel. A volunteer played with them for a few minutes, then put all the puppies back into the kennel until the afternoon, when the same feeding and handling routine occurred.

Adjacent to their kennel, separated only by a partial wall, was a warehouse area under active construction, with workers coming in and out all day and a lot of activity. When Marlene and her two preteen children arrived, just one puppy remained—the only male in the litter and a runt. That day, little Cooper had spent five hours all alone in the quarantine kennel without the comfort of his littermates.

Marlene recalls the shelter volunteer saying, "Thank goodness you're here. He's the last one, and he's really wired. You're going to have your hands full." When the volunteer brought out the pup, Marlene was smitten by this "insanely cute puppy—barrel-chested, skinny hips, blocky head. He immediately comes to the kids, and they just fall in love with him."

When the volunteer discovered the family hadn't brought a crate, she warned that the puppy was so wired, he would be a problem in the car. To be safe, Cooper was secured into a tiny harness that could be attached to a seat belt if necessary. The kids carried the pup into the car and held him close inside a jacket during the drive home. Cooper just cuddled quietly on the ride. At home, everyone was captivated. "We were struggling to understand why they were referring to him as so hyper and wired because he actually seemed really calm," Marlene says.

Once the new puppy was home for about a week, Marlene took him to join her and her husband on their regular 5:30 AM walks. At that hour, the sun wasn't up, and the weather was bitter cold. "As soon as we get out the door, Cooper starts bear hugging my legs. He's wrapping his little legs around my calf and holding on and shaking. He doesn't want to walk."

They'd never seen a dog behave like that. Marlene assumed the puppy was freezing, so she would pick him up and pop him into the front of her coat for a few minutes to warm him up, and then put him down again. They got him a little coat, but he hated wearing it. "He would pancake and freeze. And we just kept doing life with him. He didn't particularly love his morning walks, but I thought he was maybe a little nervous or unsure or whatever."

By six months old, Cooper was barking and lunging at everything. If Marlene brought him to meet kids at the bus stop, Cooper barked and lunged at neighbors and their children. Marlene thought, *This is really weird,* but she shrugged it off as "he's just going through a developmental fear phase or whatever." They also noticed that Cooper was hypersensitive to sounds. Air brakes on a truck, backup beeps from construction equipment, even tires crunching on ice sent him into a frenzy.

They began puppy classes, hoping that would help him settle. Cooper completed training exercises, but social interaction was a bust. He just wanted to go to his mat. If another dog in the class approached, Cooper began barking and snarling.

"The trainer in that initial class had the insight to say, 'Cooper seems relationally insecure. I think this is fear. I don't think it's aggression,'" recalls Marlene. That trainer suggested giving him a little more space and allowing him to observe other dogs from a distance.

From a distance, Cooper was able to watch other dogs and remain alert without barking or lunging. "The trainer also recommended positive reinforcement counterconditioning," says Marlene. This would involve taking Cooper to the bus stop at a moderately busy time and treating him every time he looked at something without barking.

But COVID hit, in-person dog classes shut down, people stopped visiting the house, and the world quieted. "Life got a little bit easier for Cooper during COVID because there weren't really any pressure points for him," Marlene says. "We didn't think about the long-term consequences of that lack of practice, but it was a good initial decompression, I guess." The family vacationed at a cabin with their two dogs during this time. One day, grandparents arrived unexpectedly, opening the cabin door with their hands full of stuff. Both dogs rushed them and jumped up. In no time, the grandmother's arm was bleeding. Everyone assumed that Cooper had bitten her.

Marlene immediately phoned a professional, who urged muzzle training for Cooper using positive reinforcement training. Days later, when they removed the grandmother's arm bandage, everyone realized this wasn't a bite, it was a scratch—and it had been caused by Conway's dewclaw, not a bite from Cooper.

Standard Solutions

But now Cooper was labeled as trouble. Marlene tried muzzle training with no success. Cooper simply couldn't tolerate the device on his head or touching his whiskers. "When anything is on his body, whether it's a coat or a muzzle, he's so focused on the physical sensation that he just can't coordinate his movements anymore." The muzzle was so distracting and distressing to him that they quit trying.

The trainer had also recommended standard protocols for reducing reactivity based on positive reinforcement, such as Leslie McDevitt's Look at That protocol and other disengagement skills. All relied on giving treats heavily. Marlene was advised to practice in the community, in areas where Cooper could have space and distance from triggers and where the family could engage him in play, so he wasn't so stressed.

"We tried some of those. But over time, he started to get more and more resistant to going out for walks," says Marlene. "Cooper was like 'Oh, you're going to take me out and expose me to the thing.'"

Once COVID eased, Marlene tried an outdoor class for reactive dogs, held in a spacious community park. Unfortunately, the area was surrounded by a perfect storm of triggers: a sound wall that shielded a major roadway plus a busy bike path and a playground full of mothers and strollers and bike commuters and families.

"We picked a space with a nice grove of trees that we could dip behind if he needed space and respite," says Marlene, who had also learned about Sarah Fisher's ACE Free Work protocol. "We brought a free work kit from home, spread soft treats on different surfaces that he could lick, scattered some in the snuffle mat, and let him forage and sniff to get him out of the car. Then the reactivity training games began. For the first two classes that worked. At the third class, we opened the back, but Cooper was not getting out."

Marlene wondered whether this class was really helpful for Cooper, but the trainer encouraged them to persevere. No matter the accommodations and adjustments Marlene made, by classes three and four, Cooper made his feelings clear: *No, thank you.* Marlene worried that maybe they were sensitizing him instead of desensitizing him.

Then one day, during a walk, a garbage truck thundered by. Cooper freaked and bolted for home. The next day he would not leave the house.

"Looking back on it, I would say we had trigger stacked him profoundly with the classes," says Marlene. "And then with this close call with a garbage truck, we had a complete shutdown. He wouldn't even go out to go to the bathroom. I had to coax him and stand there, and he would run to the dog run, pee, then race back inside and go right down into our basement, into the laundry room, into his crate. If we lifted his harness off the hook, he would run into his crate, and push himself hard into the back of the crate, like, 'I'm not going anywhere.' So we ended up with a full shutdown. At that point, we were completely lost."

Exploring Medication

By now, Marlene felt like she had read every positive reinforcement book on aggression and reactivity she could get her hands on. "I must have studied ten to fifteen different protocols on what to do to try to support him. I had all this conventional knowledge and felt like I had done everything out there as far as training."

A veterinarian in her circle helped her contemplate a pharmaceutical approach. "She gave me the same talk that I give parents about 'Don't fear meds,'" says Marlene. "When I talk to parents about meds, we talk about putting scaffolding on a building. Sometimes when you do repairs, you need to put up scaffolding so that you can reach the places that need repair. When the repairs are done, depending on the condition, sometimes you can remove the scaffolding and sometimes the scaffolding is lifelong. To help make Cooper more accessible to learning, we had that conversation about how medication doesn't have to be a forever thing."

Marlene submitted nearly forty pages of intake information for an appointment with a behavioral veterinarian, a specialist qualified to prescribe medication. "My husband and I sat in the consult room with Cooper. They were okay with us not muzzling him. The vet comes in the opposite entrance door, sits down, and has a camera to record. She doesn't make eye contact with him. She greets us, raises her eyebrows once, and Cooper loses his mind. He's barking, lunging, snarling, can't settle. Then he's pulling back and hiding. Then he's barking at her. Then he's pulling back and trying to get under our chairs. His behavior was quite dramatic."

When Cooper didn't settle after twenty minutes, the vet suggested putting him elsewhere so they could have a quiet conversation. "We couldn't put him in the car because it was in a busy strip parking lot, and he would have just barked at everyone. So the vet clears the room, gives me clear passage, and I have to put him in this awful run outside the vet's office with a whole bunch of kennel dogs going crazy. It was awful. I'm crying because it was so overwhelming. I just didn't feel good about this," recalls Marlene.

The vet reeled off diagnosis after diagnosis for Cooper, making Marlene's head swim. "By the time we left, I think we had four diagnoses plus medication prescriptions. She said, 'You've done everything you can do. You've tried all the approaches, you're actually working too hard with him at this point. You look exhausted. If he's not better in six months, I'm going to recommend you euthanize him.'"

Marlene and her husband were shell-shocked. "We were completely overwhelmed leaving that office, thinking about having to tell our kids, knowing they would be devastated. I just didn't know what to do," she says.

Reactivity and Aggression Fears

Back home, Marlene was a mess, and the dog could feel it. Cooper was chronically stressed and reacting to any sudden movement.

"I was completely dysregulated, and Cooper's behavior was actually getting worse," she says. There were worrying incidents. "Cooper had been sleeping on the foot of the bed when my husband walked in and said, 'Hey, Cooper.' The dog snapped and almost bit Steven's face. We thought, *Oh, my god, the vet was right. Look at what a mess this dog is; he's broken.* We were telling ourselves this narrative that Cooper's neurology was beyond repair—with no recognition of the fact that the whole house was upside down. Everybody's crying. Everyone's upset."

And there was the scare with their son. While the two dogs were resting on the foot of the parents' bed, the bedroom door had swung open, and thirteen-year old Thomas stomped in on boots, calling, "Mom! Dad! Look!" to show off a Halloween costume. In a split second, Cooper launched off the bed at him. The boy froze, and Cooper realized in time that this was his great buddy; fortunately, no one was injured.

The household was in turmoil. "At that point, Cooper was not in a good space," says Marlene. "We couldn't live like this. I can't be afraid he's going to bite my family. I can't be afraid he's going to bite guests in the house."

"We started his medication at that point. This was do-or-die for Cooper."

Looking Further

Marlene didn't gamble that medication alone would solve Cooper's challenges. "I felt there had to be a better answer. If this was my kid, and somebody said, 'Unfixable,' I would not give up," she says. "I would just go find the top experts in the field." So she started digging around for what she had missed.

Online searches led her to Andrew Hale's *Beyond the Operant* series, which helped her reconsider conventional positive reinforcement approaches, and Kim Brophey's applied ethology L.E.G.S. Family Dog Mediation course. Marlene e-mailed Kim, saying, "I know your course is for dog professionals, but I am so totally lost— will you accept me into your course?"

Marlene was particularly concerned about how Cooper would behave when family would arrive to stay for an upcoming holiday weekend. Cooper was too reactive to comfortably or safely remain in the home with overnight guests. To make sure everyone was safe, they undertook drastic measures. "My husband entirely renovated our backyard. He dug it up, built a parking pad, and pulled our camping trailer there so that we could stay with Cooper in a camping trailer while my brother and his partner stayed safely in our house."

During that visit, Marlene intermittently checked in with Cooper in the camping trailer and took the opportunity to pore through the applied ethology course. Soon, lightbulbs began going off.

"This was opening a whole world to me," she says. "I started thinking, *Oh, my goodness, he's environmentally sensitive. Oh, my goodness, he had stress cortisol flooding in early life. Oh, my goodness, the impact of that.* We clearly had not considered the impact of his early experiences and environment on his current presentation. And the realization that *Oh, my god, we spent the last two years not understanding who he is.*"

She ran back into the house to tell her husband, feeling a great rush of hope. "The lens had changed," she says, "the curtain was pulled back."

Marlene's next aha moment came when she discovered Laura Donaldson, who likened struggling dogs to youth from traumatic and chaotic environments. Marlene thought, *Oh, I understand this. Every kid I work with has a heightened sense of scanning for danger. They have a heightened sense of suspicion around strangers and new people and changes to routine.* All of a sudden, she saw that dogs follow the exact same template as traumatized children trying to make sense of their world.

Cooper was scared of the world. He hated going on walks. He was barking and lunging at everything and everyone except the family.

Marlene signed up for Laura's Slow Thinking Is Lifesaving for Dogs class and used the social processing games with Cooper. "I set a piece of kibble on the ground, he puts his head down to eat it. He looks up at me, I set down another piece of kibble, he looks up at me. He's lowering his head, lowering his blood pressure, and looking at me while playing this game," explains Marlene. "There are no cues, Cooper's just figuring it out. With these pattern games, dogs are in control of figuring it out. The criteria are super low. They figure out if they raise their head toward Mom, she's going to drop them a treat."

Using the Slow Thinking philosophy, Marlene no longer felt obligated to force Cooper out the front door. If he didn't want to leave the yard, she could simply load him in the car and drive somewhere nonthreatening—even if it was only three blocks away.

"I wasn't making him look at scary stuff. I wasn't forcing any desensitization," says Marlene. It was a full-on stress detox for Cooper. "After a few days of this, we were out on a walk, and the same garbage truck headed our way," she says. "I saw the truck and didn't do anything. I didn't intervene, just let him look, and gave Cooper a second to make the choice. No clicking and treating. He looks at the garbage truck. He looks up at me. He crosses the street to the side-walk where he doesn't have to see the truck. Then he shakes off and keeps walking.

"I thought, *Oh, my god.* We had been working on this for eigh-teen months with exposures and a click-and-treat agenda at a certain pace. As soon as we switched to no agenda, not pushing a timeline, not pushing an expectation, giving him space, letting him process from a safe distance, Cooper makes progress."

Making the Trauma Connection

Marlene recognized parallels to her own work with traumatized children. "I was working with a kid a few years ago who experienced sexual abuse. The offender was a family member who drove a red truck. One of her core posttraumatic symptoms was that she strug-gled to be out and about because every time she saw a red truck, she froze. She wanted to hide. Her brain globalized danger to all those trucks.

"This made it difficult for her to leave school, to hang out with her friends and be relaxed. Her brain was trying to be helpful by saying, 'If you avoid all red trucks, we can stay safe.' This is parallel to Cooper hearing loud noises. He thinks, *If I can just stay away from all loud noises, I can avoid this bad feeling inside, and I can experience relief.*"

Marlene says the solution is to help kids learn to process their en-vironment more slowly and calmly and to distinguish between safe and unsafe situations. "For kids who have experienced sexual abuse, we talk about where it happens. We help them recognize that gener-ally speaking, it happens in the secrecy and privacy of family homes, when adults in a position of trusting authority have exclusive access without supervision. We talk about when a tricky person is able to do these behaviors. How it doesn't happen when Mom's looking or Grandma's looking.

"We never have this conversation in the child's moment of fear and panic. We have it in the comfort and safety of my office. We say, 'Let's scan for signs of safety, let's do some grounding exercises, let's pay attention to the sights, smells, and sounds.' We help kids practice mindfulness skills. We help them recognize in which environments they're okay. We help them move through the fear ladder," explains Marlene. "With dogs, the principle is the same, although there's less talking and cognitive processing and more somatic and sensory assistance."

Nurturing the Relationship

Slow Thinking pattern puzzles were helping Cooper make progress outdoors, but Marlene remained concerned by his behavior in the house and with guests. When she heard a discussion on Michael Shikashio's podcast about how not all barking and lunging dogs want distance, she was led to a protocol called constructional affection.

She contacted the developers of constructional affection, Sean Will and Maasa Nishimuta, and asked for help with Cooper's sound sensitivities and social behavior. The family had gotten a SodaStream machine that puts carbonation into water, but the process was noisy. "The first time I tried to use it," says Marlene, "I pumped, pumped, pumped, released the air, and Cooper lost his mind. He was freaking out. And I thought, *Oh, my god, we can't use this ever again.* It was like I brought air brakes from a truck down inside the house."

Cooper was so distressed by the experience that if the machine was visible anywhere, he charged and started barking and lunging.

Marlene removed the SodaStream from the kitchen and said to her husband, "Sorry, you'll have to use this in the garage. I don't have the bandwidth to deal with this. It's too upsetting for Cooper."

But Sean and Maasa thought constructional affection could help Cooper shift his response and provided a plan. "I brought the machine out, without the bottle, and set it on the counter. Cooper looked at it without reacting, and I said, 'Good boy, super good boy, good boy,' and pet him several times. Then, I picked the machine up and moved it to a different section on the counter. Again, I pet, pet, pet Cooper and told him he was a good boy. Moved it to a different part of the kitchen, and again pet, pet, pet him and offered lots of soothing comfort. Eventually I went and got the Sodastream bottle and touched it to the machine. Again, Cooper received lots of petting and soothing comfort without becoming reactive.

"We didn't try to treat him," she says. "It was a completely different approach. We used affection and the relationship to offer comfort." Cooper was soothed and praised at each tiny step, and within hardly any time at all, he stood quietly as she pumped the machine. He was allowed to sniff the bottle and received petting and encouragement throughout the progression of steps up through the final carbonation process. Within two days, the family could load and carbonate bottles with no further problem.

"I was still super confused," says Marlene. "So much was going right, yet Cooper spent most of his time in the basement lying on his pillow by himself. I said to Sean, 'I really would love it if Cooper didn't choose to spend all his time downstairs by himself. The other dog sits on the couch with us.'"

Sean discussed special-needs classrooms, where a kid who constantly flicks pencils at the head of another kid isn't necessarily being aggressive. This child actually wants to connect with the other student but doesn't have the skill to achieve that in a socially comfortable way. Dogs are no different. Some bark because they truly want distance—they are not socially interested or comfortable. But other dogs want proximity and lack a social skill set.

When Sean described how constructional affection could bring Cooper closer, Marlene thought, *This is exactly what we do for withdrawn kids! Oh, my God, how did I miss this?*

"With a withdrawn kid, we use an approach called 'touch lightly.' You don't overwhelm them with an overdose of I'm-so-fun-let's-hang-out-I'm-here-to-be-your-attachment-figure! If you do that, they reject you. Instead, you approach them where they are, pay attention briefly to what they're paying attention to, and then get out of Dodge. Like, 'Oh-buddy-that's-great-that-you're-doing-that-with-the-Lego-I'm-heading-back-to-the-kitchen.' Just pepper in those light touches all day long. The more you do it, the more they start to seek you out because they develop trust."

She used a comparable approach with Cooper. "I went downstairs to where he was resting and said, 'Hey, Coops,' gave him some pats, and left. A little while later, I did it again. And so on. When he followed me somewhere, I laid it on, saying, 'Oh, buddy, we're so glad to see you. Thanks for coming upstairs,' and then I left.

"Within just two or three days, he was coming upstairs looking for us. Within a week, he was choosing to be upstairs most of the time." The process was as simple as speaking quietly to him, saying something nice, giving him a little stroke or two, and then walking away.

"Anytime he's doing something that we love, we reinforce it with affection. And he has blossomed with that approach, just blossomed," says Marlene. "It's amazing and there are no treats. And it's so common sense. It's sending the message 'I'm here when you need me.'"

Revisiting the Meds

Marlene began to joke about Cooper being officially off death row.

When he had been on medication for a year—tweaked until a combination of antidepressant and antianxiety meds proved most beneficial—it was time for a blood draw and medication review. The meds had reduced Cooper's arousal and anxiety and opened him up to learning, but the prospect of returning to that office concerned Marlene. The dog was still unsuited for a muzzle, and she didn't want to simply immobilize him.

"At that point, I felt much more equipped to advocate for his needs," says Marlene. "I decided not to take him in and have a set-back. We had made a lot of progress, so I felt ready to wean him off the meds and see what were the permanent changes for Cooper and what was med-mediated."

The vet argued against it. She believed that to get permanent change in his brain chemistry, Cooper should be on the meds for at least two years, but she agreed to give the family a plan for weaning him off them.

"I felt so good about the decision," says Marlene, "because Cooper's playfulness came back. His brain had cooled down enough to learn, but now he's silly and playful and the sensory gains are holding."

Cooper was completely weaned off the meds when he was able to make the leap to having overnight family guests stay in the house for the first time. Marlene was careful to give Cooper plenty of space to feel safe. "If we were all on the main floor, Cooper relaxed upstairs in our bedroom," she says. "We did long social walks together in a provincial park with the dogs on long lines and our guests with us. Cooper was able to observe them from a distance, and we practiced having Cooper greet the stranger from a distance. They kept walking, and he could air scent them and stand where he wanted. The stranger didn't close the gap or intrude on him. We did lots of walks like that while they were here. And when we came back in the house, he was content to go lay down in a separate space."

New Horizons

Marlene found a local dog care professional who was open to supporting Cooper's journey with the goal of eventually providing overnight dog sitting.

"We did a lot of protected contact and social walks and joint free work," Marlene says. "We started teaching him nose work in our house with Emily behind the baby gate. When Cooper got it right, she'd throw the treat. So we had this structure of games. Recently, he had his second overnight with her, and it went so smoothly that he was sleeping on the bed with her contentedly."

Then came Mother's Day, and the family arranged to bring both dogs to a private off-leash park. On arriving, they were disappointed to realize the field was bordered by two busy and noisy highways. Marlene decided to keep Cooper comfortable, give the other dog a chance to enjoy the space, and never return to this field because it was so poorly suited to Cooper's needs.

When they parked, the elder dog, Conway, jumped out of the truck and confidently began exploring the field with the two children. Cooper also jumped out but immediately scrambled low to the ground, looking for somewhere to hide, then jumped back into the truck.

"Historically, this would have felt disappointing," says Marlene. "I would have told myself a story about Cooper overreacting, a story about the facility owners needing to advertise their field transparently, maybe a story about how little progress Cooper had made in relation to his noise sensitivity. Instead, I made a conscious choice to shift my own agenda and focus to a more sensitive, flexible response to his needs.

"So I closed the vehicle doors adjacent to the roadways and opened the doors that allowed Cooper to watch everyone in the field. I sat with him quietly for a few minutes and made sure that the traffic noise wasn't too loud inside the vehicle while he observed the family's activity from a vantage point that felt comfortable for him. I returned to the vehicle intermittently, sat with him and chatted with him, offered affection—but no pressure, prompts, or lures."

After thirty minutes, Cooper jumped out of the truck and sniffed his way through a cluster of bushes and trees on the field. Marlene was amazed. "After a few laps in the trees, he ventured out into the open field to chase balls and sticks with our kids—even though cars, trucks, and motorcycles were passing noisily in plain view. This was not an expected outcome," she says. "With acceptance and understanding comes possibility."

If They Could Do It All Over Again

If Marlene had it all to do over again, what would she do? First, she would consider the dog's temperament right from the start. "I love how Suzanne Clothier talks about this idea of understanding the size of the dog's world," she says. "That's how I work with kids, right? A dog like Cooper needs to start with a very small world. They need to learn safety in that small world, before you're exposing them to the big world. We had been operating under that old wisdom that he needs all these exposures, exposures, exposures. Instead, I would keep his world very small.

"Our early intervention with him was a big piece of the problem. We kept putting him in environments that were overwhelming, like his puppy class. He nipped the fingers of a training assistant at his very first puppy class because she leaned in over him and he was stressed out. We were seeing behaviors with him by six months that were concerning. But we missed it and felt like we needed to correct his behavior. He needed a smaller world, less sensory input, and less sensory challenge.

"If we had a kid who had sensory processing issues, we wouldn't just keep pushing them ahead, we would back up to meet them where they are. For Cooper, I would not have made him try to cope with situations that were beyond his capacity. Instead, I would have done free work in our house for sensory exposures. Given him positive rituals and experiences of people coming into the house.

"I feel like we're twenty years ahead in child-rearing to where we are in dogs right now," Marlene says. "When I started my career with children and children's therapy, all this was just bubbling up. We were just starting to learn about Daniel Hughes's work and Karyn Purvis's and David Cross's work and all the attachment and trauma stuff that was coming to the forefront, changing the way we thought about meeting the child where they're at versus behavior modification.

"I just would do everything differently. Like we only walk sniffari now on fifteen-foot lines. I would sniffari Cooper in the backyard and maybe outside in the back alley, but I wouldn't try big walks. I'd let him experience sights and sounds from safe distances and give him time to process.

"Now when I foster, I see that every litter has its Cooper. They don't eat well in the facility. They're generally the smallest because they're too stressed to eat. They're constantly pressing into laps and wanting to be held when the other dogs are eating.

"When I care for a foster puppy now, I set up a free work course on our back patio. I sit with a coffee on the steps and let them hear trucks and buses and sounds of people getting ready in the morning and kids talking and they can hear it all from the safe confines of the yard with me sitting right there. That's enough exposure. Then I would graduate things so much more slowly and reduce expectation. If we had done that, we could have built Cooper differently.

"We had such avoidable disappointment with both of our dogs," says Marlene. "We felt like they were both inherently broken because they couldn't meet this standard. But having that standard was the fallacy. It's like looking at a kid who sits nicely at the table and cleans their plate and doesn't speak and saying that's the ideal child. We know that's not the ideal child—you want a child who's vibrant and creative and contributes and has a mind of their own where they can think independently and push back. We didn't used to cherish those things in kids. Now we cherish those things in balance. We want them to be respectful and pay attention to their surroundings and adjust their behavior to suit the setting. You want all those things, right, the balance of both. And I think that's the place that we're getting to now with our dogs.

"The dog industry needs permission to say, 'Look, look at the dog in front of us. Let's look at the pacing that they need. Not every dog has to follow this exact plan.' I think Cooper is such a good dog. He's probably one of the best dogs we've ever owned, at this point," Marlene says. "Because we can see him for who he is. We've adjusted our expectations, and he exists in the world in a way that is good for him. And it's the same for Conway. We no longer feel disappointed in our dogs. We're so proud of them and so happy with them and see them as so functional and capable. And we wouldn't have seen that before."

PART FIVE

Embracing
HEARTS

CHAPTER 21:
Become a Detective of Unmet Needs

THE FIRST STEP IN HELPING A DOG that struggles or in tackling unwanted behavior is sleuthing out the underlying need. This is often tricky because just like preverbal and nonverbal kids, dogs can't answer our questions directly. They speak in behaviors, which may carry varied meanings or reflect varied needs. It's up to us to figure out which one is relevant in context. For example, dogs might pull on the leash for a variety of reasons:

- they naturally move at a fast pace;
- they spotted a friend and are eager to visit;
- their predatory sequence was triggered by something in the environment;
- they have dementia and always pull to one side; or
- they are scared.

The steps we take to shift that behavior would vary based on the underlying cause and the dog's individual situation. For example, a fearful dog could stop pulling naturally once given sufficient distance from whatever disturbs him.

Make a study of watching your child's body language diagnosti-
cally, particularly for signs of fear, indications of sensory processing
dysfunction, and even subtle signs of undiagnosed seizure activity.
Ask yourself: What calms my child? What sets him or her off? Does
he seek touch, or avoid it? Is she responding positively to a certain
sound, or does she dread it? What is my child's body language
communicating?

—The Connected Child[1]

To help a dog, we need to sift through the possibilities and see what
fits.[2] Their behavior may look like aggression, but it can be coming
from a place of fear or pain or frustration or predatory sequence
or medication side effect—even a problem with their diet.[3-5] Their
behavior can look like chewing or barking, but it might be coming
from frustration, boredom, anxiety, or having no appropriate place
to channel normal energy. Their behavior can look like compulsion
or obsession, but it might be coming from a genetic cause, a medical
problem, stress, or typical canine tendencies.

reflections from the field

Veterinary behaviorist Christopher Pachel, DVM, DACVB, CABC, de-
scribes the complexity of getting to the root of behavioral issues. He says:

> I can't ask my patients specifically, "What's going
> through your head right now? What are you flashing
> back to, what really stands out to you about this experi-
> ence that makes you really emotional about it?"
>
> With dogs, we are now diagnosing a version of PTSD
> called canine posttraumatic stress disorder, or C-PTSD,
> and we're getting a better understanding of what those
> patterns really look like. For this diagnosis, the way that

I practice, we have to have a known trauma, and we have to have a difference in performance before and after.

A lot of the initial work on C-PTSD was done in military working dogs, where we had a high level of training, very specific performance criteria, experiential trauma, and degradation in performance. Being able to see the before and after relative to a time point is a really helpful part of understanding what is going on and what exactly may be feeding into some of those patterns.

It's a lot harder when we're working with animals who come to us with unknown histories, where they're showing fear, anxiety, aggression, irritable bowel disease that seems to be exacerbated by stress.

Fear-based aggression could look very similar from very different stories. It can show up because of a trauma response. We can also see cases showing up because of insufficient socialization because these animals have not experienced strangers or kids or unfamiliar dogs, for example. The brain basically says, "This is novel, this is scary, keep yourself safe."

We can also get a self-perpetuating cycle that creates trauma in the moment. If we're looking at puppies, for example, we have, as with everything, that bell curve. We may have puppies who are on the shy or timid end of the spectrum.

Well-intentioned people say, "I was told to socialize them, so here we go. We're going to the soccer game with the kids on Saturday." And there the puppy basically gets flooded and overwhelmed, and we can create a trauma experience in the name of socialization.

Being a detective means paying close attention to details of body language, environment, past learning, and the sequence of events. A veterinary specialist can also offer valuable perspective.

It can be helpful to run through the possibilities by reviewing HEARTS and needs, as shown in the summary table, to make sure we've considered all the potential underlying issues.[6]

To achieve this goal . . .		Think about the following . . .	
Heal the body	**H**	• Pain • Infection • Allergy • Optimal nutrition and digestion	• Rest and sleep • Timely food, water, and toileting
Engage and optimize the brain	**E**	• Physical activity • Mental challenges	• Sensory • Self-regulation and alert/calm balance stimulation
Appropriate environments with felt safety	**A**	• Suitable space and place • Allowed distance or escape	• Force-free handling • Does not feel threatened
Respectful and secure relationships	**R**	• Secure attachment and trust • Affectionate touch by consent • Sufficient social connection	• Limits, rules, and boundaries • Clear expectations and communication
Teach sensitively and positively	**T**	• Positive reinforcement • (Intended) Positive associations • Practice life skills	• Scaffolded guidance • Incremental goals • Social learning and synchrony
Support the individual	**S**	• Developmental phase • Express natural aptitudes • Express aspects of predatory sequence	• Individual temperament • Medical and trauma history • Realistic expectations for this dog

Avoid Jumping to Conclusions

Consider a housetrained adult dog that suddenly begins peeing indoors. It's tempting to assume the dog is being stubborn or angry, but if we turn to HEARTS, we can gain better understanding. For example, with H (heal the body), we might uncover a medical issue, such as a bladder stone, urinary infection, or tumor that is causing the urgent need to pee.

Or it could be something entirely different, as in the case of five-year-old rescue dog Rocko whose owner sought my help. Rocko only peed in the house when he and his owner stayed overnight with the owner's boyfriend, and the dog only did it when near the boyfriend. Rocko was housebroken under ordinary circumstances.

So I suggested that the boyfriend work to make friends with the dog. When the couple sat together on the couch, the boyfriend could toss bits of cheese and treats on the ground nearby for the dog. No more shouting or grabbing for the dog. At bedtime, they were to let the dog stay in a spot where the dog could always see the owner rather than lock him away in another room. Within twenty-four hours, Rocko's indoor peeing stopped.

In this case, the solution required addressing the environment and the relationship, the A and R in HEARTS. With greater sensitivity to the disruption of the animal's ordinary routine and environment, Rocko's people helped him overcome his fear.

Once we identify a dog's emotional state, we can try different strategies to increase their feeling of safety, as shown in the following table.

How to Provide Relief When Dogs Show Emotional Discomfort

POSITIVE ◀━━━━━━━━ NEUTRAL

Comfortable and relaxed	Becoming stressed/ uncomfortable
• Leaning toward or against your body • Initiating touch • Relaxed posture • Loose, fluid movements • Settling calmly nearby • Relaxed wiggling • Engaging in friendly play • Playful growl • Head down/haunches up ("play bow") • Certain wags (e.g., relaxed tail swung below horizon of back), but not all wags	• Yawning • Blinking • Tongue flicks • Licking own nose • Offering placating lick • Heavy panting (not heat related) • Turning head away • Lifting paw • Avoiding contact • Purposely focusing elsewhere • Pawing or seeking attention/ assistance • Displacement behaviors[B] • Tightening facial expression • Whites of eye extra visible ("whale eye")
To provide relief . . .	**Try this . . .**
	• Provide assistance if sought • Provide space/distance if sought • Use a soothing, quiet voice • Manage/adjust environment • Turn sideway/face away • Avoid eye contact • Slow down/wait • Redirect to something they enjoy • Rub dog's chest if that relaxes them • Gently toss treats • Disengage

A–This behavior sometimes has an unrelated medical cause
B–Examples: chewing paw, humping, snapping at tail, seeking a toy to chew, pacing

NEGATIVE

Increasing stress /fear	Fear/ panic	Extreme stress /crisis mode
INTERNALIZING		
• Tail tucked under • Pawing or seeking attention/assistance • Making self small • Crouching/creeping • Displacement behaviors[B] • Excessive shedding[A] • Dander kicking up[A]	• Trembling[A] • Pee accident[A] • Lying on back stiffly, feet in air • Pancaking • Cowering • Body odor/anal glands release[A]	• Freezing • Dissociation
EXTERNALIZING*		
• Ears flattened back • Barking to alert/warn • Snarling • Moving away	• Hard stare • Menacing growl • Air snapping[A] • Lunging	• Biting • Attacking • Fleeing
Try this . . .	**Try this . . .**	**Do this . . .**
• Provide assistance if sought • Provide space/distance if sought • Use a soothing quiet voice • Manage/adjust environment • Turn sideways/face away • Avoid eye contact • Slow down/wait • Gently toss treats • Disengage	• Back off • Give them space • Avoid eye contact • Disengage • Consult a dog behavior professional	• Back off • Give them space • Avoid eye contact • Disengage • Consult a dog behavior professional

* This is different from the predatory sequence (of searching, orienting, stalking, chasing, catching, killing, carrying, dissecting, and eating)

Look for Pain

Pain is so often involved in problem behavior that some experts recommend addressing suspected pain as a first-line treatment rather than waiting until the dog doesn't respond to behavioral interventions.[7] Many vets are willing to prescribe pain medications on a test basis to see if they give the dog relief and help resolve the behavioral issue. Specialists, such as those trained in the Dynamic Dog method, are available to do in-depth physiological assessments and provide a detailed report to your vet.[8]

When a dog suddenly stops cooperating, consider if undiagnosed pain and physical discomfort might be involved.

- A dog trained often in heeling position can get chronic neck and shoulder pain from always looking up and to the side.

- A dog may stop sitting on command due to arthritic pain or may have dysplasia, an orthopedic hip alignment issue that makes sitting painful.

- A cracked tooth, perhaps far back in the mouth and hidden from view, could cause the dog to become skittish or nippy and shy away from touch around the head.

- Collars and harnesses that snap or yank the head and neck cause chronic pain that can provoke aggressive behavior.

- Refusing to walk on a particular floor, eat a favorite food, or get in or out of a car is often a sign of pain.

- An undiagnosed infection can cause aggression and biting, including after surgery.

- Chronic skin irritations or itchiness makes dogs cranky and more prone to aggressive behavior.[9]

- Noise sensitivities and phobias can be heightened by pain.[10]

reflections from the field

Hélène Marie Lawler of Kynic Stockdogs shares her concern that sometimes, in our eagerness to heal the body, we may inadvertently contribute to future problems. She says:

For several years, I rescued border collies that had all sorts of challenges. This may be controversial, but in my personal experience—of rescuing a relatively limited number of dogs, but enough to draw general conclusions —if a dog came in to rescue and was immediately spayed or neutered, vaccinated, and given flea and tick medications, then two weeks later, we would start to see a whole bunch of behavioral problems coming up.

When I changed my approach and let the rescue dogs settle into their new home with me first, I did not see that behavioral shift. My theory is that when we take a highly stressed animal that just had a big life transition or lost their family, and we give them a major surgery that removes all their hormones, then vaccinate them— which stimulates the immune system and puts it on high alert—and then apply flea treatment which has neurochemicals, then their nervous system shorts out. That's when they start developing all these behaviors. I'm quite convinced this contributes to a lot of the problems that people experience with rescue dogs.

I was able to persuade the foster group to adopt my approach. When we took rescue dogs in, we didn't do any of those procedures or treatments right away. First, we got the dogs healthy and calm and in a good place. Then, once the dog was very comfortable, adjusted to its new life, and on good nutrition and stabilized, if it

needed spay or neuter or other medical care, we would
do just one of those things at a time and let them recover
to step back from causing a huge biological trauma.

I know this suggests that the standard practice at
most rescue organizations could be contributing to
problems instead of resolving them, but that was what I
concluded from my experience.

Recalibrate Positive Reinforcement

Positive reinforcement methods often provide excellent results,
but we can inadvertently provoke challenges or even trauma by
using positive reinforcement without sufficient sensitivity. We might
be too rigid and controlling with it, or too indulgent, and stumble
into problems. The chart below shows how positive reinforcement
might result in three different parenting styles.

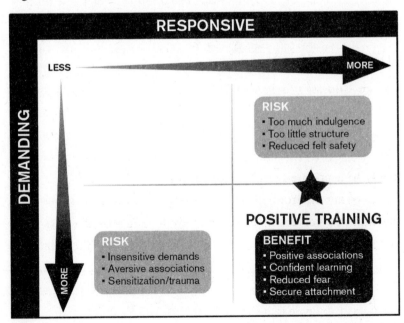

To deliver real benefit, all methods must be applied with great respect for individual needs, with an eye on maintaining healthy levels of stress, not piling on more stress. One way we can protect against causing too much stress is by inviting feedback from the learner and responding to what is communicated. The simplest way to do this is by offering choices. Even preverbal children and dogs can signal their willingness to participate or preference to stop engaging in an activity. Allowing the learner to help set the pace and giving them breaks as needed goes a long way toward keeping stress within the sweet spot and improving outcomes.

Make Allowances for Trauma

Like children with a background of deprivation or trauma, dogs from hoarding situations and other adverse early conditions suffer higher rates of chronic medical issues and other problems.[11-16] In a sense, trauma is very deep neurological learning. For some individuals, trauma reactivity becomes hardwired.[17, 18] Helping a little one heal from trauma requires creativity and all the HEARTS.[19]

We need to remember that even being "rescued" can provoke trauma. Consider, for example, a breeding female from a puppy farm who spent months or years restricted to a small pen—perhaps never even allowed to toilet elsewhere—and surrounded by cages full of other dogs and puppies. Then she gets transported to a rescue and finally to a private home where she might be the only dog. Every aspect of her environment is brand-new—from the floor on which she walks to her ability to move freely to sights overhead, sounds and smells, and even the absence of other animals. She is facing a profound change and requires time to adjust. In a similar fashion, former street dogs that are suddenly thrust into a human domestic setting can struggle in a similar way.[20]

Sherry Steinlein of Paws for Success shares an example of how mean-
ingful solutions are not one-size-fits-all. She says:

I work with a lot of trauma now. There's so much
trauma going on in our culture, in our society today.
Even if you get a lovely well-bred perfect breed or puppy,
just the puppy changing from their litter and Mama to
our homes is a trauma event, I believe. They're thinking,
Where's Mommy? Where are my siblings? even when it's
a great situation.

Then think of all these rescues and the transport
with other dogs screaming and yelling, and the change
in climate and environment from the humidity, the heat,
the different plants and grasses in the southern United
States to suburban Long Island with trucks and motorcycles and garbage trucks and delivery trucks all over
the place. People want fixes for these dogs. I'm very big
about explaining how we can't fix them, but we can help
support these dogs in these changes. That's when we'll
see good behavior change.

One family I worked with was a great example. Mom
was an art therapist, and Dad had an office job and a
degree in psychology. They had nine-year-old twin boys
and a rescue beagle-hound mix that was being aggressive with kids. There might have been a nip before I got
involved.

We discussed that this dog just didn't understand
what was going on. He had come from a transport and
shelter situation and was plopped down in their home.

He'd probably never been around children. Now he lived with nine-year-old male twins. One wanted to hug and kiss and love on this dog, and this dog just didn't understand. He just saw two nine-year-old rough-and-tumble boys coming at him, and their voices were so high pitched. These parents completely got it and were able to see it from the dog's perspective.

So we spoke about safety and management, immediately, in the first session. We talked about how this dog did not have to meet all the kids' friends. We talked about separating the dog at certain times using x-pens and baby gates. We talked about crating and stuffed Kongs and other enrichment, like snuffle mats, to give this dog more of a quality of life.

They really got on board with seeing this dog like it was a third kid and giving each kid what the kid needs. They were amazing. I gave the mom a role in doing enrichment, and I had the father look at the science stuff—the resource guarding videos I sent and protocols we were going to put in place and how important timing was with treats.

And they did fabulously; they were so clear in their age-appropriate explanations for the twins about the dog's feelings. That blew me away, how they explained the dog's feelings to nine-year-olds. This mother sent me videos for months, showing how everybody was doing great.

They learned that this dog just didn't like young kids. That was his limit—toddlers and babies. The family decided that the dog never needed to be around them. They themselves weren't going to have any more kids, and when relatives were visiting or young kids were around, the dog was separated with enrichment in a different part of the house. That was just going to be a management situation. And that was fine, and they did great.

Remember that repetitive behaviors and nervous habits are often an attempt to channel and manage stress.[21-23] Such stereotypies and displacement behaviors can occur both in children and in dogs. In children, these behaviors are worsened by a stressful environment but diminished when the child is placed in a more supportive setting and given more appropriate ways to channel anxiety.[24] The same goes for dogs, such as those removed from restrictive confinement.

reflections from the field

Denise Fenzi, founder of Denise Fenzi Dog Sports Academy, reminds us to step back and think big picture when tackling what appears to be "problem" behavior. She says:

It is helpful to start with the assumption that most dogs are normal and typical. Don't take situations which are normal and typical and make them complicated! This has nothing to do with desirable behavior. For example, I think it is perfectly typical for an eight-week-old puppy to mouth human hands and to chew random objects in the house. Typical is normal!

Having raised working-line Belgian shepherds, I consider a puppy hanging off the sleeve of my jacket to be perfectly normal, even if he redirects on me with anger when I attempt to remove him (which doesn't mean I allow it or encourage it to continue). But I find it normal. It is typical for my breed. A herding breed of dog who is reserved with strangers? Often perfectly normal. You don't need to change it! Simply accept the dog for who they are. A highly energetic young retriever? Our job is not to teach the dog to be calm; our job is to find daily routines that recognize the normalcy of that dog's temperament within the breed.

These dogs do not need to be changed. They do not need drugs or a specialist. They need a reasonable plan that can actually be put into effect! Don't make training complicated when it doesn't need to be. Maybe think of it like this: some toddlers are calm, and some are energetic! Some are outgoing, and some are shy! These are all within the range of typical, so one might ask oneself, *How does one raise a toddler?* With kindness, structure, and consistency! Ask for what is reasonable, offer choice within structure as the toddler is ready, and pick your battles. I guarantee this will set you on the right path a very high percentage of the time.

(Which doesn't necessarily mean owners will always be thrilled about the entire package, but hey, if your kid is a chess player and you wanted a football player, who should give a little?)

Normal interventions like basic training and common management strategies work for most normal dogs. But some dogs need extra help.

When a dog is atypical, we start talking about things like functional analysis, behavior modification protocols, drug therapy, and intensive management strategies. We start thinking about behavior specialists rather than dog trainers. For example, if I were working with a dog that had true separation anxiety, the atypical kind? The kind that is impacting the dog's and owner's quality of life? I am going to recommend a behavior specialist. That dog needs more than the average.

What is atypical? Atypical is what I don't expect of a given dog in a given circumstance. For example, it is atypical for a dog to bite a family member with intent to harm. It is atypical for a dog to scream and drool for hours when their needs have been taken care of. It is atypical to spin in circles when there is nothing happening. It is atypical to hide and shake when someone who is ignoring the dog comes into your house.

Atypical dogs are different. Maybe they are notably fearful in daily life situations, or sensitive, or showing neurotic behaviors, or just a really bad match for their owner and something needs to change. Those dogs are real and reasonably common these days, and then it's absolutely appropriate (and to be encouraged) to involve professional assistance, and medication, as warranted.

CHAPTER 22:
Restore Balance

WE BECOME BETTER EQUIPPED to support others when our own foundation is sturdy. So instead of powering through the day, consider whether now is the time to stop for our own food, water, rest, exercise, or a hug. If we feel tense or overwhelmed, we can take a calming breath. Let air drift into our lungs, hold it briefly, then with extra beats release it out s-l-o-w-l-y. Doing this a few times resets the nervous system. We might also:

- sit or stand up straight and think about softening the muscles around the neck and shoulders;
- tell that critical inner voice to be quiet; and
- catch ourselves doing something right and say, "Good job!"

Soothe the Inner Child

There will be times when pain or heartache from our own past haunts and distracts us and causes us to lose touch with the richness of today. Our suffering inner child may sabotage relationships and steer us down paths of which we are not fully aware. The Zen monk Thich Nhat Hanh recommends that we tend to our own inner child daily with tender care and lovingness.[1] Once our inner child is well cared for, we become more present to the little one who is standing before us.

Exercise: Seeing Yourself with Compassion

Look in the mirror.

Look with great love, tenderness, and compassion as if through the eyes of a doting grandparent or grandchild.

Gaze with delight and profound appreciation at your reflection for a few moments.

Honor the struggle, the journey, the resilience, the beauty, and the wonder you see there.

Smile gently.

Practicing mindfulness enables us to become more present in the moment and to downshift our own reactivity. In time, we become less likely to lash out in frustration and more likely to respond with calmness and clarity. Once our hearts and minds are open, we can restore balance between the dog's needs and our own. For example, you might ask yourself, *Do I walk the dog in a way that is meaningful to them or meaningful to me?*

reflections from the field

Lynne Bernfield, LMFT, practices mindfulness with her fifteen-year-old mixed breed, Rhemmy. She says:

> I have become aware, rather late in life, that I'm an impatient person and that this impatience has not served me. I often do two different things at the same time, and when I do that, I can't concentrate as well on both things. So I often make mistakes and drop things.
>
> Fortunately for me, I so love my dog that he has been

teaching me patience. I used to walk him, and when I didn't feel like walking anymore, I would make him come home. But now, I think to myself, *My God, this is all he gets. This is his joy. This is his pleasure. I don't have to give in to my impatience.*

It's also true that my dog is quite old. Having watched my father go through sundowning, I think I'm watching it in my dog. Late in the day, he begins to do things he doesn't do during the day. He'll come over and look at me, and I know that he wants something, but he seems incapable of letting me know what it is. But I'm working on patience. So I let him wander around. I ask him if he wants to go out. I ask if he wants food. I ask him if he wants to play; I ask him if he wants to come up on the couch. Sometimes he'll do it, sometimes he won't. But this is a gift I'm giving to him, and I'm getting the gift of experiencing patience.

Rebalance Structure and Nurture

Restoring balance may also involve stepping back to recalibrate our parenting style, recalling that optimal outcomes include equal parts nurture and structure. Inadvertently, we may have slipped into an excessively strict and demanding style or an excessively nurturing and permissive one. My original crisis with puppy Hazel arose when I became overly demanding and insensitive to her needs.

To rebalance my approach, I increased nurturing and adjusted my demands to be more sensitive to her situation. I slowed down and gave the puppy time to process a world that was new and stimulating. I stopped using tentative fingertip touches that irritated and excited her and switched to confidently warm, full hand strokes and petting that calmed and promoted healthy attachment. Her firecracker energy got channeled into appropriate enrichment activities and playful exercise. We tossed sticks for her out in the yard, graduated to walks across a woodsy park, and when she was big and strong enough for tennis balls, we sometimes threw one from the top of carpeted stairs to the far reach of a family room on a lower level. She bounded after it and carried it up the stairs back to us, time and again, magnificent in her youth.

In addition to being more nurturing, I needed to think about structure. This included having reasonable demands and practicing calm and centered leadership. The first step was simply not letting her lunacy ruffle me. I needed to be aware of my body language and to project neutral confidence. I treated her respectfully and expected her to reciprocate, giving her plenty of opportunities to succeed. For example, I stood and waited calmly and silently, food bowl in hand, for her to settle before she got the meal.

Greater structure also included setting physical limits, like the hinged, wooden baby gate we installed at a strategic spot in the house.

Norm modified the gate by cutting small holes so the cats could travel freely but Hazel could not get through and chase them. With bedlam reduced, the cats became more confident and occasionally ventured into the fray. One cat schooled Hazel in respectful behavior by nipping her cheek each time she stepped on his head. I can't recall exactly when it happened, but after a year or two, everyone calmed down enough that we could safely take down the baby gate.

All these techniques helped, but Hazel still had her share of puppy and adolescent destruction and mishaps. She pulverized twigs in the yard, taste-tested furniture legs, and shredded at least one pool float. Number-2 pencils must have been a rare delicacy to her, as we occasionally found a lone thin rod of graphite on the floor, surrounded by neat piles of yellow-tinged sawdust.

One day I arrived in the kitchen to discover Hazel sitting sphinx-like on the floor. The sharp tip of a carving knife glinted between her paws as she gnawed contentedly on the knife's handle. I choked back a cry of alarm and crept forward. By this time we had developed a trusting relationship, so I managed to extract the weapon without injuries. Norm and I never could figure out how she got hold of that knife. Miraculously, there was no trace of blood anywhere.

Let Go and Move On

No parent is 100 percent perfect. And none of us lives a full life without having regrets in one form or another. I remind myself of these truths when Hazel's memory drifts to mind and I cringe over less-than-ideal choices I made while raising her.

Once, while out on a walk together, she bolted for a squirrel. The auto-extension leash fed out unrestrained, she gained momentum, and when all sixty-plus pounds of her hit the end of the line, the jolt pulled me off my feet and into a furrow, nearly dislocating my shoulder. Struggling to rise and nursing my injury, I decided that both the dog and I deserved respect and something needed to change or Hazel wouldn't get walks or visits to the field where she loved to run off leash.

So I hired a trainer to come to our house. The trainer's solution was to replace Hazel's nylon collar with a pinch collar. The dog, who used to bounce along with an upright curly tail, now began stepping gingerly and cautiously, tail pulled low between her legs. I'm sorry to say we used that collar for a few months. Then one day Norm had her out for a walk and a cranky Rottweiler grabbed Hazel by the throat. She suffered a puncture wound, and based on its position and shape, I concluded the collar contributed to the injury and banished it. Instead, I found an adjustable harness and quit using the auto-extension leash. This combination served for the rest of her life, and her curly tail sprang back up with happy enthusiasm again.

Parenting, it seems, is aspirational. The best we can do, to paraphrase Karyn Purvis, is keep circling back to "What is the little one really saying?" and "What does the little one really need?" Then HEARTS can help us find a win-win solution.

Take a Tender Pause

Instead of throwing our hands up in frustration over a difficult puppy or dog, we can stop for a tender pause. Take a mental step back to regain our equilibrium.

Looking at puppies and dogs through the lens of therapeutic parenting encourages us to become more attuned and compassionate. We begin to focus less on "naughtiness" and more on their vulnerability and the need and trust placed in our care. We respond more to the actual little one in front of us and less to a preconception crafted in the imagination.

There were times when I was out walking with Hazel and, inexplicably, she would suddenly stand stock-still. At first, I was impatient to keep moving.

Then I considered Hazel's paws, which were surprisingly thin and smooth, especially for an animal of her bulk. The soles had little of that thick, horny callous most dogs have there. During dry weather, sharp thistles often got stuck between the tender pads.

So I learned to ask, "Is something in your paw?" She stood quietly while I carefully lifted each limb and probed the crevice of her paws. Eventually, I fished out all the offending thistles, and we proceeded on our way.

A famous folktale describes a traveler who hears a roaring lion and goes to investigate. Noticing a thorn in the lion's paw, he stops to remove it. Years later, the beast saves his life, honoring him with a lifetime of loyalty and affection.

We, too, can be our animal's ally. We can be alert to thorns, real or metaphorical, and do our best to remove them. In this way, we walk in the footsteps of foster parents and adoptive parents and alloparents who step up with grace on behalf of little ones in need.

I wish you and your dog great well-being on your journey together.

notes

Chapter 1

1. Purvis, K. B., Cross, D. R., & Sunshine, W. L. (2007). *The connected child: Bring hope and healing to your adoptive family.* McGraw-Hill Education, 98.
2. Firnkes, A., Bartels, A., Bidoli, E., & Erhard, M. (2017). Appeasement signals used by dogs during dog–human communication. *Journal of Veterinary Behavior*, 19 (May), 35–44. https://doi.org/10.1016/j.jveb.2016.12.012
3. Portions of this chapter originally appeared in Sunshine, W. L. n.d. Does your problem pup need a do-over? PsychologyToday.Com. Accessed September 17, 2023. https://www.psychologytoday.com/us/blog/tender-paws/202201/does-your-problem-pup-need-do-over. Used with permission.

Chapter 2

1. Grandin, T., & Johnson, C. (2009). *Animals make us human: Creating the best life for animals.* Houghton Mifflin Harcourt.
2. Woo, B. M., & Schaller, M. (2020). "Parental" responses to human infants (and puppy dogs): Evidence that the perception of eyes is especially influential, but eye contact is not. *PLOS One*, 15(5), e0232059. https://doi.org/10.1371/journal.pone.0232059
3. Prato-Previde, E., Ricci, E. B., & Colombo, E. S. (2022). The complexity of the human–animal bond: Empathy, attachment and anthropomorphism

in human–animal relationships and animal hoarding. *Animals*, 12(20), 2835. https://doi.org/10.3390/ani12202835

4. Gergely, A., Koós-Hutás, E., Filep, L. A., Kis, A., & Topál, J. (2023). Six facial prosodic expressions caregivers similarly display to infants and dogs. *Scientific Reports*, 13(1), 929. https://doi.org/10.1038/s41598-022-26981-7

5. Waller, B. M., Peirce, K., Caeiro, C. C., Scheider, L., Burrows, A. M., McCune, S., & Kaminski, J. (2013). Paedomorphic facial expressions give dogs a selective advantage. *PLOS One*, 8(12), e82686. https://doi.org/10.1371/journal.pone.0082686

6. Kaminski, J., Waller, B. M., Diogo, R., Hartstone-Rose, A., & Burrows, A. M. (2019). Evolution of facial muscle anatomy in dogs. *Proceedings of the National Academy of Sciences*, 116(29), 14677–81. https://doi.org/10.1073/pnas.1820653116

7. Packer, R. M. A., Murphy, D., & Farnworth, M. J. (2017). Purchasing popular purebreds: Investigating the influence of breed-type on the pre-purchase motivations and behaviour of dog owners. *Animal Welfare*, 26(2), 191–201. https://doi.org/10.7120/09627286.26.2.191

8. Packer, R. M. A., O'Neill, D. G., Fletcher, F., & Farnworth, M. J. (2019). Great expectations, inconvenient truths, and the paradoxes of the dog-owner relationship for owners of brachycephalic dogs. *PLOS One*, 14(7), e0219918. https://doi.org/10.1371/journal.pone.0219918

9. Paul, E. S., Packer, R. M. A., McGreevy, P. D., Coombe, E., Mendl, E., & Neville, V. (2023). That brachycephalic look: Infant-like facial appearance in short-muzzled dog breeds. *Animal Welfare*, 32 (January), e5. https://doi.org/10.1017/awf.2022.6

10. Volsche, S., Mukherjee, R., & Rangaswamy, M. (2022). The difference is in the details: Attachment and cross-species parenting in the United States and India. *Anthrozoös*, 35(3), 393–408. https://doi.org/10.1080/08927936.2021.1996026

11. Gergely, A., Gábor, A., Gácsi, M., Kis, A., Czeibert, K., Topál, J., & Andics, A. (2023). Dog brains are sensitive to infant- and dog-directed prosody. *Communications Biology*, 6(1), 1–9. https://doi.org/10.1038/s42003-023-05217-y

12. Feldman, R. (2016). The neurobiology of mammalian parenting and the biosocial context of human caregiving. *Hormones and Behavior*, 77 (January), 3–17. https://doi.org/10.1016/j.yhbeh.2015.10.001

13. Feldman, R. (2017). The neurobiology of human attachments. *Trends in Cognitive Sciences*, 21(2), 80–99. https://doi.org/10.1016/j.tics.2016.11.007

14. Shimon-Raz, O., Yeshurun, Y., Ulmer-Yaniv, A., Levinkron, A., Salomon, R., & Feldman, R. (2023). Attachment stimuli trigger widespread synchrony across multiple brains. *bioRxiv*. https://doi.org/10.1101/2023.02.10.527970

15. Lezama-García, K., Mariti, C., Mota-Rojas, D., Martínez-Burnes, J., Barrios-García, H., & Gazzano, A. (2019). Maternal behaviour in domestic dogs. *International Journal of Veterinary Science and Medicine*, 7(1), 20–30. https://doi.org/10.1080/23144599.2019.1641899

16. Porges, S. W. (2009). The polyvagal theory: New insights into adaptive reactions of the autonomic nervous system. *Cleveland Clinic Journal of Medicine*, 76 (Suppl 2), S86–90. https://doi.org/10.3949/ccjm.76.s2.17

17. Baker, E., & Lui, F. (2023). Neuroanatomy, vagal nerve nuclei. In *StatPearls*. StatPearls Publishing. http://www.ncbi.nlm.nih.gov/books/NBK545209/.

18. Taylor, S. E., Klein, L. C., Lewis, B. P., Gruenewald, T. L., Gurung, R. A., & Updegraff, J. A. (2000). Biobehavioral responses to stress in females: Tend-and-befriend, not fight-or-flight. *Psychological Review*, 107(3), 411–29. https://doi.org/10.1037/0033-295x.107.3.411

19. Kucerova, B., Levit-Binnun, N., Gordon, I., & Golland, Y. (2023). From oxytocin to compassion: The saliency of distress. *Biology*, 12(2), 183. https://doi.org/10.3390/biology12020183

20. Herbeck, Y. E., Eliava, M., Grinevich, V., & MacLean, E. L. (2022). Fear, love, and the origins of canid domestication: An oxytocin hypothesis. *Comprehensive Psychoneuroendocrinology*, 9 (February), 100100. https://doi.org/10.1016/j.cpnec.2021.100100

21. Walker, S. C., Trotter, P. D., Swaney, W. T., Marshall, A., & Mcglone, F. P. (2017). C-tactile afferents: Cutaneous mediators of oxytocin release during

affiliative tactile interactions? *Neuropeptides, SI: Neuropeptides-2015*, 64 (August), 27–38. https://doi.org/10.1016/j.npep.2017.01.001

22. Ogi, A., Mariti, C., Baragli, P., Sergi, V., & Gazzano, A. (2020). Effects of stroking on salivary oxytocin and cortisol in guide dogs: Preliminary results. *Animals*, 10(4), 708. https://doi.org/10.3390/ani10040708

23. Fairhurst, M. T., McGlone, F., & Croy, I. (2022). Affective touch: A communication channel for social exchange. *Current Opinion in Behavioral Sciences*, 43 (February), 54–61. https://doi.org/10.1016/j.cobeha.2021.07.007

24. Croy, I., Fairhurst, M. T., & McGlone, F. (2022). The role of c-tactile nerve fibers in human social development. *Current Opinion in Behavioral Sciences*, 43 (February), 20–26. https://doi.org/10.1016/j.cobeha.2021.06.010

25. Yu, H., Miao, W., Ji, E., Huang, S., Jin, S., Zhu, X., Liu, M.-Z., Sun, Y.-G., Xu, F., & Yu, X. (2022). Social touch-like tactile stimulation activates a tachykinin 1-oxytocin pathway to promote social interactions. *Neuron*, 110(6), 1051–1067.e7. https://doi.org/10.1016/j.neuron.2021.12.022

26. Kis, A., Bolló, H., Gergely, A., & Topál, J. (2022). Social stimulation by the owner increases dogs' (Canis familiaris) social susceptibility in a food choice task—the possible effect of endogenous oxytocin release. *Animals*, 12(3), 296. https://doi.org/10.3390/ani12030296

27. Kubinyi, E., Bence, M., Koller, D., Wan, M., Pergel, E., Ronai, Z., Sasvari-Szekely, M., & Miklósi, A. (2017). Oxytocin and opioid receptor gene polymorphisms associated with greeting behavior in dogs. *Frontiers in Psychology*, 8. https://www.frontiersin.org/articles/10.3389/fpsyg.2017.01520

28. Gerra, L. M., Gerra, G., Mercolini, L., Manfredini, M., Somaini, L., Pieri, C. M., Antonioni, M., Protti, M., Ossola, P., & Marchesi, C. (2017). Increased oxytocin levels among abstinent heroin addicts: Association with aggressiveness, psychiatric symptoms and perceived childhood neglect. *Progress in Neuro-Psychopharmacology and Biological Psychiatry*, 75. https://doi.org/10.1016/j.pnpbp.2017.01.005

29. MacLean, E. L., Gesquiere, L. R., Gruen, M. E., Sherman, B. L., Martin, W. L., & Carter, C. S. (2017). Endogenous oxytocin, vasopressin, and aggression

in domestic dogs. *Frontiers in Psychology*, 8. https://www.frontiersin.org/articles/10.3389/fpsyg.2017.01613

30. Kesner, A. J., Calva, C. B., & Ikemoto, S. (2022). Seeking motivation and reward: Roles of dopamine, hippocampus, and supramammillo-septal pathway. *Progress in Neurobiology*, 212 (May), 102252. https://doi.org/10.1016/j.pneurobio.2022.102252

31. Collins, A. G. E., & Shenhav, A. (2022). Advances in modeling learning and decision-making in neuroscience. *Neuropsychopharmacology*, 47(1), 104–18. https://doi.org/10.1038/s41386-021-01126-y

32. Gruber, T., Bazhydai, M., Sievers, C., Clément, F., & Dukes, D. (2022). The ABC of social learning: Affect, behavior, and cognition. *Psychological Review*, 129, 1296–318. https://doi.org/10.1037/rev0000311

33. Casado-Sainz, A., Gudmundsen, F., Baerentzen, S. L., Lange, D., Ringsted, A., Martinez-Tejada, I., Medina, S., et al. (2022). Dorsal striatal dopamine induces fronto-cortical hypoactivity and attenuates anxiety and compulsive behaviors in rats. *Neuropsychopharmacology*, 47(2), 454–64. https://doi.org/10.1038/s41386-021-01207-y

34. Eschmann, K. C. J., Pereira, D. F. M. M., Valji, A., Dehmelt, V., & Gruber, M. J. (2023). Curiosity and mesolimbic functional connectivity drive information seeking in real life. *Social Cognitive and Affective Neuroscience*, 18(1), nsac050. https://doi.org/10.1093/scan/nsac050

35. González-Martínez, A., de Miguel, S. M., Graña, N., Costas, X., & Diéguez, F. J. (2023). Serotonin and dopamine blood levels in ADHD-like dogs. *Animals*, 13(6), 1037. https://doi.org/10.3390/ani13061037

36. Casado-Sainz, A., Gudmundsen, F., Baerentzen, S. L., Lange, D., Ringsted, A., Martinez-Tejada, I., Medina, S., et al. (2022). Dorsal striatal dopamine induces fronto-cortical hypoactivity and attenuates anxiety and compulsive behaviors in rats. *Neuropsychopharmacology*, 47(2), 454–64. https://doi.org/10.1038/s41386-021-01207-y

37. Hori, Y., Kishi, H., Inoue-Murayama, M., & Fujita, K. (2013). Dopamine receptor D4 gene (DRD4) is associated with gazing toward humans in domestic dogs (Canis familiaris). *Open Journal of Animal Sciences*, 3(1). https://doi.org/10.4236/ojas.2013.31008

38. Chmelíková, E., Bolechová, P., Chaloupková, H., Svobodová, I., Jovičić, M., & Sedmíková, M. (2020). Salivary cortisol as a marker of acute stress in dogs: A review. *Domestic Animal Endocrinology*, 72 (July), 106428. https://doi.org/10.1016/j.domaniend.2019.106428

39. Wesarg, C., Van Den Akker, A. L., Oei, N. Y. L., Hoeve, M., & Wiers, R. W. (2020). Identifying pathways from early adversity to psychopathology: A review on dysregulated HPA axis functioning and impaired self-regulation in early childhood. *European Journal of Developmental Psychology*, 17(6), 808–27. https://doi.org/10.1080/17405629.2020.1748594

40. Colombel, N., Ferreira, G., Sullivan, R. M., & Coureaud, G. (2023). Dynamic developmental changes in neurotransmitters supporting infant attachment learning. *Neuroscience & Biobehavioral Reviews*, 151 (August), 105249. https://doi.org/10.1016/j.neubiorev.2023.105249

41. Prato-Previde, E., Ricci, E. B., & Colombo, E. S. (2022). The complexity of the human–animal bond: Empathy, attachment and anthropomorphism in human–animal relationships and animal hoarding. *Animals*, 12(20), 2835. https://doi.org/10.3390/ani12202835

42. Martínez-García, M., Cardenas, S. I., Pawluski, J., Carmona, S., & Saxbe, D. E. (2022). Recent neuroscience advances in human parenting. In *Patterns of parental behavior: From animal science to comparative ethology and neuroscience*, edited by Gabriela González-Mariscal, 239–67. *Advances in Neurobiology*. Springer International Publishing. https://doi.org/10.1007/978-3-030-97762-7_8

43. Kenkel, W. M., Perkeybile, A. M., & Carter, C. S. (2017). The neurobiological causes and effects of alloparenting. *Developmental Neurobiology*, 77(2), 214–32. https://doi.org/10.1002/dneu.22465

44. Kotrschal, K. (2023). Wolf–dog–human: Companionship based on common social tools. *Animals*, 13(17), 2729. https://doi.org/10.3390/ani13172729

Chapter 3

1. "Therapeutic parenting." n.d. Attachment and Trauma Network. Accessed September 14, 2023. https://www.attachmenttraumanetwork.org/parenting/

2. Greene, R. W. (2014). *The explosive child: A new approach for understanding and parenting easily frustrated, chronically inflexible children.* Fifth edition. HarperCollins Publishers.

Chapter 4

1. Carreiro, C., Reicher, V., Kis, A., & Gácsi, M. (2023). Owner-rated hyperactivity/impulsivity is associated with sleep efficiency in family dogs: A non-invasive EEG study. *Scientific Reports*, 13(1), 1291. https://doi.org/10.1038/s41598-023-28263-2

2. McAuliffe, L. R., Koch, C. S., Serpell, J., & Campbell, K. L. (2022). Associations between atopic dermatitis and anxiety, aggression, and fear-based behaviors in dogs. *Journal of the American Animal Hospital Association*, 58(4), 161–67. https://doi.org/10.5326/JAAHA-MS-7210

3. Cocco, R., Arfuso, F., Giannetto, C., Piccione, G., Cesarani, A., Pulina, G., & Sechi, S. (2023). A preliminary study on the interplay between the serum levels of neurotransmitters and thyroid hormones for the evaluation of the behavioral phenotype of dogs. *Animals*, 13(3), 411. https://doi.org/10.3390/ani13030411

4. Salat, J., & Ruzek, D. (2020). Tick-borne encephalitis in domestic animals. *Acta Virologica*, 64(2), 226–32. https://doi.org/10.4149/av_2020_212

5. Maxwell, S. P., Brooks, C., McNeely, C. L., & Thomas, K. C. (2022). Neurological pain, psychological symptoms, and diagnostic struggles among patients with tick-borne diseases. *Healthcare*, 10(7), 1178. https://doi.org/10.3390/healthcare10071178

6. Bransfield, R. C. (2018). Aggressiveness, violence, homicidality, homicide, and lyme disease. *Neuropsychiatric Disease and Treatment*, 14 (December), 693–713. https://doi.org/10.2147/NDT.S155143

7. Mills, D. S., Demontigny-Bédard, I., Gruen, M., Klinck, M. P., McPeake, K. J., Barcelos, A. M., Hewison, L., et al. (2020). Pain and problem behavior in cats and dogs. *Animals*, 10(2), 318. https://doi.org/10.3390/ani10020318

8. Collins, Anne G. E., & Shenhav, A. (2022). Advances in modeling learning and decision-making in neuroscience. *Neuropsychopharmacology*, 47(1), 104–18. https://doi.org/10.1038/s41386-021-01126-y

9. Hrach, S. (2020). *Minding bodies: How physical space, sensation, and movement affect learning*. West Virginia University Press. http://wvupressonline.com/minding-bodies

10. Paul, A. M. (2021). *The extended mind: The power of thinking outside the brain*. Houghton Mifflin Harcourt.

11. Dishman, R. K., Berthoud, H.-R., Booth, F. W., Cotman, C. W., Edgerton, V. R., Fleshner, M. R., Gandevia, S. C., et al. (2006). Neurobiology of exercise. *Obesity*, 14(3), 345–56. https://doi.org/10.1038/oby.2006.46

12. Magistro, D., Cooper, S. B., Carlevaro, F., Marchetti, I., Magno, F., Bardaglio, G., & Musella, G. (2022). Two years of physically active mathematics lessons enhance cognitive function and gross motor skills in primary school children. *Psychology of Sport and Exercise*, 63 (November), 102254. https://doi.org/10.1016/j.psychsport.2022.102254

13. Schmidt, S. K., Bratland-Sanda, S., & Bongaardt, R. (2022). Secondary school teachers' experiences with classroom-based physically active learning: "I'm excited, but it's really hard." *Teaching and Teacher Education*, 116 (August), 103753. https://doi.org/10.1016/j.tate.2022.103753

14. Pastor, D., Cervelló, E., Peruyero, F., Biddle, S., & Montero, C. (2021). Acute physical exercise intensity, cognitive inhibition and psychological well-being in adolescent physical education students. *Current Psychology*, 40(10), 5030–39. https://doi.org/10.1007/s12144-019-00454-z

15. Cook, C. J., Howard, S. J., Scerif, G., Twine, R., Kahn, K., Norris, S. A., & Draper, C. E. (2019). Associations of physical activity and gross motor skills with executive function in preschool children from low-income South African settings. *Developmental Science*, 22(5), e12820. https://doi.org/10.1111/desc.12820

16. Rodriguez-Ayllon, M., Cadenas-Sánchez, C., Estévez-López, F., Muñoz, N. E., Mora-Gonzalez, J., Migueles, J. H., Molina-García, P., et al. (2019). Role of physical activity and sedentary behavior in the mental health of preschoolers, children and adolescents: A systematic review and meta-analysis. *Sports Medicine*, 49(9), 1383–410. https://doi.org/10.1007/s40279-019-01099-5

17. Moylan, S., Eyre, H. A., Maes, M., Baune, B. T., Jacka, F. N., & Berk, M.

(2013). Exercising the worry away: How inflammation, oxidative and nitrogen stress mediates the beneficial effect of physical activity on anxiety disorder symptoms and behaviours. *Neuroscience & Biobehavioral Reviews*, 37(1), 573 84. https://doi.org/10.1016/j.neubiorev.2013.02.003

18. Tandon, P. S., Sasser, T., Gonzalez, E. S., Whitlock, K. B., Christakis, D. A., & Stein, M. A. (2019). Physical activity, screen time, and sleep in children with ADHD. *Journal of Physical Activity and Health*, 16(6), 416–22. https://doi.org/10.1123/jpah.2018-0215

19. Purvis, K. B., Cross, D. R., & Sunshine, W. L. (2007). *The connected child: Bring hope and healing to your adoptive family.* 1st edition. McGraw-Hill Education.

20. Sulkama, S., Puurunen, J., Salonen, M., Mikkola, S., Hakanen, E., Araujo, C., & Lohi, H. (2021). Canine hyperactivity, impulsivity, and inattention share similar demographic risk factors and behavioural comorbidities with human ADHD. *Translational Psychiatry*, 11(1): 1–9. https://doi .org/10.1038/s41398-021-01626-x

21. Tiira, K., & Lohi, H. (2015). Early life experiences and exercise associate with canine anxieties. *PLOS One*, 10(11), e0141907. https://doi .org/10.1371/journal.pone.0141907

22. Porges, S. W. (2009). The polyvagal theory: New insights into adaptive reactions of the autonomic nervous system. *Cleveland Clinic Journal of Medicine*, 76(Suppl 2), S86–90. https://doi.org/10.3949/ccjm.76.s2.17

23. Gothard, K. M., & Fuglevand, A. J. (2022). The role of the amygdala in processing social and affective touch. *Current Opinion in Behavioral Sciences*, 43 (February), 46–53. https://doi.org/10.1016/j.cobeha.2021.08.004

24. Lezama-García, K., Mariti, C., Mota-Rojas, D., Martínez-Burnes, J., Barrios-García, H., & Gazzano, A. (2019). Maternal behaviour in domestic dogs. *International Journal of Veterinary Science and Medicine*, 7(1), 20–30. https://doi.org/10.1080/23144599.2019.1641899

25. Gazzano, A., Mariti, C., Notari, L., Sighieri, C., & McBride, E. A. (2008). Effects of early gentling and early environment on emotional development of puppies. *Applied Animal Behaviour Science*, 110(3), 294–304. https://doi.org/10.1016/j.applanim.2007.05.007

26. Turcsán, B., Tátrai, K., Petró, E., Topál, J., Balogh, L., Egyed, B., & Kubinyi, E. (2020). Comparison of behavior and genetic structure in populations of family and kenneled beagles. *Frontiers in Veterinary Science*, 7, 183. https://doi.org/10.3389/fvets.2020.00183

27. Polgar, Z., Blackwell, E. J., & Rooney, N. J. (2019). Assessing the welfare of kennelled dogs—a review of animal-based measures. *Applied Animal Behaviour Science*, 213 (April), 1–13. https://doi.org/10.1016/j.applanim.2019.02.013

28. Nogueira, L. B., Palme, R., & Mendonça-Furtado, O. (2021). Give them a toy or increase time out of kennel at lawn areas: What is the influence of these interventions on police dogs' welfare? *Animals*, 11(8), 2264. https://doi.org/10.3390/ani11082264

29. Howard, S. J., & Williams, K. E. (2018). Early self-regulation, early self-regulatory change, and their longitudinal relations to adolescents' academic, health, and mental well-being outcomes. *Journal of Developmental and Behavioral Pediatrics*, 39(6), 489–96. https://doi.org/10.1097/DBP.0000000000000578

30. Robson, D. A., Allen, M. S., & Howard, S. J. (2020). Self-regulation in childhood as a predictor of future outcomes: A meta-analytic review. *Psychological Bulletin*, 146, 324–54. https://doi.org/10.1037/bul0000227

31. Jones, M. S., Pierce, H., & Chapple, C. L. (2022). Early adverse childhood experiences and self-control development among youth in fragile families. *Youth & Society*, 54(5), 806–32. https://doi.org/10.1177/0044118X21996378

32. Gobbo, E., and Šemrov, M. Z. (2022). Dogs exhibiting high levels of aggressive reactivity show impaired self-control abilities. *Frontiers in Veterinary Science*, 9. https://www.frontiersin.org/articles/10.3389/fvets.2022.869068

33. Moser, A. Y., Brown, W. Y., Bennett, P., Taylor, P. S., Wilson, B., & McGreevy, P. (2023). Defining the characteristics of successful biosecurity scent detection dogs. *Animals*, 13(3), 504. https://doi.org/10.3390/ani13030504

34. Stilwell, V. n.d. Touch (hand targeting). Accessed December 13, 2023.

https://positively.com/dog-training/article/canine-life-skills-touch-hand-targeting

35. Hedrick, N. G., Lu, A., Bushong, E., Singhi, S., Nguyen, P., Magaña, Y., Jilani, S., Lim, B. K., Ellisman, M., & Komiyama, T. (2022). Learning binds new inputs into functional synaptic clusters via spinogenesis. *Nature Neuroscience*, 25(6), 726–37. https://doi.org/10.1038/s41593-022-01086-6

36. Colliver, Y., Harrison, L. J., Brown, J. E., & Humburg, P. (2022). Free play predicts self-regulation years later: Longitudinal evidence from a large Australian sample of toddlers and preschoolers. *Early Childhood Research Quarterly*, 59 (April), 148–61. https://doi.org/10.1016/j.ecresq.2021.11.011

37. Clothier, S. (2023). See the dog: Temperament, training, choices & relationships. Presented at the 2023 Dog Behavior Conference, Online, April 22.

38. Schaefer, M., Kevekordes, M.-C., Sommer, H., & Gärtner, M. (2022). Of orchids and dandelions: Empathy but not sensory processing sensitivity is associated with tactile discrimination abilities. *Brain Sciences*, 12(5), 641. https://doi.org/10.3390/brainsci12050641

39. Lindaman, S., Booth, P. B., & Cockerill, G. M. (2017). Theraplay: Creating felt safety, emotional connection, and social joy in relationships. In *Attachment theory in action: Building connections between children and parents*. Rowman & Littlefield.

40. Porges, S. W. (2009). The polyvagal theory: New insights into adaptive reactions of the autonomic nervous system. *Cleveland Clinic Journal of Medicine*, 76(Suppl 2), S86–90. https://doi.org/10.3949/ccjm.76.s2.17

41. Bailey, R., Dana, D., Bailey, E., & Davis, F. (2020). The application of the polyvagal theory to high conflict co-parenting cases. *Family Court Review*, 58(2), 525–43. https://doi.org/10.1111/fcre.12485

42. Purvis, K. B., Cross, D. R., & Sunshine, W. L. (2007). *The connected child: Bring hope and healing to your adoptive family*. 1st edition. McGraw-Hill Education.

43. Collins, K., Miller, K., Zverina, L., Patterson-Kane, E., Cussen, V., & Reid, P. (2022). Behavioral rehabilitation of extremely fearful dogs: Report on

the efficacy of a treatment protocol. *Applied Animal Behaviour Science*, 254 (September), 105689. https://doi.org/10.1016/j.applanim.2022.105689

44. Battaglia, M. R., Di Fazio, C., & Battaglia, S. (2023). Activated tryptophan-kynurenine metabolic system in the human brain is associated with learned fear. *Frontiers in Molecular Neuroscience*, 16. https://www .frontiersin.org/articles/10.3389/fnmol.2023.1217090

45. Polgar, Z., Blackwell, E. J., & Rooney, N. J. (2019). Assessing the welfare of kennelled dogs—a review of animal-based measures. *Applied Animal Behaviour Science*, 213 (April), 1–13. https://doi.org/10.1016/j .applanim.2019.02.013

46. Dalla Villa, P., Barnard, S., Di Fede, E., Podaliri, M., Di Nardo, A., Siracusa, C., & Serpell, J. A. (2013). Behavioural and physiological responses of shelter dogs to long-term confinement. *Veterinaria Italiana*, 49(2), 231–41. https://doi.org/10.12834/VetIt.2013.492.231.241.

46. Mascarenhas Ladeia Dutra, L., de Souza, F. S., Schork, I. G., da Silva Vasconcellos, A., & Young, R. J. (2023). How a dog's background is related to relative telomere length (rTL). *SSRN Scholarly Paper*. Rochester, NY. https://doi.org/10.2139/ssrn.4328190

47. Scheifele, P., Martin, D., Clark, J. G., Kemper, D., & Wells, J. (2012). Effect of kennel noise on hearing in dogs. *American Journal of Veterinary Research*, 73(4), 482–89. https://doi.org/10.2460/ajvr.73.4.482

48. Baqueiro-Espinosa, U., Lo, T. H., Hunter, R., Donnelly, P., McEvoy, V., Crump, A., & Arnott, G. (2023). Positive human interaction improves welfare in commercial breeding dogs: Evidence from attention bias and human sociability tests. *Applied Animal Behaviour Science*, 262 (May), 105904. https://doi.org/10.1016/j.applanim.2023.105904

49. Foraita, M., Howell, T., & Bennett, P. (2021). Environmental influences on development of executive functions in dogs. *Animal Cognition*, 24(4), 655–75. https://doi.org/10.1007/s10071-021-01489-1

50. Hennessy, M. B., Willen, R. M., & Schiml, P. A. (2020). Psychological stress, its reduction, and long-term consequences: What studies with laboratory animals might teach us about life in the dog shelter. *Animals*, 10(11), 2061. https://doi.org/10.3390/ani10112061

51. Zaccagnino, M., Cussino, M., Preziosa, A., Veglia, F., & Carassa, A. (2015). Attachment representation in institutionalized children: A preliminary study using the child attachment interview. *Clinical Psychology & Psychotherapy, 22*(2), 165–75. https://doi.org/10.1002/cpp.1882

52. Lezama-García, K., Mariti, C., Mota-Rojas, D., Martínez-Burnes, J., Barrios-García, H., & Gazzano, A. (2019). Maternal behaviour in domestic dogs. *International Journal of Veterinary Science and Medicine, 7*(1), 20–30. https://doi.org/10.1080/23144599.2019.1641899

53. Bosmans, G., Van Vlierberghe, L., Bakermans-Kranenburg, M. J., Kobak, R., Hermans, D., & van IJzendoorn, M. H. (2022). A learning theory approach to attachment theory: Exploring clinical applications. *Clinical Child and Family Psychology Review, 25*(3), 591–612. https://doi.org/10.1007/s10567-021-00377-x

54. Wall, M. D. S., Ainsworth, M. C., Blehar, E., & Waters, S. (2014). *Patterns of attachment: A psychological study of the strange situation.* Psychology Press. https://doi.org/10.4324/9781315802428

55. Madigan, S., Pasco Fearon, R. M., van IJzendoorn, M. H., Duschinsky, R., Schuengel, C., Bakermans-Kranenburg, M. J., Ly, A., et al. (2023). The first 20,000 strange situation procedures: A meta-analytic review. *Psychological Bulletin, 149*(1–2), 99–132. https://doi.org/10.1037/bul0000388

56. Yang, Y., & Perkins, D. R. (2021). Association between childhood adversity and criminal thinking: The role of attachment. *Psychology, Crime & Law, 27*(8), 796–814. https://doi.org/10.1080/1068316X.2020.1850724

57. Tiira, K., & Lohi, H. (2015). Early life experiences and exercise associate with canine anxieties. *PLOS One, 10*(11), e0141907. https://doi.org/10.1371/journal.pone.0141907

58. Buttner, A. P., Awalt, S. L., & Strasser, R. (2023). Early life adversity in dogs produces altered physiological and behavioral responses during a social stress-buffering paradigm. *Journal of the Experimental Analysis of Behavior, 120*(1), 6–20. https://doi.org/10.1002/jeab.856

59. Buttner, A. P., & Strasser, R. (2022). Extreme life histories are associated with altered social behavior and cortisol levels in shelter dogs.

Applied Animal Behaviour Science, 256 (November), 105693. https://doi
.org/10.1016/j.applanim.2022.105693

60. Smith, J. G., & Katz, J. S. (2023). Measuring the dog side of the dog-human
bond. In *Canine Cognition and the Human Bond*, edited by Jeffrey R. Ste-
vens, 37–62. Nebraska Symposium on Motivation. Springer International
Publishing. https://doi.org/10.1007/978-3-031-29789-2_3

61. Carreiro, C., Reicher, V., Kis, A., & Gácsi, M. (2022). Attachment towards
the owner is associated with spontaneous sleep EEG parameters in family
dogs. *Animals*, 12(7), 895. https://doi.org/10.3390/ani12070895

62. Ainsworth, M. D., & Bell, S. M. (1970). Attachment, exploration, and separation: Illustrated by the behavior of one-year-olds in a strange situation.
Child Development, 41(1), 49–67. https://doi.org/10.2307/1127388

63. Prato-Previde, E., Custance, D. M., Spiezio, C., & Sabatini, F. (2003). Is the
dog-human relationship an attachment bond? An observational study
using Ainsworth's strange situation. *Behaviour*, 140(2), 225–54.

64. Solomon, J., Beetz, A., Schöberl, I., Gee, N., & Kotrschal, K. (2019). Attachment security in companion dogs: Adaptation of Ainsworth's strange
situation and classification procedures to dogs and their human caregivers. *Attachment & Human Development*, 21(4), 389–417. https://doi
.org/10.1080/14616734.2018.1517812

65. Seim, A. R., Jozefiak, T., Wichstrøm, L., Lydersen, S., & Kayed, N. S.
(2022). Reactive attachment disorder and disinhibited social engagement
disorder in adolescence: Co-occurring psychopathology and psychosocial problems. *European Child & Adolescent Psychiatry*, 31(1), 85–98.
https://doi.org/10.1007/s00787-020-01673-7

66. Gábor, A., Andics, A., Miklósi, A., Czeibert, K., Carreiro, C., & Gácsi,
M. (2021). Social relationship-dependent neural response to speech in
dogs. *NeuroImage*, 243 (November), 118480. https://doi.org/10.1016/j
.neuroimage.2021.118480

67. Souza, P., Guo, K., Mills, D. S., Resende, B., & Albuquerque, N. (2023). How
do dogs behave when presented with situations of different emotional valences? *Animals*, 13(6), 1027. https://doi.org/10.3390/ani13061027

68. Fonseca, M. L. A., & Vasconcellos, A. S. (2021). Can dogs' origins and

interactions with humans affect their accomplishments? A study on the responses of shelter and companion dogs during vocal cue training. *Animals*, 11(5), 1360. https://doi.org/10.3390/ani11051360

69. Girme, Y. U., Jones, R. E., Fleck, C., Simpson, J. A., & Overall, N. C. (2021). Infants' attachment insecurity predicts attachment-relevant emotion regulation strategies in adulthood. *Emotion*, 21(2), 260–72. https://doi.org/10.1037/emo0000721

70. Strathearn, L., Giannotti, M., Mills, R., Kisely, S., Najman, J., & Abajobir, A. (2020). Long-term cognitive, psychological, and health outcomes associated with child abuse and neglect. *Pediatrics*, 146(4), e20200438. https://doi.org/10.1542/peds.2020-0438

71. van der Voort, A., Juffer, F., & Bakermans-Kranenburg, M. J. (2014). Sensitive parenting is the foundation for secure attachment relationships and positive social-emotional development of children. Edited by Jane Barlow. *Journal of Children's Services*, 9(2), 165–76. https://doi.org/10.1108/JCS-12-2013-0038

72. Barnard, S., Flint, H., Diana, A., Shreyer, T., Arrazola, A., Serpell, J., & Croney, C. (2023). Management and behavioral factors associated with rehoming outcomes of dogs retired from commercial breeding kennels. *PLOS One*, 18(3), e0282459. https://doi.org/10.1371/journal.pone.0282459

73. Bennett, M. S. (2017). *Connecting paradigms: A trauma-informed and neurobiological framework for motivational interviewing implementation.* Bennett Innovation Group, L3C.

74. Runcan, P. L., Constantineanu, C., Ielics, B., & Popa, D. (2012). The role of communication in the parent-child interaction. *Procedia—Social and Behavioral Sciences, 4th World Conference on Educational Sciences (WCES-2012) 02–05 February 2012 Barcelona, Spain*, 46(January), 904–8. https://doi.org/10.1016/j.sbspro.2012.05.221

75. Donaldson, L., n.d. The cognitive revolution and everyday dog training: The case of "look at that." The IAABC Journal (blog). Accessed March 26, 2023. https://iaabcjournal.org/cognitive-revolution-dog-training-lat/

76. Hunger, C. (2021). *How Stella learned to talk: The groundbreaking story of the world's first talking dog.* HarperCollins Publishers.

77. Hyde, L. W., Waller, R., Trentacosta, C. J., Shaw, D. S., Neiderhiser, J. M., Ganiban, J. M., Reiss, D., & Leve, L. D. (2016). Heritable and non-heritable pathways to early callous-unemotional behaviors. *American Journal of Psychiatry,* 173(9), 903–10. https://doi.org/10.1176/appi.ajp.2016.15111381

78. Starling, M. J., Branson, N., Cody, D., & McGreevy, P. D. (2013). Conceptualising the impact of arousal and affective state on training outcomes of operant conditioning. *Animals,* 3(2), 300–317. https://doi.org/10.3390/ani3020300

79. Smith, M. L. (2021). *The connected therapist: Relating through the senses.* Marti Smith Seminars.

80. The neurosequential model of therapeutics (NMT): Helping clients move beyond trauma. 2019. SocialWorker.Com. January 14, 2019. https://www.socialworker.com/api/content/eaa838c8-0a21-11e9-aba9-120e7ad5cf50/

81. Pryor, K. (1984). *Don't shoot the dog, the art of teaching and training: The secrets to changing behavior in pets, kids, and yourself.* Simon & Schuster.

82. Katz, M., & Rosales-Ruiz, J. (2022). Constructional fear treatment: Teaching fearful shelter dogs to approach and interact with a novel person. *Journal of the Experimental Analysis of Behavior,* 118(2), 278–91. https://doi.org/10.1002/jeab.784

83. Zurlinden, S., Spano, S., Griffith, E., & Bennett, S. (2022). Impact of classical counterconditioning (quiet kennel exercise) on barking in kenneled dogs—a pilot study. *Animals,* 12(2), 171. https://doi.org/10.3390/ani12020171

84. Riemer, S. (2020). Effectiveness of treatments for firework fears in dogs. *Journal of Veterinary Behavior,* 37 (May), 61–70. https://doi.org/10.1016/j.jveb.2020.04.005

85. Collins, K., Miller, K., Zverina, L., Patterson-Kane, E., Cussen, V., & Reid, P. (2022). Behavioral rehabilitation of extremely fearful dogs: Report on the efficacy of a treatment protocol. *Applied Animal Behaviour Science,* 254 (September), 105689. https://doi.org/10.1016/j.applanim.2022.105689

86. Rooney, N. J., Clark, C. C. A., & Casey, R. A. (2016). Minimizing fear and anxiety in working dogs: A review. *Journal of Veterinary Behavior*, 16 (November), 53–64. https://doi.org/10.1016/j.jveb.2016.11.001

87. Sandoval-Norton, A. H., Shkedy, G., & Shkedy, D. (2019). How much compliance is too much compliance: Is long-term ABA therapy abuse? Edited by Jacqueline Ann Rushby. *Cogent Psychology*, 6(1), 1641258. https://doi.org/10.1080/23311908.2019.1641258

88. Tottenham, N., Hertzig, M. E., Gillespie-Lynch, K., Gilhooly, T., Millner, A. J., & Casey, B. J. (2014). Elevated amygdala response to faces and gaze aversion in autism spectrum disorder. *Social Cognitive and Affective Neuroscience*, 9(1), 106–17. https://doi.org/10.1093/scan/nst050

89. Madipakkam, A. R., Rothkirch, M., Dziobek, I., & Sterzer, P. (2017). Unconscious avoidance of eye contact in autism spectrum disorder. *Scientific Reports*, 7(1), 13378. https://doi.org/10.1038/s41598-017-13945-5

90. Hadjikhani, N., & Johnels, J. A. (2023). Overwhelmed by the man in the moon? Pareidolic objects provoke increased amygdala activation in autism. *Cortex*, 164 (July), 144–51. https://doi.org/10.1016/j.cortex.2023.03.014

91. McGill, O., & Robinson, A. (2020). "Recalling hidden harms": Autistic experiences of childhood applied behavioural analysis (ABA). *Advances in Autism*, 7(4), 269–82. https://doi.org/10.1108/AIA-04-2020-0025

92. Bowlby, J. (1984). Violence in the family as a disorder of the attachment and caregiving systems. *American Journal of Psychoanalysis*, 44(1), https://www.proquest.com/openview/eb355bc234212e93883a74511f590a6c/1?pq-origsite=gscholar&cbl=1818460

93. Avezum, M. D. M. de M., Altafim, E. R. P., & Linhares, M. B. M. (2022). Spanking and corporal punishment parenting practices and child development: A systematic review. *Trauma, Violence, & Abuse*, September, 15248380221124243. https://doi.org/10.1177/15248380221124243

94. Visser, L. N., van der Put, C. E., & Assink, M. (2022). The association between school corporal punishment and child developmental outcomes: A meta-analytic review. *Children*, 9(3), 383. https://doi.org/10.3390/children9030383

95. Joyner, B., & Beaver, K. M. (2022). Unpacking the association between corporal punishment and criminal involvement. *Criminal Justice and Behavior*, 49(12), 1845–63. https://doi.org/10.1177/00938548221107874

96. Duong, H. T., & Sirohi, A. (2023). Where do perceived norms supporting child corporal punishment come from? A study of low-income parents. *Health Communication*, 1–12. https://doi.org/10.1080/10410236.2023.2193754

97. Vieira de Castro, A. C., Fuchs, D., Morello, G. M., Pastur, S., de Sousa, L., & Olsson, I. A. S. (2020). Does training method matter? Evidence for the negative impact of aversive-based methods on companion dog welfare. *PLOS One*, 15(12). https://doi.org/10.1371/journal.pone.0225023

98. Ziv, G. (2017). The effects of using aversive training methods in dogs—a review. *Journal of Veterinary Behavior*, 19 (May), 50–60. https://doi.org/10.1016/j.jveb.2017.02.004.95

99. Grohmann, K., Dickomeit, M. J., Schmidt, M. J., & Kramer, M. (2013). Severe brain damage after punitive training technique with a choke chain collar in a German shepherd dog. *Journal of Veterinary Behavior*, 8(3), 180–84. https://doi.org/10.1016/j.jveb.2013.01.002

100. Mejdell, C. M., Basic, D., & Bøe, K. E. (2017). A review on the use of electric devices to modify animal behaviour and the impact on animal welfare; opinion of the Panel on Animal Health and Welfare of the Norwegian Scientific Committee for Food and Environment. ISSN: 2535-4019. Norwegian Scientific Committee for Food and Environment. https://nmbu.brage.unit.no/nmbu-xmlui/bitstream/handle/11250/2474441/Mejdell_2017_Are.pdf

101. Hiby, E. F., Rooney, N. J., & Bradshaw, J. W. S. (2004). Dog training methods: Their use, effectiveness and interaction with behaviour and welfare. *Animal Welfare*, 13(1), 63–69. https://doi.org/10.1017/S0962728600026683

102. Blackwell, E., & Casey, R. (2009). *The use of shock collars and their impact on the welfare of dogs: A review of the current literature*. Petprofessionalguild.com. www.petprofessionalguild.com/resources/No%20Shock%20Coalition/The-Use-of-Shock-Collars-and-Their-Impact-on-the-Welfare-of-Dogs.pdf

103. Arhant, C., Bubna-Littitz, H., Bartels, A., Futschik, A., & Troxler, J. (2010). Behaviour of smaller and larger dogs: Effects of training methods, inconsistency of owner behaviour and level of engagement in activities with the dog. *Applied Animal Behaviour Science*, 123(3), 131–42. https://doi.org/10.1016/j.applanim.2010.01.003

104. Casey, R. A., Naj-Oleari, M., Campbell, S., Mendl, M., & Blackwell, E. J. (2021). Dogs are more pessimistic if their owners use two or more aversive training methods. *Scientific Reports*, 11(1), 19023. https://doi.org/10.1038/s41598-021-97743-0

105. Herron, M. E., Shofer, F. S., & Reisner, I. R. (2009). Survey of the use and outcome of confrontational and non-confrontational training methods in client-owned dogs showing undesired behaviors. *Applied Animal Behaviour Science*, 117(1/2), 47–54.

106. Hunsley, J., Crawley, R., & Call, C. (2021). The pilot of a therapeutic family camp intervention to improve adoptive family functioning. *Adoption Quarterly*, 25 (November), 1–24. https://doi.org/10.1080/10926755.2021.2005728

107. Lee, K. (2023). Effects of formal center-based care and positive parenting practices on children in foster care. *Child Abuse & Neglect, Learning in the Context of Adversity*, 142 (August), 105946. https://doi.org/10.1016/j.chiabu.2022.105946

108. Jylänki, P., Mbay, T., Hakkarainen, A., Sääkslahti, A., & Aunio, P. (2022). The effects of motor skill and physical activity interventions on preschoolers' cognitive and academic skills: A systematic review. *Preventive Medicine*, 155 (February), 106948. https://doi.org/10.1016/j.ypmed.2021.106948

109. Purvis, K. B., Razuri, E. B., Howard, A. R. H., Call, C. D., DeLuna, J. H., Hall, J. S., & Cross, D. R. (2015). Decrease in behavioral problems and trauma symptoms among at-risk adopted children following trauma-informed parent training intervention. *Journal of Child & Adolescent Trauma*, 8(3), 201–10. https://doi.org/10.1007/s40653-015-0055-y

110. Mills, D., & Zulch, H. (2023). Veterinary assessment of behaviour cases in cats and dogs. *In Practice*, October. https://doi.org/10.1002/inpr.359

111. Collins, K., Miller, K., Zverina, L., Patterson-Kane, E., Cussen, V., & Reid, P. (2022). Behavioral rehabilitation of extremely fearful dogs: Report on the efficacy of a treatment protocol. *Applied Animal Behaviour Science*, 254 (September), 105689. https://doi.org/10.1016/j.applanim.2022.105689.

112. Wells, D. L. (2022). Factors influencing the expression of behavior in the domestic dog. In T. Grandin (ed.), *Genetics and the behavior of domestic animals* (3rd ed.) (229–52). Academic Press. https://doi.org/10.1016/B978-0-323-85752-9.00011-1

113. Purvis, K. B., Cross, D. R., & Sunshine, W. L. (2007). *The connected child: Bring hope and healing to your adoptive family.* 1st edition. McGraw-Hill Education, p. 2.

Chapter 5

1. Smith, K. E., Landry, S. H., & Swank, P. R. (2000). The influence of early patterns of positive parenting on children's preschool outcomes. *Early Education and Development*, 11(2), 147–69. https://doi.org/10.1207/s15566935eed1102_2

2. Sanvictores, T., & Mendez, M. D. (2022). Types of parenting styles and effects on children. In *StatPearls*. StatPearls Publishing. http://www.ncbi.nlm.nih.gov/books/NBK568743/

3. van Herwijnen, I. R., van der Borg, J. A. M., Naguib, M., & Beerda, B. (2018). The existence of parenting styles in the owner-dog relationship. *PLOS One*, 13(2), e0193471. https://doi.org/10.1371/journal.pone.0193471

4. van Herwijnen, I. R., van der Borg, J. A. M., Naguib, M., & Beerda, B. (2020). Dog-directed parenting styles mirror dog owners' orientations toward animals. *Anthrozoös*, 33(6), 759–73. https://doi.org/10.1080/08927936.2020.1824657

5. van Herwijnen, I. R., van der Borg, J. A. M., Naguib, M., & Beerda, B. (2020). Dog-directed parenting styles predict verbal and leash guidance in dog owners and owner-directed attention in dogs. *Applied Animal Behaviour Science*, 232 (November), 105131. https://doi.org/10.1016/j.applanim.2020.105131

6. van Herwijnen, I. R. (2021). Contribution to the special issue on

clinical ethology: Educating dog owners: How owner–dog interactions can benefit from addressing the human caregiving system and dog-directed parenting styles. *Behaviour*, 1, 1–22. https://doi.org/10.1163/1568539X-bja10066

7. Singh, C., & Sihag, J. n.d. The effects of parenting style on children's behavior: A systematic literature review. *The Pharma Innovation Journal*, SP-11(11), 1695–702.

8. Stinnett, L. (2017). Taking the veterinary practice: Prong collar free. *NAVTA Journal*, December/January, 58–62.

9. Masson, S., de la Vega, S., Gazzano, A., Mariti, C., Da Graça Pereira, G., Halsberghe, C., Leyvraz, A. M., McPeake, K., & Schoening, B. (2018). Electronic training devices: Discussion on the pros and cons of their use in dogs as a basis for the position statement of the European Society of Veterinary Clinical Ethology. *Journal of Veterinary Behavior*, 25 (May), 71–75. https://doi.org/10.1016/j.jveb.2018.02.006

10. Sung, W., & Radosta, L. (2023). Unruly and destructive behaviors—canine. In *Behavior Problems of the Dog and Cat*. Elsevier Health Sciences. (includes photo of prong collar injury).

11. Ziv, G. (2017). The effects of using aversive training methods in dogs—A review. *Journal of Veterinary Behavior*, 19 (May), 50–60. https://doi.org/10.1016/j.jveb.2017.02.004

12. Vieira de Castro, A. C., Fuchs, D., Morello, G. M., Pastur, S., de Sousa, L., & Olsson, I. A. S. (2020). Does training method matter? Evidence for the negative impact of aversive-based methods on companion dog welfare. *PLOS One*, 15(12). https://doi.org/10.1371/journal.pone.0225023

13. Sanvictores, T., & Mendez, M. D. (2022). Types of parenting styles and effects on children. In *StatPearls*. StatPearls Publishing. http://www.ncbi.nlm.nih.gov/books/NBK568743/

14. van Herwijnen, I. R., Corbee, R. J., Endenburg, N., Beerda, B., & van der Borg, J. A. M. (2020). Permissive parenting of the dog associates with dog overweight in a survey among 2,303 Dutch dog owners. *PLOS One* 15 (8): e0237429. https://doi.org/10.1371/journal.pone.0237429.

15. Suchman, N. E., Rounsaville, B., DeCoste, C., & Luthar, S. (2007). Parental control, parental warmth, and psychosocial adjustment in a sample

of substance-abusing mothers and their school-aged and adolescent children. *Journal of Substance Abuse Treatment*, 32(1), 1–10. https://doi .org/10.1016/j.jsat.2006.07.002

16. Volsche, S., & Gray, P. (2016). "Dog moms" use authoritative parenting styles. *Human-Animal Interaction Bulletin*, 4(2). https://doi.org/10.1079 /hai.2016.0008

17. Brubaker, L., & Udell, M. A. R. (2023). Does pet parenting style predict the social and problem-solving behavior of pet dogs (Canis lupus familiaris)? *Animal Cognition*, 26(1), 345–56. https://doi.org/10.1007 /s10071-022-01694-6

18. Querdasi, F. R., Enders, C., Karnani, N., Broekman, B., Seng, C. Y., Gluckman, P. D., Daniel, L. M., et al. (2023). Multigenerational adversity impacts on human gut microbiome composition and socioemotional functioning in early childhood. *Proceedings of the National Academy of Sciences*, 120(30), e2213768120. https://doi.org/10.1073/pnas.2213768120

19. Rowell, T., & Neal-Barnett, A. (2022). A systematic review of the effect of parental adverse childhood experiences on parenting and child psychopathology. *Journal of Child & Adolescent Trauma*, 15(1), 167–80. https:/ /doi.org/10.1007/s40653-021-00400-x

20. Hanh, T. N. (2010). *Reconciliation: Healing the inner child*. Parallax Press.

Chapter 6

1. Johnson, A. C., & Wynne, C. D. L. (2023). Training dogs with science or with nature? An exploration of trainers' word use, gender, and certification across dog-training methods. *Anthrozoös*, 36(1), 35–51. https://doi.org/10 .1080/08927936.2022.2062869

2. Walmsley, D. W., Day, S. K., & Nash, K. J. (2022). Management of a skin wound associated with use of an electronic anti-barking collar in a dog. *Australian Veterinary Practitioner*, 52(1). https://www.ava.com.au/siteassets /library/journal/australian-veterinary-practitioner/archive/avp-vol-52 -issue-1-march--2022.pdf

3. Straub, R. H. (2023). What is a child's psychological trauma? In *Early trauma as the origin of chronic inflammation: A psychoneuroimmunological perspective* (R. H. Straub, ed.), 13–70. Springer. https://doi .org/10.1007/978-3-662-66751-4_2

4. Grohmann, K., Dickomeit, M. J., Schmidt, M. J., & Kramer, M. (2013). Severe brain damage after punitive training technique with a choke chain collar in a German shepherd dog. *Journal of Veterinary Behavior*, 8(3), 180–84. https://doi.org/10.1016/j.jveb.2013.01.002

5. Kim, S.-A., & Bain, M. J. (2022). Animal behavior case of the month—Shiba Inu C-PTSD. *Journal of the American Veterinary Medical Association*, 260(12), 1463–65. https://doi.org/10.2460/javma.22.03.0132

6. Ziv, G. (2017). The effects of using aversive training methods in dogs—a review. *Journal of Veterinary Behavior*, 19 (May), 50–60. https://doi.org/10.1016/j.jveb.2017.02.004

7. Vieira de Castro, A. C., Fuchs, D., Morello, G. M., Pastur, S., de Sousa, L., & Olsson, I. A. S. (2020). Does training method matter? Evidence for the negative impact of aversive-based methods on companion dog welfare. *PLOS One*, 15(12). https://doi.org/10.1371/journal.pone.0225023

8. Wells, D. L. (2022). Factors influencing the expression of behavior in the domestic dog. In T. Grandin (ed.), *Genetics and the behavior of domestic animals* (3rd ed.) Academic Press, 229–52. https://doi.org/10.1016/B978-0-323-85752-9.00011-1

9. Starling, M. J., Branson, N., Cody, D., & McGreevy, P. D. (2013). Conceptualising the impact of arousal and affective state on training outcomes of operant conditioning. *Animals*, 3(2), 300–317. https://doi.org/10.3390/ani3020300

10. China, L., Mills, D. S., & Cooper, J. J. (2020). Efficacy of dog training with and without remote electronic collars vs. a focus on positive reinforcement. *Frontiers in Veterinary Science*, 7, 508. https://doi.org/10.3389/fvets.2020.00508

11. Cooper, J. J., Mills, D. S., & China, L. (2021). Response: Commentary: Remote electronic training aids; efficacy at deterring predatory behavior in dogs and implications for training and policy. *Frontiers in Veterinary Science*, 8. https://www.frontiersin.org/articles/10.3389/fvets.2021.675005

12. Statement—American College of Veterinary Behaviorists. n.d. Accessed September 20, 2023. https://www.dacvb.org/page/sep2023statement

Chapter 7

1. Feldman, R. (2017). The neurobiology of human attachments. *Trends in Cognitive Sciences*, 21(2), 80–99. https://doi.org/10.1016/j.tics.2016.11.007

2. Barnard, S., Flint, H., Diana, A., Shreyer, T., Arrazola, A., Serpell, J., & Croney, C. (2023). Management and behavioral factors associated with re-homing outcomes of dogs retired from commercial breeding kennels. *PLOS One*, 18(3), e0282459. https://doi.org/10.1371/journal.pone.0282459.x

3. Pierantoni, L., Amadei, E., & Pirrone, F. (2022). Factors to consider when selecting puppies and preventing later behavioral problems. *Advances in Small Animal Care*, 3(1), 1–11. https://doi.org/10.1016/j.yasa.2022.05.001

4. Evans, K. M., & Adams, V. J. (2010). Proportion of litters of purebred dogs born by Caesarean section. *Journal of Small Animal Practice*, 51(2), 113–18. https://doi.org/10.1111/j.1748-5827.2009.00902.x

5. Boone, G., Romaniuk, A. C., Barnard, S., Shreyer, T., & Croney, C. (2023). The effect of early neurological stimulation on puppy welfare in commercial breeding kennels. *Animals*, 13(1), 71. https://doi.org/10.3390/ani13010071

6. Levine, P. A., & Kline, M. (2006). *Trauma through a child's eyes*. North Atlantic Books and ERGOS Institute Press, 314.

7. Davis, K. M., Partin, A. M., Burghardt, G. M., Springer, C. M., & Albright, J. D. (2023). A descriptive methodology for studying the ontogeny of object play and breed differences in dogs (Canis lupus familiaris). *Animals*, 13(8), 1371. https://doi.org/10.3390/ani13081371

8. Whitehead, S. n.d. Help with puppy biting. Accessed September 10, 2023. https://sarahwhitehead.thinkific.com/courses/help-with-puppy-biting

9. Asher, L., England, G. C. W., Sommerville, R., & Harvey, N. D. (2020). Teenage dogs? Evidence for adolescent-phase conflict behaviour and an association between attachment to humans and pubertal timing in the domestic dog. *Biology Letters*, 16(5), 20200097. https://doi.org/10.1098/rsbl.2020.0097

Chapter 8

1. Duong, T. H., Jansson, U.-B., Holmdahl, G., Sillén, U., & Hellström, A. L. (2013). Urinary bladder control during the first 3 years of life in healthy

children in Vietnam—a comparison study with Swedish children. *Journal of Pediatric Urology*, 9(6, Part A), 700–706. https://doi.org/10.1016/j .jpurol.2013.04.022

2. Thorpe, M. (2014). The psychological advantages of enhanced sensitive attunement through nappy-free elimination communication. *Journal of Psychotherapy Aotearoa New Zealand, Special Issue: The Essence of Psychotherapy*, 18(2), https://doi.org/10.9791/ajpanz.2014.12

3. Aloff, B. (2005). *Canine body language, a photographic guide: Interpreting the native language of the domestic dog*. TFH Publications, Inc.

4. Stilwell, V. (2016). *The secret language of dogs: Unlocking the canine mind for a happier pet*. Ten Speed Press.

5. Rugaas, T. (1997). *On talking terms with dogs: Calming signals*. Dogwise Publishing.

6. Firnkes, A., Bartels, A., Bidoli, E., & Erhard, M. (2017). Appeasement signals used by dogs during dog–human communication. *Journal of Veterinary Behavior*, 19 (May), 35–44. https://doi.org/10.1016/j.jveb.2016.12.012

7. Maglieri, V., Zanoli, A., Mastrandrea, F., & Palagi, E. (2022). The relaxed open mouth is a true signal in dogs: Demonstrating Tinbergen's ritualization process. *Animal Behaviour*, 188 (June), 65–74. https://doi.org /10.1016/j.anbehav.2022.03.015

8. Mota-Rojas, D., Marcet-Rius, M., Ogi, A., Hernández-Ávalos, I., Mariti, C., Martínez-Burnes, J., Mora-Medina, P., et al. (2021). Current advances in assessment of dog's emotions, facial expressions, and their use for clinical recognition of pain. *Animals*, 11(11), 3334. https://doi.org/10.3390 /ani11113334

9. Correia-Caeiro, C., Guo, K., & Mills, D. (2021). Bodily emotional expressions are a primary source of information for dogs, but not for humans. *Animal Cognition*, 24(2), 267–79. https://doi.org/10.1007/s10071 -021-01471-x

10. Correia-Caeiro, C., Guo, K., & Mills, D. S. (2020). Perception of dynamic facial expressions of emotion between dogs and humans. *Animal Cognition*, 23(3), 465–76. https://doi.org/10.1007/s10071-020-01348-5

11. Győri, B., Gácsi, M., & Miklósi, A. (2010). Friend or foe: Context dependent sensitivity to human behaviour in dogs. *Applied Animal Behaviour Science*, 128(1), 69–77. https://doi.org/10.1016/j.applanim.2010.10.005

12. Topál, J., Miklósi, A., & Csányi, V. (1997). Dog-human relationship affects problem solving behavior in the dog. *Anthrozoös*, 10(4), 214–24. https://doi.org/10.2752/089279397787000987

13. Albuquerque, N., & Resende, B. (2023). Dogs functionally respond to and use emotional information from human expressions. *Evolutionary Human Sciences*, 5 (January), e2. https://doi.org/10.1017/ehs.2022.57

14. Karl, S., Boch, M., Zamansky, A., van der Linden, D., Wagner, I. C., Völter, C. J., Lamm, C., & Huber, L. (2020). Exploring the dog–human relationship by combining fMRI, eye-tracking and behavioural measures. *Scientific Reports*, 10(1), 22273. https://doi.org/10.1038/s41598-020-79247-5

15. McConnell, P. (2002). *The other end of the leash*. Ballantine Books.

16. Correia-Caeiro, C., Guo, K., & Mills, D. (2021). Bodily emotional expressions are a primary source of information for dogs, but not for humans. *Animal Cognition*, 24(2), 267–79. https://doi.org/10.1007/s10071-021-01471-x

17. Hecht, J., & Horowitz, A. (2015). Introduction to dog behavior. In *Animal behavior for shelter veterinarians and staff* (1st ed.). John Wiley & Sons.

18. Coppinger, R., & Coppinger, L. (2001). *Dogs: A startling new understanding of canine origin, behavior, & evolution*. Scribner.

19. Lenkei, R., Faragó, T., Bakos, V., & Pongracz, P. (2021). Separation-related behavior of dogs shows association with their reactions to everyday situations that may elicit frustration or fear. *Scientific Reports*, 11 (September), 19207. https://doi.org/10.1038/s41598-021-98526-3

20. Pedretti, G., Canori, C., Marshall-Pescini, S., Palme, R., Pelosi, A., & Valsecchi, P. (2022). Audience effect on domestic dogs' behavioural displays and facial expressions. *Scientific Reports*, 12(1), 9747. https://doi.org/10.1038/s41598-022-13566-7

21. Correia-Caeiro, C., Guo, K., & Mills, D. S. (2020). Perception of dynamic facial expressions of emotion between dogs and humans. *Animal Cognition*, 23(3), 465–76. https://doi.org/10.1007/s10071-020-01348-5

22. Kuhne, F., Hößler, J. C., & Struwe, R. (2014). Behavioral and cardiac responses by dogs to physical human–dog contact. *Journal of Veterinary Behavior*, 9(3), 93–97. https://doi.org/10.1016/j.jveb.2014.02.006

23. Dorrigiv, I., Hadian, M., & Bahram, M. (2023). Comparison of volatile compounds of anal sac secretions between the sexes of domestic dog (Canis lupus familiaris). *Veterinary Research Forum*, 14(3), 169–76. https://doi.org/10.30466/vrf.2023.1983063.3714

24. Sunshine, W. L. n.d. Dog owner questionnaire. Accessed September 22, 2023. https://form.jotform.com/211695765089167

25. Eisenberg, N., Cumberland, A., Spinrad, T. L., Fabes, R. A., Shepard, S. A., Reiser, M., Murphy, B. C., Losoya, S. H., & Guthrie, I. K. (2001). The relations of regulation and emotionality to children's externalizing and internalizing problem behavior. *Child Development*, 72(4), 1112–34. https://doi.org/10.1111/1467-8624.00337

26. Purvis, K. B., Cross, D. R., & Sunshine, W. L. (2007). *The connected child: Bring hope and healing to your adoptive family* (1st ed.). McGraw-Hill Education.

27. Behavior Checklist (BCL) Definitions English Version (V9, updated June 2022). (2022). International Working Dog Registry. https://www.iwdr.org/master-knowledge-base/bcl-definitions-download/

28. Shepherd, K. (2021). The ladder of aggression. In *Demystifying dog behaviour for the veterinarian*. CRC Press.

29. Fox, R., Charles, N., Smith, H., & Miele, M. (2023). "Imagine you are a dog": Embodied learning in multi-species research. *Cultural Geographies*, 30(3), 429–52. https://doi.org/10.1177/14744740221102907

30. Yin, S. 2002. A new perspective on barking in dogs (Canis familiaris). *Journal of Comparative Psychology*, 116, 189–93. https://doi.org/10.1037/0735-7036.116.2.189

31. Yin, S., & McCowan, B. (2004). Barking in domestic dogs: Context specificity and individual identification. *Animal Behaviour*, 68(2), 343–55. https://doi.org/10.1016/j.anbehav.2003.07.016

32. Dombrowski, S. C., Timmer, S. G., Blacker, D. M., & Urquiza, A. J. (2005). A positive behavioural intervention for toddlers: Parent–child

attunement therapy. *Child Abuse Review*, 14(2), 132–51. https://doi
.org/10.1002/car.888

33. Di Lorenzo, M. G., Bucsea, O., Rumeo, C., Waxman, J. A., Flora, D. B.,
Schmidt, L. A., & Riddell, R. P. (2022). Caregiver and young child biological attunement in distress contexts: A systematic review and narrative
synthesis. *Neuroscience & Biobehavioral Reviews*, 132 (January), 1010–36.
https://doi.org/10.1016/j.neubiorev.2021.10.045

Chapter 9

1. Levine, P. A., & Kline, M. (2006). *Trauma through a child's eyes*. North
Atlantic Books and ERGOS Institute Press.

2. Buttner, A. P., & Strasser, R. (2022). Extreme life histories are associated with altered social behavior and cortisol levels in shelter dogs. *Applied Animal Behaviour Science*, 256 (November), 105693. https://doi
.org/10.1016/j.applanim.2022.105693

3. Purvis, K. B., Cross, D. R., & Sunshine, W. L. (2007). *The connected child:
Bring hope and healing to your adoptive family* (1st ed.). McGraw-Hill Education, 43.

4. Portions of this section appeared in Sunshine, W. L. (2021). What dog
trainers can teach us about coping. PsychologyToday.com. https://www
.psychologytoday.com/us/blog/tender-paws/202107/what-dog-trainers
-can-teach-us-about-coping. Used with permission.

5. Wever, M. C. M., van Houtum, L. A. E. M., Janssen, L. H. C., Wentholt, W.
G. M., Spruit, I. M., Tollenaar, M. S., Will, G.-J., & Elzinga, B. M. (2022).
Neural and affective responses to prolonged eye contact with one's own adolescent child and unfamiliar others. *NeuroImage*, 260 (October), 119463.
https://doi.org/10.1016/j.neuroimage.2022.119463

6. Akechi, H., Senju, A., Uibo, H., Kikuchi, Y., Hasegawa, T., & Hietanen, J. K.
(2013). Attention to eye contact in the west and east: Autonomic responses
and evaluative ratings. *PLOS One*, 8(3), e59312. https://doi.org/10.1371
/journal.pone.0059312

7. Daily, R. S., Vana, G., Andrade, J. K. L., & Pruett, J. (2022). Evaluating native youth: Issues and considerations in clinical evaluation and treatment.
Child and Adolescent Psychiatric Clinics, 31(4), 779–88. https://doi.org
/10.1016/j.chc.2022.06.008

8. Hadjikhani, N., Johnels, J. A., Lassalle, A., Zürcher, N. R., Hippolyte, L., Gillberg, C., Lemonnier, E., & Ben-Ari, Y. (2018). Bumetanide for autism: More eye contact, less amygdala activation. *Scientific Reports*, 8(1), 3602. https://doi.org/10.1038/s41598-018-21958-x

9. Clin, E., & Kissine, M. (2023). Neurotypical, but not autistic, adults might experience distress when looking at someone avoiding eye contact: A live face-to-face paradigm. *Autism*, January, 13623613221148553. https://doi.org/10.1177/13623613221148553

10. Kleberg, J. L., Högström, J., Sundström, K., Frick, A., & Serlachius, E. (2021). Delayed gaze shifts away from others' eyes in children and adolescents with social anxiety disorder. *Journal of Affective Disorders*, 278 (January), 280–87. https://doi.org/10.1016/j.jad.2020.09.022

11. Anunciação, L., Cito, L., Pessoa, L., Squires, J., Murphy, K., & Landeira-Fernandez, J. (2023). Lack of voluntary interest and difficulty making eye contact are the most discriminative behaviors of the ASQ:SE and might suggest delays: Results from a large-scale assessment. *Applied Neuropsychology: Child*, 1–9. https://doi.org/10.1080/21622965.2022.2156795

12. Rees, C. (2020). Children's attachments. *Pediatrics and Child Health*, 30(5), 162–68. https://doi.org/10.1016/j.paed.2020.02.002

13. Oláh, K., Topál, J., Kovács, K., Kis, A., Koller, D., Park, S.-Y., & Virányi, Z. (2017). Gaze-following and reaction to an aversive social interaction have corresponding associations with variation in the OXTR Gene in dogs but not in human infants. *Frontiers in Psychology*, 8 (December), 2156. https://doi.org/10.3389/fpsyg.2017.02156

14. Riemer, S., Heritier, C., Windschnurer, I., Pratsch, L., Arhant, C., & Affenzeller, N. (2021). A review on mitigating fear and aggression in dogs and cats in a veterinary setting. *Animals*, 11(1), 158. https://doi.org/10.3390/ani11010158

15. Kim, S.-A., & Bain, M. J. (2022). Animal behavior case of the month—Shiba Inu C-PTSD. *Journal of the American Veterinary Medical Association*, 260(12), 1463–65. https://doi.org/10.2460/javma.22.03.0132

16. Gähwiler, S., Bremhorst, A., Tóth, K., & Riemer, S. (2020). Fear expressions of dogs during New Year fireworks: A video analysis. *Scientific Reports*, 10(1), 16035. https://doi.org/10.1038/s41598-020-72841-7

17. Blackwell, E. J., Bradshaw, J. W. S., & Casey, R. A. (2013). Fear responses to noises in domestic dogs: Prevalence, risk factors and co-occurrence with other fear related behaviour. *Applied Animal Behaviour Science*, 145(1), 15–25. https://doi.org/10.1016/j.applanim.2012.12.004

18. Fish, R. E., Foster, M. L., Gruen, M. E., Sherman, B. L., & Dorman, D. C. (2017). Effect of wearing a telemetry jacket on behavioral and physiologic parameters of dogs in the open-field test. *Journal of the American Association for Laboratory Animal Science*, 56(4), 382–89.

19. Riemer, S. (2020). Effectiveness of treatments for firework fears in dogs. *Journal of Veterinary Behavior*, 37 (May), 61–70. https://doi.org/10.1016/j.jveb.2020.04.005

20. Purvis, K. B., Cross, D. R., & Sunshine, W. L. (2007). *The connected child: Bring hope and healing to your adoptive family* (1st ed.). McGraw-Hill Education, 76.

Chapter 10

1. Purvis, K. B., Cross, D. R., & Sunshine, W. L. (2007). *The connected child: Bring hope and healing to your adoptive family* (1st ed.). McGraw-Hill Education, 151.

2. Buckwalter, K. D., Reed, D., & Sunshine, W. L. (2021). *Raising the challenging child: How to minimize meltdowns, reduce conflict, and increase cooperation*. Revell, 17.

3. Thielke, L. E., & Udell, M. A. R. (2019). Evaluating cognitive and behavioral outcomes in conjunction with the secure base effect for dogs in shelter and foster environments. *Animals*, 9(11), 932. https://doi.org/10.3390/ani9110932

4. Kis, A., Bolló, H., Gergely, A., & Topál, J. (2022). Social stimulation by the owner increases dogs' (Canis familiaris) social susceptibility in a food choice task—the possible effect of endogenous oxytocin release. *Animals*, 12(3), 296. https://doi.org/10.3390/ani12030296

5. Tellington TTouch Worldwide. (2023). Tellington TTouch® training. Santa Fe, NM. July 29, 2023. https://ttouch.com/our-method-for/dogs/

6. Lloyd, J. K. F., & Roe, E. (2012). Integrating the Tellington TTouch method in guide dog training. In *Proceedings of the 14th International Mobility Conference*. https://ttouch.com/images/links/2940-Dogs_2013-GuideDog.pdf

7. Hupfeld, J., Dölle, D., Volk, H. A., & Rieder, J. (2023). A qualitative analysis of the impact of canine hypoadrenocorticism on the quality of life of owners. *BMC Veterinary Research*, 19(1), 152. https://doi.org/10.1186/s12917-023-03716-y

8. The Feldenkrais Method, dir. (2021). Tellington-TTOUCH and the Feldenkrais Method: An interview with Linda Tellington Jones. https://www.youtube.com/watch?v=pfDlq4KI7jE

9. Feldenkrais Guild of North America. n.d. Feldenkrais Method awareness through movement. Feldenkrais Method (blog). Accessed September 24, 2023. https://feldenkrais.com/

10. Anat Baniel Method NeuroMovement. 2015. Anat Baniel Method NeuroMovement (blog). December 14, 2015. Accessed September 24, 2023. https://www.anatbanielmethod.com/about/

11. Elgelid, S., & Kresge, C. (2021). *The Feldenkrais Method: Learning Through movement*. Jessica Kingsley Publishers.

12. Faramarzi, H. (2018). Effectiveness of Anat Baniel's method for neuromotor therapy on motor skills and social skills of children with high-functioning autism spectrum disorder. *Empowering Exceptional Children*, 9(1), 99–112.

13. Anat Baniel, dir. (2013). Anat Baniel Method NeuroMovement: Lessons for Isabel with cerebral palsy and brain injury. https://www.youtube.com/watch?v=k4R_5Y17Zfs

14. Feuerbacher, E. N., & Wynne, C. D. L. (2015). Shut up and pet me! Domestic dogs (Canis lupus familiaris) prefer petting to vocal praise in concurrent and single-alternative choice procedures. *Behavioural Processes, New Directions in Canine Behavior*, 110 (January), 47–59.

15. Owens, C. n.d. Constructional affection—becoming best friends. Accessed May 17, 2023. http://www.constructionalaffection.com/

16. Katz, M., & Rosales-Ruiz, J. (2022). Constructional fear treatment: Teaching fearful shelter dogs to approach and interact with a novel person. *Journal of the Experimental Analysis of Behavior*, 118(2), 278–91. https://doi.org/10.1002/jeab.784

Chapter 11

1. Missildine, W. H. (1962). The "mutual respect" approach to child guidance: A report of ninety-seven cases from private practice. *American Journal of Diseases of Children*, 104(2), 116–21. https://doi.org/10.1001/archpedi.1962.02080030118003

2. Buckwalter, K. D., Reed, D., & Sunshine, W. L. (2021). *Raising the challenging child: How to minimize meltdowns, reduce conflict, and increase cooperation*. Revell.

3. Purvis, K. B., Cross, D. R., & Sunshine, W. L. (2007). *The connected child: Bring hope and healing to your adoptive family* (1st ed.). McGraw-Hill Education, 91.

Chapter 12

1. Riemer, S. (2020). Effectiveness of treatments for firework fears in dogs. *Journal of Veterinary Behavior*, 37 (May), 61–70. https://doi.org/10.1016/j.jveb.2020.04.005

2. Patel, C., dir. (2015). The bucket game introduction part 1. https://www.youtube.com/watch?v=GJSs9eqi2r8

3. Swenson, S., Ho, G. W. K., Budhathoki, C., Belcher, H. M. E., Tucker, S., Miller, K., & Gross, D. (2016). Parents' use of praise and criticism in a sample of young children seeking mental health services. *Journal of Pediatric Health Care, Behavioral Health Care*, 30(1), 49–56. https://doi.org/10.1016/j.pedhc.2015.09.010

Chapter 13

1. Putnick, D. L., Trinh, M.-H., Sundaram, R., Bell, E. M., Ghassabian, A., Robinson, S. L., & Yeung, E. (2023). Displacement of peer play by screen time: Associations with toddler development. *Pediatric Research*, 93(5), 1425–31. https://doi.org/10.1038/s41390-022-02261-y

2. Mehrkam, L. R., & Wynne, C. D. L. (2021). Owner attention facilitates

social play in dog–dog dyads (Canis lupus familiaris): Evidence for an interspecific audience effect. *Animal Cognition*, 24(2), 341–52. https://doi.org/10.1007/s10071-021-01481-9

3. Terradas, M. M., & Asselin, A. (2022). Episodic experiences of child physical abuse, early relational trauma and post-traumatic play: Theoretical considerations and clinical illustrations. *Journal of Child & Adolescent Trauma*, September. https://doi.org/10.1007/s40653-022-00489-8

4. Pursi, A., Lipponen, L., & Sajaniemi, N. K. (2018). Emotional and playful stance taking in joint play between adults and very young children. *Learning, Culture and Social Interaction*, 18 (September), 28–45. https://doi.org/10.1016/j.lcsi.2018.03.002

5. Landreth, G. L. (2012). *Play therapy: The art of the relationship* (3rd ed.). Routledge. https://doi.org/10.4324/9780203835159

6. Ray, D. C., Burgin, E., Gutierrez, D., Ceballos, P., & Lindo, N. (2022). Child-centered play therapy and adverse childhood experiences: A randomized controlled trial. *Journal of Counseling & Development*, 100(2), 134–45. https://doi.org/10.1002/jcad.12412

7. Heshmati, R., Esmailpour, K., Hajsaghati, R., & Barenji, F. A. (2023). The effect of child-centered play therapy (CCPT) on the symptoms of oppositional defiant disorder in preschool children. *International Journal of Play*, 12(2), 193–205. https://doi.org/10.1080/21594937.2023.2209240

8. Purrington, J., Glover-Humphreys, E., Edwards, H., & Hudson, M. (2022). The impact of a brief neuro-collaborative play-based intervention on the presentations of developmental trauma and attachment difficulties in adopted children: A service evaluation. *International Journal of Play Therapy*, 31(4), 237–47. https://doi.org/10.1037/pla0000182

9. Booth, P. B., & Jernberg, A. M. (2009). *Theraplay: Helping parents and children build better relationships through attachment-based play*. John Wiley & Sons.

10. Money, R., Wilde, S., & Dawson, D. (2021). Review: The effectiveness of theraplay for children under 12—a systematic literature review. *Child and Adolescent Mental Health*, 26(3), 238–51. https://doi.org/10.1111/camh.12416

11. Hiles Howard, A. R., Lindaman, S., Copeland, R., & Cross, D. R. (2018). Theraplay impact on parents and children with autism spectrum disorder: Improvements in affect, joint attention, and social cooperation. *International Journal of Play Therapy*, 27, 56–68. https://doi.org/10.1037/pla0000056

12. McMillan, T., & Cook, A. (2023). Play way live chat—shelter behavior hub. August 7, 2023. https://trish-s-school-bcb6.thinkific.com/courses/take/live-chat-recordings/lessons/47429714-live-chat-recording-play-way-with-amy-cook

13. Rooney, N. J., Bradshaw, J. W. S., & Robinson, I. H. (2001). Do dogs respond to play signals given by humans? *Animal Behaviour*, 61(4), 715–22. https://doi.org/10.1006/anbe.2000.1661

14. Horowitz, A., & Hecht, J. (2016). Examining dog–human play: The characteristics, affect, and vocalizations of a unique interspecific interaction. *Animal Cognition*, 19(4), 779–88. https://doi.org/10.1007/s10071-016-0976-3

15. Donaldson, L. n.d. Slow thinking is lifesaving for dogs. Accessed September 6, 2023. https://fourpawsfourdirections.com/slow-thinking

16. Stevens-Smith, D. A. (2020). Brain-based teaching: Differentiation in teaching, learning, and motor skills. *Journal of Physical Education, Recreation & Dance*, 91(7), 34–42. https://doi.org/10.1080/07303084.2020.1781717

17. DeBenedet, A. T., & Cohen, L. J. (2011). *The art of roughhousing: Good old-fashioned horseplay and why every kid needs it*. Quirk Books.

18. Schilder, M. B. H., van der Borg, J. A. M., & Vinke, C. M. (2019). Intraspecific killing in dogs: Predation behavior or aggression? A study of aggressors, victims, possible causes, and motivations. *Journal of Veterinary Behavior*, 34 (November), 52–59. https://doi.org/10.1016/j.jveb.2019.08.002

19. L.E.G.S. Applied Ethology Family Dog Mediation Professional Course. n.d. Kim Brophey L.E.G.S. courses. Accessed September 18, 2023. https://kimbropheylegscourses.thinkific.com/courses/legs-applied-ethology-family-dog-mediation-professional-course

20. Hembree-Kigin, T. L., McNeil, C. B., & Eyberg, S. (1995). *Parent-child interaction therapy* (1st ed.). Springer.

21. Nash, J. B. (2021). Doll play. In *Play Therapy with Children: Modalities for Change*, 25–37. American Psychological Association. https://psycnet.apa.org/doiLanding?doi=10.1037%2F0000217-003

22. Hashmi, S., Vanderwert, R. E., Price, H. A., & Gerson, S. A. (2020). Exploring the benefits of doll play through neuroscience. *Frontiers in Human Neuroscience*, 14, 413. https://doi.org/10.3389/fnhum.2020.560176

23. Bolouki, A. (2023). Neurobiological effects of urban built and natural environment on mental health: Systematic review. *Reviews on Environmental Health*, 38(1), 169–79. https://doi.org/10.1515/reveh-2021-0137

24. Bratman, G. N., Anderson, C. B., Berman, M. G., Cochran, B., de Vries, S., Flanders, J., Folke, C., et al. (2019). Nature and mental health: An ecosystem service perspective. *Science Advances*, 5(7), eaax0903. https://doi.org/10.1126/sciadv.aax0903

25. Whitebread, D. (2017). Free play and children's mental health. *The Lancet Child & Adolescent Health*, 1(3), 167–69. https://doi.org/10.1016/S2352-4642(17)30092-5

26. Veiga, G., Neto, C., & Rieffe, C. (2016). Preschoolers' free play: Connections with emotional and social functioning. *International Journal of Emotional Education*, 8(1). https://www.um.edu.mt/library/oar/handle/123456789/9993

27. Hewes, J. (2014). Seeking balance in motion: The role of spontaneous free play in promoting social and emotional health in early childhood care and education. *Children*, 1(3), 280–301. https://doi.org/10.3390/children1030280

28. Colliver, Y., Harrison, L. J., Brown, J. E., & Humburg, P. (2022). Free play predicts self-regulation years later: Longitudinal evidence from a large Australian sample of toddlers and preschoolers. *Early Childhood Research Quarterly*, 59 (April), 148–61. https://doi.org/10.1016/j.ecresq.2021.11.011

29. Gray, P. (2011). The decline of play and the rise of psychopathology in children and adolescents. *American Journal of Play*, 3(4), 443–63.

30. Gray, P. (2019). Evolutionary functions of play: Practice, resilience, innovation, and cooperation. In *The Cambridge handbook of play: Developmental and disciplinary perspectives*, 84–102. Cambridge University Press.

31. Panksepp, J. (1998). *Affective neuroscience: The foundations of human and animal emotions.* Oxford University Press.

32. Fisher, S. n.d. Animal centred education overview. Animal Centred Education. Accessed September 5, 2023. https://animalcentrededucation .teachable.com/p/home

33. Fisher, S. (2023). Patterns, habits, and familiarity. Presented at the 2023 Dog Behavior Conference, online, April 22.

Chapter 14

1. Ward, K. P., Lee, S. J., Grogan-Kaylor, A. C., Ma, J., & Pace, G. T. (2022). Patterns of caregiver aggressive and nonaggressive discipline toward young children in low- and middle-income countries: A latent class approach. *Child Abuse & Neglect*, 128 (June), 105606. https://doi.org/10.1016/j .chiabu.2022.105606

2. Buckwalter, K. D., Reed, D., & Sunshine, W. L. (2021). *Raising the challenging child: How to minimize meltdowns, reduce conflict, and increase cooperation.* Revell.

Chapter 15

1. Brophey, K., Coppinger, R., & Hewitt, J. (2018). *Meet your dog: The game-changing guide to understanding your dog's behavior* (Illustrated ed.). Chronicle Books LLC.

2. Dutrow, E. V., Serpell, J. A., & Ostrander, E. A. (2022). Domestic dog lineages reveal genetic drivers of behavioral diversification. *Cell*, 185(25), 4737–4755.e18. https://doi.org/10.1016/j.cell.2022.11.003

3. Morrill, K., Hekman, J., Li, X., McClure, J., Logan, B., Goodman, L., Gao, M., et al. (2022). Ancestry-inclusive dog genomics challenges popular breed stereotypes. *Science*, 376(6592), eabk0639. https://doi.org/10.1126 /science.abk0639

4. Mikkola, S., Salonen, M., Puurunen, J., Hakanen, E., Sulkama, S., Araujo, C., & Lohi, H. (2021). Aggressive behaviour is affected by demographic,

environmental and behavioural factors in purebred dogs. *Scientific Reports*, 11(1), 9433. https://doi.org/10.1038/s41598-021-88793-5

Chapter 16

1. Bender, A., & Strong, E. (2021). Treating aggression through an enrichment framework. Presented at the Aggression in Dogs Conference.

2. Harvey, N. D., Christley, R. M., Giragosian, K., Mead, R., Murray, J. K., Samet, L., Upjohn, M. M., & Casey, R. A. (2022). Impact of changes in time left alone on separation-related behaviour in UK pet dogs. *Animals*, 12(4), 482. https://doi.org/10.3390/ani12040482

3. It's Me or the Dog, dir. (2022). When the dream of a perfect puppy turns into a nightmare | It's me or the dog. https://www.youtube.com/watch?v=Xn0tCeTdp1E

4. Purvis, K. B., Cross, D. R., & Sunshine, W. L. (2007). *The connected child: Bring hope and healing to your adoptive family* (1st ed.). McGraw-Hill Education, 101.

5. Collins, K., Miller, K., Zverina, L., Patterson-Kane, E., Cussen, V., & Reid, P. (2022). Behavioral rehabilitation of extremely fearful dogs: Report on the efficacy of a treatment protocol. *Applied Animal Behaviour Science*, 254 (September), 105689. https://doi.org/10.1016/j.applanim.2022.105689

6. Bell, M. A. (2020). Mother-child behavioral and physiological synchrony. In J. Benson (ed.), *Advances in child development and behavior*, 58, 163–88. JAI. https://doi.org/10.1016/bs.acdb.2020.01.006

7. Gruber, T., Bazhydai, B., Sievers, C., Clément, F., & Dukes, D. (2022). The ABC of social learning: Affect, behavior, and cognition. *Psychological Review*, 129, 1296–318. https://doi.org/10.1037/rev0000311

8. Wilson, C., Campbell, K., Petzel, Z., & Reeve, C. (2022). Dogs can discriminate between human baseline and psychological stress condition odours. *PLOS One*, 17(9), e0274143. https://doi.org/10.1371/journal.pone.0274143

9. Souza, P., Guo, K., Mills, D. S., Resende, B., & Albuquerque, N. (2023). How do dogs behave when presented with situations of different emotional valences? *Animals*, 13(6), 1027. https://doi.org/10.3390/ani13061027

10. Buttner, A. P., Thompson, B., Strasser, R., & Santo, J. (2015). Evidence for a synchronization of hormonal states between humans and dogs during

competition. *Physiology & Behavior*, 147 (August), 54–62. https://doi
.org/10.1016/j.physbeh.2015.04.010

11. Sundman, A.-S., Van Poucke, E., Holm, A.-C. S., Faresjö, A., Theodorsson, E., Jensen, P., & Roth, L. S. V. (2019). Long-term stress levels are synchronized in dogs and their owners. *Scientific Reports*, 9(1), 7391. https://doi.org/10.1038/s41598-019-43851-x

12. Fugazza, C., Temesi, A., Coronas, R., Uccheddu, S., Gácsi, M., & Pogány, A. (2023). Spontaneous action matching in dog puppies, kittens and wolf pups. *Scientific Reports*, 13(1), 2094. https://doi.org/10.1038/s41598-023-28959-5

13. Duranton, C., Courby-Betremieux, C., & Gaunet, F. (2022). One- and two-month-old dog puppies exhibit behavioural synchronization with humans independently of familiarity. *Animals*, 12(23), 3356. https://doi.org/10.3390/ani12233356

14. Duranton, C., & Gaunet, F. (2015). Canis sensitivus: Affiliation and dogs' sensitivity to others' behavior as the basis for synchronization with humans? *Journal of Veterinary Behavior*, 10(6), 513–24. https://doi.org/10.1016/j.jveb.2015.08.008

15. Holcova, K., Koru, E., Havlicek, Z., & Rezac, P. (2021). Factors associated with sniffing behaviors between walking dogs in public places. *Applied Animal Behaviour Science*, 244 (November), 105464. https://doi.org/10.1016/j.applanim.2021.105464

16. Gruber, T., Bazhydai, M., Sievers, C., Clément, F., & Dukes, D. (2022). The ABC of social learning: Affect, behavior, and cognition. *Psychological Review*, 129, 1296–318. https://doi.org/10.1037/rev0000311

Chapter 17

1. Flint, H. E., Atkinson, M., Lush, J., Hunt, A. B. G., & King, T. (2023). Long-lasting chews elicit positive emotional states in dogs during short periods of social isolation. *Animals*, 13(4), 552. https://doi.org/10.3390/ani13040552

2. Hunter, A., Blake, S., & De Godoy, R. F. (2019). Pressure and force on the canine neck when exercised using a collar and leash. *Veterinary and Animal Science*, 8 (December), 100082. https://doi.org/10.1016/j.vas.2019.100082

3. Carter, A., McNally, D., & Roshier, A. (2020). Canine collars: An investigation of collar type and the forces applied to a simulated neck model. *Veterinary Record*, 187(7), e52–e52. https://doi.org/10.1136/vr.105681

4. Steinker, A., & Tudge, N. (2012). Choke & prong collars: Health concerns prompt changing dog training equipment. *Barks from the Guild*. The Pet Professional Guild, October 2012.

5. Grohmann, K., Dickomeit, M. J., Schmidt, M. J., & Kramer, M. (2013). Severe brain damage after punitive training technique with a choke chain collar in a German shepherd dog. *Journal of Veterinary Behavior*, 8(3), 180–84. https://doi.org/10.1016/j.jveb.2013.01.002

6. Cooper, J. J., Cracknell, N., Hardiman, J., Wright, H., & Mills, D. (2014). The welfare consequences and efficacy of training pet dogs with remote electronic training collars in comparison to reward based training. *PLOS One*, 9(9), e102722. https://doi.org/10.1371/journal.pone.0102722

7. Shih, H.-Y., Georgiou, F., Curtis, R. A., Paterson, M. B. A., & Phillips, C. J. C. (2020). Behavioural evaluation of a leash tension meter which measures pull direction and force during human–dog on-leash walks. *Animals*, 10(8), 1382. https://doi.org/10.3390/ani10081382

8. Haug, L. I, Beaver, B. V., & Longnecker, M. T. (2002). Comparison of dogs' reactions to four different head collars. *Applied Animal Behaviour Science*, 79(1), 53–61. https://doi.org/10.1016/S0168-1591(02)00115-6

9. Townsend, L., Dixon, L., & Buckley, L. (2022). Lead pulling as a welfare concern in pet dogs: What can veterinary professionals learn from current research? *Veterinary Record*, 191(10), e1627. https://doi.org/10.1002/vetr.1627

10. How to leash belay—revolutionary new dog walking technique. n.d. Grisha Stewart Academy. Accessed May 6, 2023. https://school.grishastewart.com/courses/belaypractice

11. Polsky, R. (2000). Can aggression in dogs be elicited through the use of electronic pet containment systems? *Journal of Applied Animal Welfare Science*, 3(4), 345–57. https://doi.org/10.1207/S15327604JAWS0304_6

12. DeGreeff, L. E., & Schultz, C. A. (eds.). (2022). Training considerations for operational performance: Train the handler, train the dog, train the team. In *Canines: The Original Biosensors*. CRC Press.

13. Collins, K., Miller, K., Zverina, L., Patterson-Kane, E., Cussen, V., & Reid, P. (2022). Behavioral rehabilitation of extremely fearful dogs: Report on the efficacy of a treatment protocol. *Applied Animal Behaviour Science*, 254 (September), 105689. https://doi.org/10.1016/j.applanim.2022.105689

14. Cuaya, L. V., Hernández-Pérez, R., Boros, M., Deme, A., & Andics, A. (2022). Speech naturalness detection and language representation in the dog brain. *NeuroImage*, 248 (March), 118811. https://doi.org/10.1016/j.neuroimage.2021.118811

Chapter 21

1. Purvis, K. B., Cross, D. R., & Sunshine, W. L. (2007). *The connected child: Bring hope and healing to your adoptive family* (1st ed.). McGraw-Hill Education, 9.

2. Gerken, A. (2023) All body systems affect behavior. In *Behavior problems of the dog and cat* (4th ed.). Elsevier.

3. Suñol, A., Perez-Accino, J., Kelley, M., Rossi, G., & Schmitz, S. S. (2020). Successful dietary treatment of aggression and behavioral changes in a dog. *Journal of Veterinary Behavior*, 37 (May), 56–60. https://doi.org/10.1016/j.jveb.2020.04.009

4. Cocco, R., Arfuso, F., Giannetto, C., Piccione, G., Cesarani, A., Pulina, G., & Sechi, S. (2023). A preliminary study on the interplay between the serum levels of neurotransmitters and thyroid hormones for the evaluation of the behavioral phenotype of dogs. *Animals*, 13(3), 411. https://doi.org/10.3390/ani13030411

5. Notari, L., Kirton, R., & Mills, D. S. (2022). Psycho-behavioural changes in dogs treated with corticosteroids: A clinical behaviour perspective. *Animals*, 12(5), 592. https://doi.org/10.3390/ani12050592

6. Sung, W., & Radosta, L. (2023). Unruly and destructive behaviors—canine. In *Behavior problems of the dog and cat*. Elsevier Health Sciences.

7. Mills, D. S., Demontigny-Bédard, I., Gruen, M., Klinck, M. P., McPeake, K. J., Barcelos, A. M., Hewison, L., et al. (2020). Pain and problem behavior in cats and dogs. *Animals*, 10(2), 318. https://doi.org/10.3390/ani10020318

8. Home | Dynamic Dog. n.d. Accessed May 1, 2023. https://www.dynamicdog.co.uk/

9. McAuliffe, L. R., Koch, C. S., Serpell, J., & Campbell, K. L. (2022). Associations between atopic dermatitis and anxiety, aggression, and fear-based behaviors in dogs. *Journal of the American Animal Hospital Association*, 58(4), 161–67. https://doi.org/10.5326/JAAHA-MS-7210

10. Fagundes, L., Luisa, A., Hewison, L., McPeake, K. J., Zulch, H., & Mills, D. S. (2018). Noise sensitivities in dogs: An exploration of signs in dogs with and without musculoskeletal pain using qualitative content analysis. *Frontiers in Veterinary Science*, 5 (February), 17. https://doi.org/10.3389/fvets.2018.00017

11. Straub, R. H. (2023). What is a child's psychological trauma? In R. H. Straub (ed.), *Early trauma as the origin of chronic inflammation: A psychoneuroimmunological perspective*. Springer, 13–70. https://doi.org/10.1007/978-3-662-66751-4_2

12. Rowell, T., & Neal-Barnett, A. (2022). A systematic review of the effect of parental adverse childhood experiences on parenting and child psychopathology. *Journal of Child & Adolescent Trauma*, 15(1), 167–80. https://doi.org/10.1007/s40653-021-00400-x

13. Buttner, A. P., Awalt, S. L., & Strasser, R. (2023). Early life adversity in dogs produces altered physiological and behavioral responses during a social stress-buffering paradigm. *Journal of the Experimental Analysis of Behavior*, 120(1), 6–20. https://doi.org/10.1002/jeab.856

14. Hennessy, M. B., Willen, R. M., & Schiml, P. A. (2020). Psychological stress, its reduction, and long-term consequences: What studies with laboratory animals might teach us about life in the dog shelter. *Animals*, 10(11), Article 11. https://doi.org/10.3390/ani10112061

15. Tiira, K., & Lohi, H. (2015). Early life experiences and exercise associate with canine anxieties. *PLOS One*, 10(11), e0141907. https://doi.org/10.1371/journal.pone.0141907

16. McMillan, F. D., Vanderstichel, R., Stryhn, H., Yu, J., & Serpell, J. A. (2016). Behavioural characteristics of dogs removed from hoarding situations. *Applied Animal Behaviour Science*, 178, 69–79. https://doi.org/10.1016/j.applanim.2016.02.006

17. Levine, P. A., & Kline, M. (2006). *Trauma through a child's eyes*. North Atlantic Books and ERGOS Institute Press.

18. Vieira de Castro, A. C., Fuchs, D., Morello, G. M., Pastur, S., de Sousa, L., & Olsson, I. A. S. (2020). Does training method matter? Evidence for the negative impact of aversive-based methods on companion dog welfare. *PLOS One*, 15(12). https://doi.org/10.1371/journal.pone.0225023

19. Wells, D. L. (2022). Factors influencing the expression of behavior in the domestic dog. In T. Grandin (ed.), *Genetics and the behavior of domestic animals* (3rd ed.). Academic Press , 229–52. https://doi.org/10.1016/B978-0-323-85752-9.00011-1

20. Meyer, I., Forkman, B., Fredholm, M., Glanville, C., Guldbrandtsen, B., Izaguirre, E. R., Palmer, C., & Sandøe, P. (2022). Pampered pets or poor bastards? The welfare of dogs kept as companion animals. *Applied Animal Behaviour Science*, 251 (June), 105640. https://doi.org/10.1016/j.applanim.2022.105640

21. Bos, K. J., Zeanah, C. H., Jr., Smyke, A. T., Fox, N. A., & Nelson, C. A., III. (2010). Stereotypies in children with a history of early institutional care. *Archives of Pediatrics & Adolescent Medicine*, 164(5), 406–11. https://doi.org/10.1001/archpediatrics.2010.47

22. Péter, Z., Oliphant, M. E., & Fernandez, T. V. (2017). Motor stereotypies: A pathophysiological review. *Frontiers in Neuroscience*, 11. https://www.frontiersin.org/articles/10.3389/fnins.2017.00171

23. Pecora, G., Addessi, E., Schino, G., & Bellagamba, F. (2014). Do displacement activities help preschool children to inhibit a forbidden action? *Journal of Experimental Child Psychology*, 126 (October), 80–90. https://doi.org/10.1016/j.jecp.2014.03.008

24. Pretlow, R., & Glasner, S. (2022). Reconceptualization of eating addiction and obesity as displacement behavior and a possible treatment. *Eating and Weight Disorders—Studies on Anorexia, Bulimia and Obesity*, 27(7), 2897–903. https://doi.org/10.1007/s40519-022-01427-1

Chapter 22

1. Hanh, T. N. (2010). *Reconciliation: Healing the inner child*. Parallax Press.

acknowledgments

THANKS FIRST AND FOREMOST to marvelous editor Darcie Abbene and the entire team at HCI for believing in my book and helping coax out its best. Art director Larissa Henoch worked magic on its cover and interior, Christian Blonshine catalyzed the audio version, and Lindsey Triebel introduced the final product into the world. Partnering with you all has been an absolute pleasure.

I am forever grateful to the late Karyn Purvis and David Cross of Texas Christian University for inviting me on their journey of compassion and hope; it was a privilege to partner with such exceptional educators devoted to the welfare and secure attachment of children and families. Thanks also to Karen Doyle Buckwalter and the late Debbie Reed of Chaddock for strengthening my connection with the subject material and for sharing their book journey and wisdom with me.

Tender Paws has been enriched and buoyed by the expertise, input, and generous participation of many. My deep thanks to Temple Grandin, Kim Brophey, Victoria Stilwell, Katrien De Clercq, Kelley Bollen, Christopher Pachel, Hélène Marie Lawler, Denise Fenzi, Suzanne Clothier, Lynne Bernfield, Marlene O'Neill LaBerge, Andrew Hale, Justine Schuurmans, Roman Gottfried, Stephie Guy,

Michelle Stern, Sherry Steinlein, Linda Keehn, Irith Bloom, Tara Stillwell, Christina Waggoner, Abigail Witthauer, Jodie Forbes, Kathy Callahan, Debbie Sheridan, and Oliver Ringrose. All your contributions are appreciated.

Thank you as well to Ethan Kocak for lovely drawings, Nancy Guth for the magical cover photo, and early readers who provided input on the proposal and manuscript. These included Kate Hopper, Jane Friedman, Rachel Weingarten, Jody Lyons Gallagher, the Splinters (Lynne Bernfield, Vivien Kalvaria, and Jackie Fenn), and Naomi Sunshine, aka Mrs. Language Person.

Humble gratitude to my mother, Judy, and late father, Allan, for persevering and planting the seeds of creativity and intellectual exploration, and to my sister, Jody, for bringing humor and spirit to our journey. I treasure your love, support, and encouragement.

Finally, deep appreciation to Norm for serenades and story time, for embracing Meal Plan, and for making home a happy place. You are the wind beneath my seagull.

about the author

WENDY LYONS SUNSHINE is an award-winning writer and journalist who co-authored *The Connected Child: Bring Hope and Healing to Your Adoptive Family*, a bestseller that has been translated into multiple languages, and *Raising the Challenging Child: How to Minimize Meltdowns, Reduce Conflict, and Increase Cooperation*. She blogs about animal welfare and the human-dog bond for PsychologyToday.com and has contributed to the *New York Times, Fort Worth Star-Telegram, Fort Worth Weekly,* and many other publications. Wendy has trained in the L.E.G.S. applied ethology model of Family Dog Mediation and assisted at a local animal shelter. She and her husband live with a rescue dog on an overgrown acre where they all enjoy watching wildlife.